POEMS

BY CHRISTOPHER SMART

Christopher Smart, from the portrait
in Pembroke College Library

POEMS

by Christopher Smart

EDITED WITH AN INTRODUCTION

AND NOTES BY

ROBERT BRITTAIN

PRINCETON, NEW JERSEY

PRINCETON UNIVERSITY PRESS

1950

PRINTED IN THE UNITED STATES OF AMERICA
BY PRINCETON UNIVERSITY PRESS AT PRINCETON, NEW JERSEY

Preface

THE poems in this volume constitute a small fraction of the total literary production of Christopher Smart, a poet whose finest work, with the exception of one great and famous poem, has been virtually unobtainable by the general reader and unknown but to a few scholars and devotees. Ironically, much of Smart's inferior hack work is easily available in the standard collections of minor English poets, because his first editor carefully gathered it up and presented it as his "Collected Poems." The present volume is an attempt to remedy the situation, by offering an introduction to that part of Smart's work which seems to have permanent value. For this purpose, I have selected poems which I hope will give a fair representation of his better volumes. In addition, I have included a few short pieces which, while inferior as poetry, have a biographical interest and offer some indication of the journalism on which he wasted so much of his energy.

The texts have been taken, wherever possible, from the editions published in Smart's lifetime, particularly those that may have had his supervision through the press. Since most of the poems are here reprinted for the first time, there are few textual variations to be accounted for, but I have indicated in footnotes the principal variants in poems that have been previously reprinted. The occasional brief annotations are Smart's. In spelling, I have followed the eighteenth-century texts, except on the rare occasions where an original spelling would be misleading or confusing to a modern reader, in which instances I have silently used a modern spelling. In matters of punctuation, I have in general taken the text as I found it, but frequently I have been obliged to dispense with the original printer's marks and supply others in order to make clear the meaning. This again I have done without the distraction of footnotes, on the assumption that the average reader will require a clear and readable text, and will not wish to be annoyed by reminders of the confusions in admittedly badly printed books.

My thanks are due to most of the little company of admirers of Smart, with whom I have had much profitable correspondence during the years. Especially, I am indebted to Dean Roland B. Botting, Mr. William Force Stead, Mr. Edmund Blunden, the late Professor E. G. Ainsworth, Jr., Mr. C. D. Abbott, Professor Raymond D. Havens, and Mr. Charles E. Noyes, all of whom have given me encouragement and help, and all of whom have made genuine contributions to the literature on Christopher Smart. I must likewise acknowledge the kindly assistance of the Librarians and staff members of Princeton University Library, the Bodleian, the American Antiquarian Society Library, the Yale University Library, the New York Public Library, and the Library of Congress. The staff of the Reading Museum, who gave me access to the papers relating to the Smart family in their collection, are especially my creditors.

And most of all, I am deeply indebted to Professor Robert K. Root, who first introduced me to the poetry of Smart and has, with unfailing courtesy and kindness, placed at my disposal again and again the rich resources of his scholarship. Without his friendly encouragement, I doubt that this book would have been done.

ROBERT BRITTAIN

Contents

HYMNS FOR THE AMUSEMENT
OF CHILDREN, 1770

Notes on the Poems

Illustrations

POEMS

BY CHRISTOPHER SMART

Introduction

THE story of Christopher Smart's reputation is one of the oddest chapters in English literary history. In the first half of his career, during which he spent his energies almost entirely on hack work, he was regarded as an ingenious and pleasant, if minor, poet. In the latter part of his life he published volumes of poetry, much of it first rate, but because he had had the misfortune to lose his mind for a time this later poetry was assumed to be inferior by his contemporaries and they scarcely bothered to read it at all. When he died in the rules of the King's Bench Prison in 1771, he was remembered for a few years as a kindly but eccentric little man, and his poetry, good and bad, sank quickly into oblivion. Twenty years later his nephew, Christopher Hunter, tried to resuscitate his memory by publishing a two-volume collection of his poetry, but he carefully selected for this project only the early verse and omitted nearly everything that raises Smart above the rank of mediocrity. By means of reprints of this collection in the bulky anthologies of Chalmers and Anderson, Smart maintained for a century a precarious foothold on the nether rim of literature. "Sir, there can be no question of precedence between a louse and a flea."

In the early years of the nineteenth century, Smart's masterpiece, *A Song to David*, was rediscovered, but although Southey, Wordsworth, and others knew at least parts of it and quoted it on occasion, the poem did not receive any wide attention and Smart's reputation was not materially improved. Finally, a full century after Smart's death, Robert Browning read the *Song* and was overwhelmed, as many readers have been since, by its splendor. He immediately set about to find what else such a master had written, but all he could discover, apparently, was Hunter's collection. And here there was nothing to suggest that Smart could write greatly. Knowing that Smart had been confined for madness for several years just before the *Song* was published, Browning jumped to the natural but quite erroneous conclusion that the great lyric was a miracle of insanity. With dramatic skill he presented this theory in his "Parleying with Christopher Smart."

It was an exciting theory: a mediocre poet laboriously grinding out reams of dull and uninspired verse suddenly loses his mind, and in a burst of insane genius scrawls upon the walls of his cell a superb lyric ode worthy to be ranked with those of Milton and Keats; then sanity returns, genius departs, and the sobered poet resumes his patient production of trash. How such nonsense could impose itself on a mind as intelligent as Browning's can only be understood if one remembers the limited evidence he had at his disposal. If one reads only Hunter's edition and *A Song to David* the situation is very puzzling, to say the least.

At any rate, when Browning's poem was published, the literary world was dazzled by the reappearance of a brilliant star. Oliver Wendell Holmes inquired timidly about "the wonderful poem"; Rossetti roundly declared it "the only great *accomplished* poem of the last century" (Pope presumably belonged to no century); Sir Edmund Gosse rhapsodized about the "inestimable jewel buried in an ash-heap"; and even Dr. Furnivall brought his rich scholarship to bear on some of the puzzling lines. Editions and reprints of *A Song to David* began to appear and have continued with frequency up to the present time. Even the bibliophiles discovered Smart, and one of the four known copies of the first edition of his masterpiece has fetched as much as £600.

The astonishing thing about all this activity is that until quite recently no very serious attempt has been made to investigate the rest of Smart's total production. Readers of poetry and students of literature have been so under the spell of Browning's theories that they have concentrated their effort almost entirely on the *Song* or on Smart's life, with especial attention, of course, to the period of insanity. Only two books have attempted to survey his life and work as a whole (McKenzie's *Christopher Smart: Sa Vie et Ses Oeuvres*, Paris 1925, and Ainsworth and Noyes: *Christopher Smart, A Biographical and Critical Study*, University of Missouri, 1943) and only Mr. Edmund Blunden has made available to the modern reader a few of Smart's later poems.

When one has read through a fair selection chosen from the whole of Christopher Smart's poetry, much of the mystery disappears. The poet who in a lifetime of dullness had one incomprehensible moment of insane genius is found to be a figment of the Romantic imagination. In his place there emerges a quite understandable man, compounded of tragic weaknesses and sturdy virtues, and a lyric poet whose clear and ringing voice, although muffled again and again by the exigencies of a most difficult life, was stilled only by death. *A Song to David* is no longer an isolated miracle. It is still Smart's greatest production, but it is surrounded by a mass of lyric poetry that will bear favorable comparison with it. The poet himself is no longer a minor hack who wrote one great piece: he is a religious lyricist whose talents may be enjoyed and studied in scores of poems, and whose work may be ranked with the best of its kind in English.

I

Christopher Smart was born in the village of Shipbourne, Kent. Although he could boast among his ancestry such well-known people as Bernard Gilpin, the beloved "Apostle of the North," and Peter Smart, the Puritan proto-martyr of the seventeenth century, his immediate forebears were people of no great importance. His father was another Peter Smart (1687-1733) who had come down from Durham to act as steward of Fairlawn, the estate of William, Viscount Vane.[1] Christopher Hunter, the poet's nephew and first

---

[1] This William was the younger son of Christopher Vane, Baron Barnard (1653-1723) and the brother of Gilbert Vane, Baron Barnard (1678-1753). The seat of the Barons Barnard was Raby Castle in Durham. It descended, along with the title, to Henry Vane, son of Gilbert (c. 1705-1758), who became the patron of Smart. (See below p. 18.) The relationships of this family and those of the Dukes of Cleveland, one of whom was also a patron of Smart, are best understood from the following table:

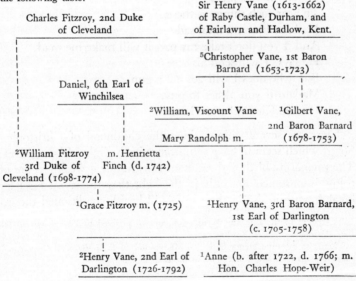

Charles Fitzroy, 2nd Duke of Cleveland

Sir Henry Vane (1613-1662) of Raby Castle, Durham, and of Fairlawn and Hadlow, Kent.

5Christopher Vane, 1st Baron Barnard (1653-1723)

Daniel, 6th Earl of Winchilsea

2William, Viscount Vane

1Gilbert Vane, 2nd Baron Barnard (1678-1753)

Mary Randolph m.

2William Fitzroy 3rd Duke of Cleveland (1698-1774)

m. Henrietta Finch (d. 1742)

1Grace Fitzroy m. (1725)

1Henry Vane, 3rd Baron Barnard, 1st Earl of Darlington (c. 1705-1758)

2Henry Vane, 2nd Earl of Darlington (1726-1792)

1Anne (b. after 1722, d. 1766; m. Hon. Charles Hope-Weir)

biographer, says that this Peter Smart had been intended for holy orders, and that he had "a better taste for literature than is commonly found in country gentlemen."[2] Of Mrs. Smart little is known beyond the fact that she had been Miss Winifred Griffiths of Radnorshire and that she had married Peter Smart about 1720.

The first child of this couple was Christopher, who was born prematurely on the eleventh of April, 1722, and was baptized in the parish church at Shipbourne one month later. From birth his constitution was delicate, and it is natural that, being denied participation in many of the activities of childhood, he should have exhibited a certain precociousness in mental growth. Mrs. LeNoir, the poet's daughter, tells an amusing story of his lisping in numbers ". . . when about the same age as Dr. S. Johnson (4 years old) when he was inspired by the lame duck. The occasion was somewhat more serious. The young rhymester was very fond of a lady of about three times his own age who used to notice and caress him. A gentleman old enough to be her father to teaze the child would pretend to be in love with his favorite and threatened to take her for his wife—'You are too old,' said little Smart; the rival answered, if that was an objection he would send his son; he answered in verse as follows, addressing the lady.

> Madam if you please
> To hear such things as these.
> Madam, I have a rival sad
> And if you don't take my part it will make me mad;
> He says he will send his son;
> But if he does I will get me a gun.
> Madam if you please to pity,
> O poor Kitty, O poor Kitty!"[3]

There are several things about the childhood of Christopher Smart which seem to have significance in the light of later events. The premature birth and resultant constitutional weakness are of prime importance, not only in the light they throw on his later breakdown but also in the way his ill health conditioned the ex-

[2] "Account of the Life and Writings of Smart" prefixed to *The Poems of the Late Christopher Smart*, Reading, 1791.

[3] Letter to Edmund Henry Barker in MS. volume of *E. H. Barker's Correspondence*, vol. 3, 1832-1838, fol. 245 ff., in the Bodleian Library.

periences of his early years. Many of his hours were spent in solitary ramblings in the Kentish fields and along the banks of the Medway. The intimate association with nature which he had in his childhood offers certainly the simplest and most natural explanation for the brilliant clarity of observation that makes his greater work so startlingly beautiful.

A much less fortunate result of illness was the cultivation of a taste for strong drink. Hunter, in commenting on Smart's character, remarks that "his chief fault, from which most of his other faults proceeded, was his deviations from the rules of sobriety; of which the early use of cordials in the infirm state of his childhood and his youth, might perhaps be one cause."

Another fact about his early years which seems to have considerable importance is the preponderance of feminine company which he had. He was an only son, but he was soon joined by two sisters, Margaret and Marianne, who must have been his principal companions. From all we can gather, these two girls were the sort who lead their older brothers by the nose. There is a lively picture of Marianne, the younger, in *The Hop Garden*:

> . . . Oft her command
> Has sav'd the pillars of the hop-land state,
> The lofty poles, from ruin, and sustain'd,
> Like Anna, or Eliza, her domain,
> With more than manly dignity. Oft I've seen,
> Ev'n at her frown the boist'rous uproar cease,
> And the mad pickers, tam'd to diligence,
> Cull from the bin the sprawling sprigs, and leaves
> That stain the sample, and its worth debase.
>
> Bk. ii, 91 ff.

Of Margaret only one event of her girlhood is recorded, an incident which occurred after the three children had been sent to Raby Castle, Durham, and she had apparently got on the nerves of young Henry Vane. Mrs. LeNoir gives the story: "The young Lord a little superior in years was not so in understanding; he had been so often twitted with the quicker progress in learning of Peggy Smart that he once made a desperate attempt at putting an end to it in a huge water tub that was in the stable yard. Her cries brought the servants to her assistance or it is probable that she would never have eclipsed him again."[4] One wonders whether her brother had ever felt the impulse to put an end to her in the Medway.

At any rate, the feminine influence in Smart's early life is significant. He was fondled and petted by girls, and he responded with a love poem at the age of four. When he was thirteen he was writing erotic verses to another young charmer, and was even caught in the act of eloping with her. (See below, p. 9.) If there is any truth in the theory of psychological conditioning, the events of his later life can only cause us to wonder that they were not more erratic than they were.

Finally, the economic condition of the Smart family during their son's early years may explain something of his improvident nature. Peter Smart was not a wealthy man, but his employment at Fairlawn evidently brought him a very comfortable income, for in 1726 he purchased from Richard Webb, gent., the mansion of Hall-Place in the parish of East Barming.[5] The interest in this estate was worth about three hundred pounds a year, according to Hunter, which in the monetary values of that time was a considerable fortune. Furthermore, when Peter Smart died in 1733, the eleven-year-old Christopher was sent with his two sisters to Raby Castle near Durham where they were taken under the protection of the Vane family. During the years he remained there (1733-1739), he met the Duchess of Cleveland, mother-in-law of the third Baron Barnard,[6] and made such an impression on her that she allowed him an annuity of forty pounds a year, which was continued after her death in 1742 by her husband. There was no real financial crisis in the Smart family, from all we can learn, until 1746, when Smart was a man of twenty-four, a fellow of the university of Cambridge, and had already begun to make a name for himself in the literary world. It would seem that during all the

---

[4] Elizabeth LeNoir, *loc.cit.*

[5] Abbott, p. 2, citing Halsted's *History of Kent*, ii, 150. "Abbott," here and hereafter, refers to an unpublished thesis on Smart by Mr. C. D. Abbott, who has very kindly allowed me to make use of it.

[6] The duchess was born Henrietta Finch, daughter to the 6th Earl of Winchilsea, who had succeeded to that title on the death of the 5th Earl, the husband of the charming Lady Anne. It is pleasant to note this faint connection between the fair Ardelia and young Mr. Smart.

years when a boy might learn something of managing financial affairs, the future poet was under the care of indulgent people of means; perhaps the desultory habits of his later life need no further explanation.

Not very much actual detail is known concerning the first seventeen years of Christopher Smart's life. Christopher Hunter supplies a few names and dates, and Mrs. LeNoir a few intimate and revealing anecdotes. While the children were in Kent with their parents the boy received the elements of his formal education in the school at Maidstone. His training was continued in Durham school under the tutelage of the Rev. Mr. Dongworth. Here he began to develop the great interest in classical literature which bore such excellent fruit in later life. Here, too, he began to attract attention with his Latin and English verses. Hunter hints that other students relied on his superior abilities when they were forced to versify, and one who knows students can have no doubt they did. Not many of his early efforts have survived, but those which have demonstrate the boy's talent.[7] The verses "To Ethelinda," written when he was thirteen, are clearly the work of a boy who has practiced versification considerably.

These verses "To Ethelinda" recall the most exciting episode of Smart's boyhood. Mrs. LeNoir tells it in delightfully ungrammatical fashion: "The young ladies of the family [the Vane family] were not all so cruel [as Henry Vane had been to Peggy Smart]; one of them, the Lady Anne who is the person addressed under the name of Ethelinda when the poet was no more than [twelve *canceled*] thirteen years old and the lady still younger, [and *canceled*] this very spirited ode had taken such effect that these young lovers had actually set off on a runaway match together; they were however timely prevented and saved as oppor-

[7] Since Smart had the habit of printing pieces which had been written years before their publication, it is impossible to date the composition of many of his early verses. "To Ethelinda" is dated by him, "written at thirteen"; "Fanny Blooming Fair, Translated into Latin" is signed "C. S. *Aetat.*, 16" (*Gentleman's Magazine*, April 1754, p. 185). In the *Universal Visiter* (no. 1, p. 42, January 1756) Smart printed some Latin verses entitled "Arion. By a Boy of Fourteen." The "Epigram by Sir Thomas More, translated" ("The Long-Nosed Fair") was first printed in the *Midwife* (ii, 259) and was there attributed to "Master Christopher Midnight, my great-grandson," which would suggest that it is a survival from Smart's school days.

tunely from sinister accident as Peggy Smart had been from drowning."[8]

The Lady Anne quickly outgrew this childhood romance. She was twice married, first to the Hon. Charles Hope-Weir and, when that union ended in divorce, to George Monson. With her second husband she went to India, where she was an ornament of English social life until her death in 1776. Smart, however, never forgot her; during the troubled years of his illness her image flitted again and again across his memory, and in *Rejoice in the Lamb* he faithfully recorded these visitations:

"God be gracious to Anne Hope" (xvii, 22)
"God be gracious to the house of Vane, especially Anne"
    (xxii, 24)
"Let Constant, house of Constant, rejoice with the Musk-goat.
I bless God for two visions of Anne Hope's being in Charity
    with me." (xxx, 25)
"For I saw a blush in Staindrop Church, which was of God's
    own colouring.
"For it was the benevolence of a virgin shewn to me before
    the whole congregation" (xix, 22-23).

From the number of references to her in Smart's strange manuscript, it seems that Anne Vane remained more constantly in his thoughts than any other woman.

After the attempted elopement, nothing further is recorded of Smart until in his seventeenth year he matriculated at Pembroke Hall, Cambridge (Oct. 10, 1739). This was to be his home for the next ten years of his life, and he was finally to emerge from it not as a young graduate but as a mature man with several years' experience as teacher and amateur writer. Toward the end of the period, it is true, he got himself into rather serious trouble, but on the whole his Cambridge career was a very successful one.

His ability in the composition of Latin verses was the means by which he first began to attract the attention of the academic world he had entered. Within his first year at college he was selected to write the Tripos Verses, an honor which was repeated in 1741 and again in 1742.[9] That the college valued his academic

[8] LeNoir, *loc.cit.*
[9] These compositions were highly regarded at the time. Francis Fawkes of Jesus

work quite as highly as his literary accomplishments is evidenced
by his receiving in 1742 the title "Scholar of the University" with a
stipend of £20, an honor for which he competed with the entire
university and which was rarely given to a student still in his third
year. In the following year he published his Latin version of Pope's
"Ode on St. Cecilia's Day." This piece attracted the attention of
William Murray, later the Earl of Mansfield, who was a friend
of Pope's. At Murray's suggestion, Smart wrote to Pope proposing
to translate the *Essay on Man*. The great poet answered with a
charming note in which he suggested that Smart try the *Essay on
Criticism* instead, and this advice the young man hastened to follow.[10] The translation was not published, however, until 1752.

College translated them into English, and the curious will find both the originals
and the translations in his *Original Poems and Translations* (1761), as well as in
Smart's *Poems on Several Occasions* (1752) and in Hunter's edition. Further evidence of Smart's ability in Latin verse may be found in the "Part of the First Canto
of Hudibras translated into Latin Doggerel by a Freshman of Pembroke College,
Christopher Smart," a MS. in the Pembroke College Library (excerpts printed in
the *Museum*, ii, 21-22; *Midwife*, ii, 35; *Student*, i, 358, and ii, 39). More important
are the translations of Milton's "L'Allegro" and of Pope's "Ode on St. Cecilia's
Day" and the "Essay on Criticism." According to McKenzie, *op.cit.*, there is in the
British Museum a MS. of an "Ode on St. David's Day, 1753" in Latin.

    [10] Smart's letter is printed in *The Life of William, late Earl of Mansfield*, by John
Holliday (London, 1797), p. 25. Since it has never been noticed by writers on
Smart, I give it here:

Pem. Hall, Cambridge, the 6th of Nov. 1743

Sir,
Mr. Murray having told me that it would, he thought, be agreeable to you to see
a good Latin version of your Essay on Man, and advised me to undertake it,
though I know myself vastly unfit for such a task, I will attempt to render any
number of lines that you shall be pleased to select from any part of the work, and
as you approve, or dislike them, will pursue or drop the undertaking.
    I am, Sir, with the utmost respect, yours,

C. Smart.

To Alexander Pope, Esq.
I should not have presumed to have given you this trouble had not Mr. Murray
assured me that I might safely venture. I have made bold likewise to send you a
specimen of a translation of your Essay on Criticism, verse the 339th.

Smart enclosed for Pope's approval some forty or fifty lines of the translated *Essay*,
and also, apparently, sent the Latin version of the "Ode on St. Cecilia's Day."
Pope's answer is printed by Hunter, although it is not included in the Elwin-
Courthope edition of Pope's works:

Twickenham, Nov. 18th.

Sir,
I thank you for the favour of yours; I would not give you the trouble of translating the whole Essay you mention; the two first Epistles are already well done,

During the Christmas season of 1743 Pembroke College celebrated the four hundredth anniversary of its founding, and young
Mr. Smart wrote a rather pompous "Secular Ode" on the occasion, his first attempt at one of the longer forms in English.[11]
Finally, a few weeks later, Smart received his B.A. degree (January, 1744), another event which he celebrated with a charming
little ode (see p. 76). With the attainment of his degree, the first
period of his residence at Cambridge comes to a close.

Exactly what happened to him during the next year and a half
is not clear. He was absent from his college several times, and it
is possible that he may have been already thinking of a literary
life in London and on some of these occasions may have visited
the metropolis. However, from the college library records (printed
by McKenzie, *op.cit.*) it is evident that he was doing a formidable
amount of reading. He read everything—poetry, theology, classics,
scientific treatises, "natural philosophy"—and stored away in his
remarkable memory a prodigious collection of facts and fancies.
It was this fund of knowledge, constantly supplemented during

and, if you try, I could wish it were on the last, which is less abstracted, and
more easily falls into poetry and common place. A few lines at the beginning and
the conclusion, will be sufficient for a trial whether you yourself can like the
task or not. I believe the Essay on Criticism will in general be the more agreeable, both to a young writer, and to the majority of readers. What made me wish
the other well done, was the want of a right understanding of the subject, which
appears in the foreign versions, in two Italian, two French, and one German.
There is one indeed in Latin verse printed at Wirtemberg, very faithful, but in-
elegant; and another in French prose; but in these the spirit of Poetry is as much
lost, as the sense and system itself in the others. I ought to take this opportunity
of acknowledging the Latin Translation of my Ode, which you sent me, and in
which I could see little or nothing to alter, it is so exact. Believe me, Sir, equally
desirous of doing you any service, and afraid of engaging you in an art so little
profitable, tho' so well deserving, as good poetry.

I am,

Your most obliged

and sincere humble servant,

A. Pope.

Smart quite naturally treasured this graceful compliment from England's most distinguished poet. In the portrait of himself that is said to be by Reynolds, the letter
is prominently displayed on the writing table at which he sits.

[11] For an interesting discussion of this celebration, see Leonard Whibley, "The
Jubilee at Pembroke Hall in 1743," *Blackwood's Magazine*, January, 1927. The
"Secular Ode" was apparently not printed until 1756, when Smart used it to eke
out his contributions to *The Universal Visiter*. The Cambridge University Press
reprinted it in 1927.

the succeeding years at Cambridge, that he drew upon in his work as a teacher; and, much more surprisingly, it was a thousand glittering fragments from his vast reading that came back to haunt his sick mind when he was under confinement. *Rejoice in the Lamb* (see below, p. 41.) is dotted with completely accurate references to a host of books he had not seen for over fifteen years.

The first tangible result of all this study was his appointment on July 3, 1745, as a Fellow of Pembroke Hall. Three months later, the college made him Praelector in Philosophy. He was also elected Keeper of the Common Chest, that is to say treasurer, an office which brought him a small additional income. The following year, both these appointments were renewed, together with the additional one of Praelector in Rhetoric. He was evidently settling down to the making of a successful academic career.

But in the meantime, other events were transpiring. Up to this time, his few publications had been poems in Latin, of which the most important was the translation of Pope's "Ode on St. Cecilia's Day." In the summer of 1746, however, when a second edition of this translation was published, Smart appended to it his own "Ode for Music on St. Cecilia's Day." This was apparently his first publication in English, and almost immediately it received a valuable bit of attention. Robert Dodsley had recently begun the publication of his magazine, *The Museum, or Literary and Historical Register*, and here, as soon as the poem was out, appeared "Warlike Music and Church Music. The two last stanzas from Mr. Smart's Ode on St. Cecilia's Day." This was the first appearance of any of Smart's verse in a magazine, and apparently his first recognition outside the university.

He must have felt that his career as a poet had begun. He immediately followed up his advantage, and the issue of the *Museum* for September contained two more of his poems. One was "Six lines extempore from *Hudibras*," some Latin doggerel which, according to a MS. in the Pembroke College Library, he had written when he was a freshman. Of much greater interest is the other, "On Seeing Miss H[arriet] P[rat]t in an Apothecary's Shop" for it is the earliest in print of some dozen poems that tell us nearly all we know about the lady for whom, as Hunter relates, Smart "entertained a long and unsuccessful passion."

Jermyn Pratt, of Downham in Norfolk, was at Caius College

from 1741 to 1746, and at any time during that period he may have introduced his friend Smart to his sister. The dates of the poems, however, make it seem likely that Smart did not become seriously interested until 1746. It was in this year, incidentally, that Smart's childhood sweetheart, Anne Vane, was married to the Hon. Charles Hope-Weir, thus effectively putting an end to any hopes he may have had of marrying into her exalted station. He never forgot Anne Vane, but it seems clear that from 1746, at least, his amorous attentions were for five or six years centered on Miss Pratt.

How much of the charm attributed to her in the poems must be discounted as the stuff of romance is an open question, but altogether there emerges the picture of a gracious and attractive young woman endowed with a lively wit. She and Smart apparently had much in common: if one can believe the poems, they read Sidney's *Arcadia* together, they strolled in the woods, they fished, and they danced; he sent her music, and what he seems to have found most attractive was her voice.

> You of the music common weal
> Who borrow, beg, compose, or steal
>   Cantata, air, or ariet,
> You'd burn your cumb'rous works in score,
> And sing, compose, and play no more
>   If once you heard my Harriet.

Smart wrote a poem on her birthday ("Ode on the Fifth of December"); he made a "crambo song" on "Lovely Harriote";[12] he wrote her an ode, "Lady Harriot,"[13] which no less a composer than Dr. William Boyce set to music years later. I have found in the *Gentleman's Magazine*, among several other pieces which, though clearly Smart's, had not previously been attributed to him, a poem called "To Miss H—— . . . with some Musick, written by a poet outragiously in love." Here her accomplishments as a vocalist and as a performer on some keyboard instrument, probably a harpsichord, are praised. It seems likely that their mutual love of music formed the strongest bond between them.

[12] The British Museum Catalogue of Printed Music lists this as a song, but without the name of a composer.

[13] Printed in the *Gentleman's Magazine*, April, 1755.

What happened to separate this obviously congenial pair, or when their romance came to an end, we have no way of knowing. When he collected his early poems in 1752, Smart included a ballad called "The Lass with the Golden Locks," the most charming of his poems to Anna Maria Carnan, whom he married. It begins

> No more of my Harriot, of Polly no more,
> Nor all the bright beauties that charmed me before.

With these words, he bade farewell to the accomplished Miss Pratt. She drifted across his memory again when he was in the midst of his afflictions, but among the hundreds of people who haunted his mind she seems but a faint ghost, remembered for a moment with kindness as the sister of a college friend. He did not dream of her as he dreamed of Anne Vane; he did not think of her as often as he thought of the unknown Polly; and he did not pray for her as he dutifully prayed for his wife. Yet of all the women to whom Smart was at one time or another attracted, Harriet Pratt seems the one with whom he might have had the happiest life. Certainly, to judge from the poems, she was the most charming.

It was probably to Harriet Pratt that Smart sent the delightful ode in which "The Author Apoligizes to the Lady for his being a little man" (*q.v.*). The amusing description of his appearance given there is supplemented by a contemporary reference to him as "a little, smart, black-eyed man . . . abnormally nervous and retiring, but when his shyness was overcome particularly amiable,"[14] and by the recently discovered portrait of the poet in cap and gown.

Sometime in 1746 occurred another event which was to have serious consequences for Christopher Smart. Hunter suggests that from the beginning of his career at Cambridge the poet had rather limited funds at his disposal. He writes: "His allowance from home was scanty; for as his father had died suddenly, and in embarrassed circumstances, his mother had been compelled to sell the largest part of the family estate at considerable loss." Hunter is, however, usually quite vague about dates, and the evi-

14 Quoted by Whibley, *loc.cit.*

dence indicates that up to 1746 Smart never felt any serious lack of funds. After all, he had his annuity from the Duchess of Cleveland, his scholarship, and later his salaries from his college posts. This may quite well have been supplemented by money from his father's estate, for it was not until 1746 that Mrs. Smart and the children sold their interest in the Kent property to one John Cale, Esq.[15] This sale may have cut off a part of his income, for despite the fact that he had still over £140 a year, Smart was soon in financial difficulties.

In the spring of 1747, the word got abroad that he was considerably in debt, and his colleagues and friends began to be worried about it. Gray, who can hardly be called a friend but who was sufficiently interested in any sort of college gossip to take note of this affair, gives the first definite record of the young poet's financial difficulties, in a letter to Wharton conjecturally dated March 17, 1747: "as to Sm:, he must necessarily be abîmé, in a very short Time. his Debts daily increase (you remember the State they were in, when you left us) Addison, I know, wrote smartly to him last Week; but it has had no Effect, that signifies. only I observe he takes Hartshorn from Morning to Night lately."[16] The cause of Smart's mounting indebtedness was simply extravagance, and it must have been going on for some little time before it became a matter for public concern. Dr. Charles Burney, the music historian who was a real friend to Smart during the later years of his life, wrote, long after the poet's death: "While he was the pride of Cambridge, and the chief poetical ornament of that university, he ruined himself by returning the tavern-treats of strangers, who had invited him as a wit, and an extraordinary personage, in order to boast of his acquaintance. This social spirit of retaliation, involving him in debt with vintners and college cooks, oc-

[15] Abbott cites Halsted's *History of Kent*, ii, 150, as authority for the date of this transaction.

[16] *Correspondence of Thomas Gray*, ed. Toynbee and Whibley, Oxford, 1935, letter No. 135, i, 272 ff. Gray and Smart were an ill-assorted pair, temperamentally unsuited for friendship, yet each apparently recognizing something of the other's ability. Smart could and did praise the poetry of "our great Augustan," but his uncontrollable sense of humor prompted him to remark of the man himself, "Gray walks as if he had fouled his small clothes, and looks as if he smelt it." When such a jest got back to him, as it must surely have done sooner or later, it could hardly amuse a man of Gray's temperament. It may account for the rather acid tone of his comments about Smart.

casioned his fellowship to be sequestered, obliged him to quit the university, and crippled him for the rest of his life."[17]

The dire results which Burney mentions did not happen immediately, however. During the spring of 1747 Smart seems to have been extraordinarily busy, and when one considers his activities there seems little doubt that he was trying to pull himself out of the hole. His M.A. was conferred, and he continued with his usual teaching assignments. But Gray's mention of hartshorn indicates that overwork was telling on his nerves. In addition to his academic work, he was trying feverishly to make some money from his writing, as may be seen from the continuation of Gray's letter quoted above: "in the meantime he is amuseing himself with a Comedy of his own Writeing, wch he makes all the Boys of his Acquaintance act, & intends to borrow the Zodiack Room, & have it performed publickly. our Friend Lawman, the mad Attorney, is his Copyist; & truly the Author himself is to the full as mad as he. his Piece (he says) is inimitable, true Sterling Wit, & Humour by God; and he can't hear the Prologue without being ready to die with Laughter. He acts five Parts himself, & is only sorry, he can't do all the rest. he has also advertised a Collection of Odes; & for his Vanity & Faculty of Lyeing, they are come to their full Maturity. all this, you see, must come to a Jayl, or Bedlam, & that without any help, almost without Pity."

The play was called *A Trip to Cambridge, or The Grateful Fair*, and although only two fragments from it have survived, the summary of the plot given in Hunter's Introduction indicates that it was sprightly and amusing. The modern reader may not be "ready to die with laughter" over the Prologue, but he can understand Smart's pride in having written it. The play was given a performance in April, with the author, despite Gray's malicious comments, appearing in only one role. It may be worth noting that at least two other members of the cast (Randall and Stonhewer) remained Smart's friends, and were active in his behalf in the later days of his illness and poverty.

Thus Smart seems to have staved off his creditors during the spring term, but when he returned to Cambridge in October after the long vacation the blow fell. The fellows refused to reappoint

[17] *Monthly Review* (Jan. 1792), ser. 2, vii, 36-43. In Griffiths' copy this article is signed "Dr. B———y."

him to any of his offices, and the creditors descended to grab him up. Gray writes to Wharton on November 30: "your Mention of Mr Vane, reminds me of poor Smart (not that I, or any other Mortal, pity him) about three Weeks ago he was arrested here at the Suit of a Taylor in London for a Debt of about 50 £ of three Years standing. [One wonders if this was Banks, from whom Smart had commissioned his Bachellor's cap and gown. See "On Taking a Bachellor's Degree." £50 would account for a great deal of finery.] the College had about 28 £ due to him in their Hands, the rest (to hinder him from going to the Castle, for he could not raise a Shilling) Brown, May, & Peele, lent him upon his Note. upon this he remain'd confined to his Room, lest his Creditors here should snap him; & the Fellows went round to make out a List of his Debts, wch amount in Cambridge to above 350 £. that they might come the readier to some Composition, he was advised to go off in the Night, & lie hid somewhere or other. he has done so, & this has made the Creditors agree to an assignment of 50 £ per ann: out of his Income, wch is above 140 £, if he lives at Cambridge (not else). but I am apprehensive, if this come to the Ears of Mr Vane he may take away the 40 £ hitherto allowed him by the Duke of Cleveland; for before all this (last Summer) I know they talk'd of doing so, as Mr Smart (they said) was settled in the World. if you found an Opportunity, possibly you might hinder this (wch would totally ruin him now) by representing his Absurdity in the best Light it will bear: but at the same time they should make this a Condition of its Continuance; that he live in the College, soberly, & within Bounds, for that upon any Information to the Contrary it shall be absolutely stop'd. this would be doing him a real Service, tho' against the Grain: yet I must own, if you heard all his Lies, Impertinence, & Ingratitude in this Affair, it would perhaps quite set you against him, as it has his only Friend (Mr Addison) totally. & yet one would try to save him, for Drunkenness is one great Source of all this, & he may change it."[18]

The college records show that Smart was "absent" from November 13 to December 31. Where he was we do not know, but it is possible that he went to London and began to consider the

[18] Toynbee & Whibley, *op.cit.*, letter 143.

possibility of abandoning his academic career and setting up as a professional writer. This conjecture is suggested by the fact that in January, 1748, he made his first appearance in the *London Magazine* when his poem "Idleness" was printed with a pretty musical setting by the great Dr. William Boyce.[19] Furthermore, he may have gone to see Dodsley about the "Collection of Odes" which Gray had mentioned, for on January 7 he wrote to Dodsley:

"Sir, I beg the favour you'll advertise my Proposals six or seven Times in the papers you think best and make the following addition viz: There will be [no] more copies printed, than what are subscribed for, and if there shou'd ever be occasion for a second impression nothing will be abated the original price. Yrs. etc.

C. Smart

Please to advertise immediately on the receipt of this."[20]

This letter is dated from Pembroke Hall. Although we have no information concerning Smart's activities for the rest of the academic year, the likeliest assumption is that he remained in the college "soberly and within bounds," and made a sincere attempt to get back into the good graces of the Fellows. He succeeded admirably, for on October 10, 1748, he was reappointed to all his former offices, including that of Keeper of the Common Chest, and was given an extra job as a catechist. He moved into cheaper rooms and remained at his work through the academic year, that is, until June 8, 1749.

From these facts it becomes clear that Burney was mistaken when he said that Smart's debts "occasioned his fellowship to be sequestered" and "obliged him to quit the university." If he had been forced to leave for this reason he would have done so in the autumn of 1747. When he finally left almost two years later he may still have had debts, but he certainly had as well the respect and friendship of the Fellows. This is evident from the treatment accorded him by the college after his withdrawal: they allowed him to remain a Fellow, continued to pay the dividend on his fellowship, and for three years gave him a sum in addition "in

[19] In 1749, Boyce made a setting for Mason's ode on the installation of the Duke of Newcastle as Chancellor of the University, which was performed on July 1st.
[20] Quoted by Sir Edmund Gosse, *TLS*, May 27, 1926, p. 355.

lieu of the Commons" (that is, the equivalent of his board in the college). It was not until 1753, when he had been married over a year, that the dividend was finally withheld, and even then it was voted that Smart should be allowed to keep his name on the books free of charge so long as he should continue to write for the Seaton prize. It is perfectly evident that he was regarded, despite Gray's remarks, as the "pride of Cambridge and the chief poetical ornament of that university."

Nevertheless, he must, in the two years of his "penance," have grown tired of what seemed the narrow restrictions of his life. He had discovered that he wanted to be a poet, not a teacher, and he had probably also discovered some of the charms of London. When he finally left Cambridge for good in the summer of 1749 he went straight to the city, as so many have done before and since, to begin the difficult and exciting struggle of the literary life.

How he fared during the first year in London we do not know, but if we are to judge by the scope of his acquaintance later on we must conclude that he had no difficulty in establishing contacts with people of position and influence. He would of course call upon Dodsley, but the *Museum* had ceased publication and there is no record of any relations between the poet and the publisher until many years later. A far more likely medium for Smart's introduction into the artistic and literary circles of mid-century London is the composer, Boyce. This would account for the fact that by June, 1750, Smart was having pieces of his produced at Vauxhall Gardens. They were set to music by Dr. Thomas Arne, the friend and fellow-composer of Boyce, who presided over much of the musical entertainment at Vauxhall.

The friends Smart made at Vauxhall remained friends through all the difficult years of his later life. They were an interesting group, whose diverse talents were united by their common desire to make money out of entertaining the public. The famous park was owned and managed by Jonathan Tyers, who had opened the gardens in 1732 and by 1750 had developed it into the most popular "resort" of the city. His eldest son, Thomas, was first introduced to Johnson, whose friend and biographer he was to become, by Christopher Smart (see below, p. 25(. The chief attractions of the gardens were the music, and the paintings and statuary with which the various buildings were adorned. Through his ability to write lyrics for the performance Smart was brought into contact not only with Dr. Arne and his talented family, but also with such lesser composers as Worgan and Arnold, and with singers like Lowe who performed some of his works. He formed a lasting friendship with Richard Rolt, a hack writer who is said to have "composed more than a hundred cantatas, songs, and other pieces, for Vauxhall, Sadler's Wells, and the theatres" (*D.N.B.*), and with whom Smart was later engaged in several enterprises. It may well have been through his connections at Vauxhall that he became acquainted with Roubilliac, the sculptor, whose statue of Handel was one of the features of the gardens, and with Francis Hayman and William Hogarth, both of whom contributed to the pictorial decorations.

It was probably through Arne, also, that Smart met Dr. Charles Burney, Arne's former pupil and a well-known organist and composer who was to acquire fame later on with his brilliant history of music. According to the tradition, Burney is the man who introduced the young poet to John Newbery, with whose fortunes Smart's were to be entangled for many strange and unhappy years. Since Newbery plays such an important role in the drama of Smart's life in London, some account of his character and activities will make more clear the events that followed upon their meeting.

The story of Newbery's rise to "fame and fortune" is the typical success story of a businessman in the early period of capitalist expansion. He was the son of a small farmer, but he early went to work for William Carnan, the proprietor of the Reading *Mercury*, one of the first of the provincial newspapers. When Carnan died, leaving a widow and three small children, Newbery succeeded to the management of the business as co-legatee under Carnan's will. After a decent interval, he acquired the business outright by the simple expedient of marrying Mrs. Carnan. To the business of printer he added a variety of other "lines," becoming a kind of general merchant dealing in virtually anything out of which he could make a profit, but especially such patent medicines as Dr. Hooper's Female Pills. So briskly did he flourish that by 1744 he was able to move to London, where he established himself in the odd double capacity of bookseller and dealer in

patent medicines, retaining the *Mercury* as an additional source
of income. His most profitable ware, however, was Dr. James'
Fever Powders, one of the most famous of eighteenth-century
panaceas; the other undertaking for which he is chiefly remembered today was the remarkable series of children's books he later
published. His personal character fitted in well with his occupa-
tion: Austin Dobson, in one of his charming *Eighteenth-Century
Vignettes*, describes him as "a bustling, multifarious, and not un-
kindly personage, essentially commercial, essentially enterprising,
rigorously exacting his money's worth of work, keeping prudent
record of all casual cash advances, but, on the whole, not unbenefi-
cent in his business fashion to the needy brethren of the pen by
whom he was surrounded." The irony of such phrases as the last
will be worth remembering in the investigation of his relations
with Christopher Smart.

The thing that made Newbery see the possibilities in Smart's
pen was probably the poem *On the Eternity of the Supreme Being*. Under the will of one Thomas Seaton there was offered at
Cambridge in the spring of 1750 a prize for a poem on some attribute of the Supreme Being (see Notes, p. 269). Smart's interest
in religious poetry and his need of money prompted him to enter
the competition, and on March 25 he received the prize. This
award brought him about £30, and considerable attention from
the literary world. In the next five years, he won the Seaton prize
four more times, and with these poems he began to achieve a
reputation.

When the *Eternity* was published at Cambridge in April, the
little pamphlet contained a set of proposals for printing a collection of Smart's poems by subscription. Newbery, who finally published the collection two years later, is not mentioned in this announcement, but his interest in Smart's potentialities must have
been attracted soon after, for by June he was launching Smart
as one of his authors.

In January, Newbery had begun to handle the London end of
an enterprise called *The Student, or the Oxford Monthly Miscel-
lany*, to which Bonnell Thornton and George Colman seem to
have been the principal contributors. With the issue of June 30,
1750, "Oxford" in the subtitle was changed to "Oxford and Cambridge," and Christopher Smart's contributions began to appear;

he contributed heavily to its pages from that date until it ceased publication in July, 1751.

Smart's regular feature in the magazine was a long humorous essay, printed serially under the title "Introduction to a New System of Castle-Building," and signed by "Chimaericus Cantabrigiensis." Each issue also included several of his poems. Some of them he signed with his own name, but lest the venture should seem a closed corporation he invented a variety of whimsical pseudonyms. "Ebeneazer Pentweazle, an old gentleman of Truro in the county of Cornwall," "Miss Nellie Pentweazle, a young lady of fifteen years," "Mr. Lun," "Zosimus Zephyr," and several completely anonymous persons all submitted Smart's compositions at one time or another.

In the same month that Smart started writing for the *Student*, Newbery published *The Horatian Canons of Friendship*, an imitation of Horace's Satire III, Book I, signed by Ebeneazer Pentweazle. This rather mild, generalized satire, embellished with the moralizing commonplaces of the day, must have seemed to Newbery an auspicious piece with which to launch his new poet. It was a pleasant and inoffensive poem with the right admixture of "wit" and proper sentiments. It contained several graceful compliments, and the satiric portraits were so generalized and so concealed under the usual eighteenth-century disguises as to be rendered harmless. I doubt that Newbery was pleased when he was informed that "sordid interest" was "the mother of our customs and our laws," but youthful poets making such discoveries can always be smilingly dismissed as "impractical idealists." However that may be, both he and Smart must have sent forth their first joint effort with high hopes.

Unfortunately, so far as we know, the poem attracted little attention. I have found no reviews of it; and Smart himself, although he printed an extract from it in *The Midwife* a year after its publication (ii, 169, July 1751), did not include it in the handsome volume of 1752 where most of his early work was collected. Nevertheless it is not destitute of interest. It is the only poem of its kind that Smart ever wrote, and displays him therefore in a rather unusual light. Such work was not native to his genius, and the poem has none of the fire and brilliance of his mature productions. But its smoothness and ease give proof of his talent for versification. Heroic couplets are rarely used by Smart (this and "The Hilliad" are the only poems of any length in that form), and it is interesting that his model seems to have been Dryden rather than Pope.

With his contributions to *The Student*, Smart became established as one of Newbery's hacks. There is some evidence to indicate that he was put to work upon such undertakings as *The History of Jack the Giant-Killer* by nine-year-old "Master Billy Pentweazle";[21] when Newbery's character is considered one can be sure the poet was not allowed to idle away his time writing religious lyrics.

Soon the publisher and the poet embarked on a more lucrative venture: a magazine which they initiated on October 16, 1750. It was called *The Midwife, or the Old Woman's Magazine*, and was designed to contain (according to the flamboyant title-page) "all the Wit, and all the Humour, and all the Learning, and all the Judgement, that has ever been or ever will be inserted in all the other Magazines, or the Magazine of Magazines, or the Grand Magazine of Magazines, or any other Book whatsoever; so that those who buy this Book will need no other." Smart, who is usually credited with being the editor and principal contributor, now had his hands full. His pseudonymous friends again came to his aid, and were joined by such droll assistants as "Quinbus Flestrin, the unborn poet."

Walter Graham has said of *The Midwife* that it "should entitle Smart to a place in the front rank of humorists of his century" (*A Survey of English Periodicals*), and this praise is not too high. The delightful nonsense of many of its pages and the caustic wit of others provide ample evidence for the contemporary opinion of Smart as a wit and a lively companion. The magazine was popular, and deservedly so; it appeared fairly regularly until May or June of 1752, and there was a final issue in the spring of 1753.

From *The Midwife* comes further evidence of the expanding

---

[21] *The Horatian Canons* had been signed by "Ebeneazer Pentweazle," and Smart used this pseudonym, "Nelly Pentweazle," and others similar in both *The Student* and *The Midwife*. For a fuller discussion of this point see the excellent article by Roland B. Botting, "Christopher Smart in London," *Research Studies of the State College of Washington*, vii, 9.

circle of Smart's acquaintanceship. From its first issue the magazine included each month a paper selected from *The Rambler*, with a discreet advertisement of the paper Johnson had begun in the previous March tucked into a footnote. There are also in *The Midwife* frequent complimentary references to Fielding and to Garrick, couched in such language as to suggest that "Mrs. Midnight" was on a footing of friendliness with those distinguished men. Smart must have been an attractive personality to win the attention and regard of such a variety of people as those whom we know to have been his friends at various periods of his life. Thomas Tyers, in his "Biographical Sketch of Dr. Samuel Johnson" (*Gentleman's Magazine*, 1785) has given us a pleasant glimpse of the poet in the early days in London: "Christopher Smart was *at first* (the italics are mine) well received by Johnson. This writer owed his first acquaintance with our author, which lasted thirty years, to the introduction of that bard. . . . Johnson had been much indisposed all that day, and repeated a Psalm he had just translated, during his affliction, into verse, and did not commit to paper. . . . Smart, in return recited some of his own Latin compositions. . . . Poet Smart used to relate, 'that the first conversation with him [Johnson] was of such variety and length, that it began with poetry, and ended at fluxions.'" As long as Smart remained well and financially successful, Johnson apparently continued to enjoy such conversations with him.

Another person of quite a different character who is mentioned in the *Midwife* was William Kenrick, a hack writer who had long disliked Fielding and who now began to attack Smart, for what reason we do not know. In the magazine for December Mrs. Midnight announced that Kenrick would receive his due in an "Old Woman's Dunciad" which she would shortly publish. Before this promised work could appear, however, Kenrick himself published a satire under the same name and purporting to be the piece itself. In it Smart was the object of the jokes, together with Rolt and others who had contributed to the *Midwife* and the *Student*. Smart, having been worsted, withdrew from the field, and through the following year (1751) pursued his various enterprises unmolested by literary warfare.[22]

[22] For a full account of this "war," see Botting, *loc.cit.*, and Ainsworth & Noyes, *op.cit.*, pp. 43 ff. It seems to me quite probable that this affair was not a real literary

His work on the two magazines and on any other odd jobs Newbery found for him to do kept him busy during the spring of 1751, but he found time for various other writing as well. In March he wrote a prologue and an epilogue for a performance of *Othello* given by some young people of fashion,[23] and when these poems were printed they went into three editions within four months. Frederick, Prince of Wales, died on March 20, and Smart immediately wrote a *Solemn Dirge* on the occasion which was performed by a group of singers at Vauxhall, one of the favorite haunts of the prince, to music by Worgan. Newbery also printed three editions of the text. The most important accomplishment of that spring, from a literary point of view, was his receipt on April 20 of the second of his Seaton prizes, this time for the poem "On the Immensity of the Supreme Being." He must have gone up to Cambridge to receive it, for on May 5 he wrote the "Ode to an Eagle Confined in a College Court" in which one can feel his glorying in his own release from the narrow confines of academic life.

Meantime, it looks as if spring had got into his blood again. The June issue of the *Midwife* is very largely devoted to the subject of love: there is an essay on love, one on matrimony, an assortment of model love letters, and some amorous verses. The fact that one of these, "The Power of Innocence," was to reappear a year later in the collected poems with slight changes and a specific dedication "To Miss C———" indicates that the object of Smart's attentions was already Miss Anna Maria Carnan, Newbery's step-daughter and the future Mrs. Smart.

The *Student* ceased publication in July, but Smart carried on with the *Midwife* through the October issue. Then he laid it aside for a more exciting undertaking. He and his friend Rolt, with the

....

battle at all, but an elaborate publicity scheme entered into by all the parties concerned with no intention of harming one another but simply with the desire of increasing the circulation of the *Midwife*, the *Student*, Kenrick's *Kapelion*, and of the *Old Woman's Dunciad* itself. Certainly if Kenrick was a real enemy he did not remain one permanently, for when Smart's great *Translation of the Psalms* was published by subscription fourteen years later, Kenrick put himself down for eight copies, an extraordinary gesture of friendship for a poor author to make to a fellow author.

[23] Smart wrote these pieces at the request of John Blake Delaval, whom he had tutored at Cambridge. Delaval played Iago, and his brother, Sir Francis, played Othello. Their patronage of Smart continued many years (see below, p. 313).

financial backing of Newbery, embarked on a theatrical production. On the third of December, 1751, they produced the first of a series of "entertainments" at the Castle Tavern in Pater-Noster Row. Evidently these performances were lucrative, for on December 27 they were removed to the New Theatre in the Haymarket where they were continued until the following May. They were not straightforward dramas; from the excerpts that have survived it would seem that they were more or less music hall "concerts" similar to those which had been given for several years by the notorious Samuel Foote. There were songs, orations, speeches, and dancing acts, and when the project was revived in the winter of 1752 the featured attraction appears to have been a troupe of performing animals. The whole series was called "Mother Midnight's Entertainments or The Old Woman's Oratory," and it is probable that Smart himself appeared on the stage as the venerable midwife. No doubt he enjoyed his part in them immensely (he had certainly enjoyed *A Trip to Cambridge*), and the long run indicates that they were financially profitable. Newbery was no man to put his money into a failing enterprise.

On the surface of things, one might suppose that Smart's life at this time was as happy as mortals have a right to expect their lives to be. His connection with a successful bookseller was established, his magazine had had a reasonable success, his theatrical productions were supplying him with money, and he probably was, or fancied himself to be, in love with his master's daughter. It is true that he had given up his chances for academic distinction, but so long as he carried off the Seaton prize year after year the college must perforce remain proud of him, and if he saw very little of the old friends at Pembroke he had in their stead a host of new ones in London. The daughter of one of those friends, Miss Frances Burney who was one day to be a famous novelist, describes the poet at this stage of his career as "a man then in equal possession of those finest ingredients for the higher call of his art, fire and fancy, and, for its comic call, of sport and waggery. No indication, however, of such possession was granted to his appearance; not a grace was bestowed on his person or manners; and his physiognomy was of that round and stubbed form that seemed appertaining to a common dealer behind a common counter, rather than to a votary of the muses." Older acquaintances were less critical of his looks than Miss Burney, no doubt; to all intents and purposes he seemed a highly successful young man, which was all the sober world of the eighteenth century demanded. Yet if his life had ended here, at the height of his success, no one today would take the trouble to chronicle it.

In the spring of 1752 comes the first recorded indication that all was not well with him. He had obviously been working too hard: in addition to the labors which have already been mentioned, he had turned out for Newbery two little compilations or commonplace books of witty or wise sayings, *The Nutcracker* and *An Index to Mankind*. Just when he broke down under the strain of his multifarious activity we do not know; the *Midwife* appeared in single issues in January and again in May or June, but "Mother Midnight's Entertainments" went on through the season to close in May. On the twenty-eighth of April the *London Daily Advertiser* announced that "the ingenious Mr. Smart who has been very seriously ill of a Fever is now in a fair way of Recovery." Although it is quite likely that he had suffered such attacks earlier in his life, this is the first record we have of the series of illnesses which were eventually to culminate in insanity.

As soon as he was apparently well, Smart pulled his affairs together and prepared to take a vacation. The theatrical season was over, and he once again laid aside the *Midwife*. The collection of his poems which he and Newbery had been advertising for two years was at last ready for publication, and *Poems on Several Occasions* made its appearance in June. It was a handsome volume, beautifully printed and decorated with some excellent plates, and supplied with a long list of distinguished subscribers.

There is no record of Smart's activities between June and August of 1752; the negative evidence points to a cessation in his labors, and there is good reason to believe that the vacation was occasioned by his marriage. The precise date of this event has never been determined; Hunter says, "In 1753 he quitted College, on his marriage to Miss Anna Maria Carnan." Beyond this we have nothing except a story in Surtees' *History of Durham* (iv, 142) to the effect that it was a "Fleet Street marriage," performed secretly at St. Bride's in 1753. Abbott has pointed out (*loc.cit.*) that if this legend is to be believed then we must conclude it was a forced wedding, for Smart's eldest daughter was born May 3,

1753. Furthermore, the parish register at St. Bride's contains no reference to it. Abbott then writes, "It seems to me more probable, in view of Smart's intimate relationship with Newbery, that it took place some time in 1752, and that it was kept secret as long as possible in order that Smart might maintain his dignity as fellow of Pembroke. The college heard of it in November, 1753, and from that time the poet's official connection with Pembroke ceased." Surely this is the logical assumption to make: everything we know of the entire Newbery-Carnan family, to say nothing of the Smart family, indicates that they would be among the last people in the world to countenance a forced marriage. Of Mrs. Smart herself every scrap of evidence which has survived proves her to have been a woman of the most uncompromising respectability. Smart had even described her as a maiden of "adamantine innocence." The suggestion that her marriage was in any way irregular is preposterous.

If we may accept the summer of 1752 as the time of the marriage, Mrs. Smart was twenty-one years old and her husband was thirty. From the success of his recent ventures it would seem that he had as much money at this period as at any time of his life. Mrs. LeNoir, in the letter from which I have already quoted, gives a pleasant account of the newly married poet: "After Mr. Smart's marriage with the daughter-in-law [sic!] of Mr. Newbery the well known philanthropic bookseller with the red pimpled face (for so he is described by Dr. Goldsmith in his Vicar of Wakefield) he resided for some time with his wife in apartments at Canonbury House belonging to Mr. Newbery. It was here that the writer of this article his youngest daughter was born and that she and her sister spent their earliest years under the care of Mrs. Fleming of whom the apartments were held. I well remember the high trees that screened the back of the dwelling, and the very old house they partly concealed, the habitation of the justice of the peace whose name was Booth: the out-door guard was a large, lean mastiff, in very ill condition, whose howlings were a great annoyance to the neighbors. One morning Mr. Smart going as usual to read the newspapers at the Public house, meeting there with Justice Booth, was accosted by him with, 'So, Mr. Smart, the dog's dead.' 'I am glad of it,' he replied. 'Why so, Mr. Smart?'— 'Why because he was half starved and always howling: I had thought of being at the expense of a brace of pistols myself, to put him out of his misery.' 'Pooh, pooh,' exclaimed the Justice—'not my dog—I mean the dog of Venice!'"

For several years the Smarts continued to live at Canonbury House (or Canbury, as it is sometimes called), and the poet was reasonably happy there. There are several references to the house and to friends he had among the other residents in *Rejoice in the Lamb* (*q.v.*), the most touching of which is this: "I bless God for my retreat at CANBURY, as it was the place of the nativity of my children."

In the late summer of 1752 Smart was again drawn into one of those literary mud-slingings which were so regrettably common in the eighteenth century. William Kenrick, who seems to have spent his life making enemies, had for several years been attacking Henry Fielding, from some obscure motive, and for his pains had been treated with contempt in *The Jacobite's Journal*. When Fielding began his *Covent-Garden Journal* in January, 1752, Kenrick made it the occasion of another attack. He was ignored, but in a few days Fielding launched the "Paper-War," as it is called, by a humorous assault upon the Grub Street army, led by "His Lowness, the Prince of Billingsgate." This worthy was not Kenrick, but a notorious quack and hack-writer named Dr. John Hill. All of Grub Street rushed into battle: Hill, Kenrick, Smollett, and Bonnell Thornton, along with several anonymous contributors, flung charges and countercharges. There was at least one attempt to draw Smart into it, but probably illness prevented him from entering the fray. By the middle of May the "war" had dribbled out, and Grub Street settled into an uneasy armistice. Nothing more happened until August 13, when Hill, upon apparently no provocation, suddenly levelled his guns at Fielding and Smart. The latter paid no immediate attention, although his friend Johnson undertook to censure Hill for his remarks. But the poet began to meditate revenge, although this time he was not so indiscreet as to advertise that another imitation of the *Dunciad* was contemplated. He said nothing, and all that the literary world received from him in the following months was the poem "On the Omniscience of the Supreme Being," with which he won the Seaton prize for the third time on November 2.

In December, Hill, perhaps having got wind that Smart was

writing a satire against him, proceeded to attack the poet again, this time including Newbery as well in his charges. Newbery, in righteous indignation, published in the newspapers an elaborate testimonial to the sterling qualities of his character, signed by four of his business friends; at the same time both he and Smart published categorical denials of Hill's charges (which, after all, were mild enough). Meanwhile, the projected satire was growing. Smart had as his collaborator another of those literary friends who was to stand by him through thick and thin. This was the journalist and playwright, Arthur Murphy, whose biographer gives a pleasant picture of the two friends gleefully at work upon *The Hilliad*, "Mr. Smart walking up and down the room, speaking the Verses, and Mr. Murphy writing the notes to them."[24] In February *The Hilliad* was published, and Hill immediately retorted with a *Smartiad*, a piece so destitute of merit that it made Smart's satire seem all the more effective. There the quarrel ended. It had been of little profit to Smart or to anyone else; on the whole, one can only regret that so much of his energies should have been wasted on it.

The next three years saw a steady decline in Smart's fortunes, brought about by periodic returns of his "fever" in increasingly severe attacks. The "Old Woman's Oratory," which had been revived in December, 1752, was concluded in the following March. In April or May another issue of the *Midwife* (the final one) appeared. It is a patched-up affair, containing only pieces which had been used at the "Oratory," a reprint from *The Craftsman*,[25] and a number of poems which had in all probability been written at earlier periods. This suggests that Smart was again ill and unable to work. Furthermore, there is no record of any activity on his part until December 5, 1753, when he again won the Seaton prize, this time for "On the Power of the Supreme Being." Of course he may have been engaged on some anonymous undertaking for Newbery, but if so we have no evidence of it. The "Ode

[24] Jesse Foot, *The Life of Arthur Murphy, Esq.* (London, 1811), p. 106, as quoted by Botting, "Christopher Smart's Association with Arthur Murphy," *JEGP*, xliii, 52. Foot's description, incidentally, is another of several indications that Smart did much of his work extempore.

[25] This is one of Arthur Murphy's pieces from his "Gray's Inn Journal" in *The Craftsman*. It contains a "puff" of the "Old Woman's Oratory," and is another indication of the mutual assistance the two writers gave each other.

to a Virginia Nightingale," which was printed in March, 1754, mentions an illness from which the poet thinks he has recovered, but since Smart had the habit of printing things long after they were written this may possibly refer back to the "fever" of 1752.

At any rate, whether he was ill or not, 1754 was another lean year. During that entire year nothing of Smart's was published except twenty-three short poems in various issues of the *Gentleman's Magazine*. Of these, four were reprints and certain of the others (such as a verse addressed to Harriet Pratt, and one signed "C.S. Aetat. 16") had obviously been lying in his desk for some time. The *Gentleman's Magazine*, when it announced the publication of the Seaton prize poem for that year, which had been written by one G. Bally, was careful to inform its readers that "this prize has for many years been constantly assigned to the ingenious Mr. Christopher Smart, who was not this year among the competitors."

Through the spring and summer of 1755, the poet's production was even more meager. Two poems appeared in the *Gentleman's Magazine* for February: one was a fable and the other "Lady Harriot"; this last, which had been written years before for Miss Pratt, reappeared in the magazine for April in a musical setting by Dr. Boyce, evidently an act of kindly assistance on the part of the composer. In April there was another fable, and in June the "Epitaph on Mrs. Rolt."

By autumn, however, Smart was able to work again. His poem "On the Goodness of the Supreme Being" (the poorest of the five) was rushed to Cambridge barely in time to receive the Seaton prize on October 28. From then until the end of the year Smart was apparently working on his prose translation of the complete work of Horace, which Newbery published in December.

There is a curious story about this Horace which may throw some light on Smart's private affairs during this period of his life. Nine years later Hawkesworth found that the poet was still indignant over Newbery's treatment of him. (See the letter quoted below, p. 47.) The publisher, it seems, agreed to pay a hundred pounds for the book, but he handed over only thirteen pounds to Smart "because the rest had been advanced for his family." This indicates quite clearly that, with a wife and two children to support after two years of intermittent illnesses, the poet was once again in debt, and this time the indebtedness was to his father-in-law. From this time on, Newbery's primary effort, so far as Smart was concerned, was to get out of his work enough to keep his family. The legend of the "philanthropic book-seller" will have to be revised by the addition of Dobson's phrase, "in his business fashion." Smart was seriously and dangerously ill, with an illness that was to drive him into insanity, yet in order that Mrs. Smart and the children should not be a charge upon the publisher himself Newbery drove him as long as he could be driven, and when he was no longer able to work at all he had him committed to a public asylum and washed his hands of him. The account of later events will be seen to bear out this analysis.[26]

There can be little doubt that by the autumn of 1755 exploitation by Newbery became as galling to Smart as the academic life had formerly been. In November, he and his friend Richard Rolt concocted a scheme which must have seemed to offer a means of escape. They agreed with two booksellers, Gardner and Allen, to supply the material for a six-penny monthly magazine to be called *The Universal Visiter and Monthly Memorialist*. The booksellers were to bear the expenses of the undertaking, and any profits were to be divided equally among the four parties. The contract was to remain in force for ninety-nine years (!), during which time none of the parties was "either directly or indirectly" to "engage

[26] In his "Gray's Inn Journal" in *The Craftsman*, Smart's friend, Arthur Murphy, had written several years earlier: "It has been the Fate of many, endowed perhaps with Parts not very inferior to *Addison*, to droop in Indigence, their Poetic Fires totally extinguished, and I make no Manner of Doubt, but in the present Age, there are those that might become shining Ornaments of the Republic of Letters, were there any Incitement to spur the Muses Steed. But a Treatise on *Cribidge*, or a Calculation of the Chances at Whist, is sure of being better received at present, than such a performance as the *Analysis of Beauty*, or any other work of distinguished Genius. While a *Smart* subsists among us, I cannot help thinking it an indelible Reproach to the Age, that he has not any where found a *Mecaenas* [The 1786 version has here this insertion: "A bookseller [Newbery] is his only friend, but for that bookseller, however liberal, he must toil and drudge."], and that he is suffered to draw his Pen in the Praises of his Maker, without receiving any other Reward, than a small Premium at *Cambridge*, and that Portion of Fame, which, in Spight of Malice and Envy, he will be always sure to enjoy." I quote this whole passage from Mr. Botting's article, "Christopher Smart's Association with Arthur Murphy," *JEGP*, xliii, 49-56. Along with many other of Murphy's remarks which Botting quotes, as well as Murphy's lines on Smart's illness (see below, p. 38, n.), it shows unmistakably both the esteem in which Smart was held by his real friends and their opinion of Newbery's dealings with him.

or concern himself in any work or undertaking of the like nature
or kind." Of course Smart was only leaping desperately from the
frying pan into the fire; one thing, however, was definitely accomplished: he would never again write a *Midwife* for Newbery.
Since this contract has been sometimes referred to as an example
of Smart's lack of practical judgment, the other provisions ought
to be noted. Each of the contracting parties was prohibited from
selling or giving away his share or part, but if either of the writers
should be unable, by reason of illness or other cause, to supply his
material, he was to see that some one else did. Finally, it was provided that if the undertaking should not be sufficiently profitable,
any one or all of the contracting parties could, by giving the others
notice, be freed from the contract. On the whole, it was about as
good a contract as a magazine writer was likely to get at the time,
and the ninety-nine year provision must have seemed to Smart
to guarantee both a permanent escape from Newbery and a certain indication of security.

This contract must have infuriated Newbery. It is true that he
continued for several years to print Smart's work, but this was
almost certainly done only for Mrs. Smart's benefit. The poet had
previously written for various magazines a number of fables, and
during the winter of 1755-1756 Newbery repeatedly advertised a
collection of "Tales and Fables in Verse" as "speedily to be published." The volume never appeared, however, possibly because
Smart refused to write enough additional ones to fill it out. With
the exception of the "Hymn to the Supreme Being," which, after
all, was an elaborate advertisement of Dr. James' fever powders,
Newbery henceforth printed nothing by his son-in-law except
reprints of work previously issued; that is, pieces on which he
already owned the copyright. One should remember, in considering Newbery's frequent editions of Smart's works, that eighteenth-
century writers received no royalties. They got only a lump sum
for the original manuscript. The publisher received the entire
proceeds from all subsequent printings.

During this winter (1755-1756), Smart had the last respite from
ill health that he was to enjoy for seven years. He wrote a few
occasional verses for the theaters, notably an epilogue to *The Ap-
prentice* (produced January 2, 1756) by his friend, Arthur Murphy, who had supplied the notes for *The Hilliad*. The *Universal*

Visiter made its first appearance on February 2, and Smart was able to produce his share of it for the first three issues, contributing both poetry and essays in prose. After April, however, nothing of his appeared in it except a few verses, some of which had been written and even published long before. Once more he had fallen ill.

Certain friends came loyally to his aid. Garrick repaid a number of complimentary references to himself in the *Midwife* by supplying a prose essay and four poems. Percy and "Dr. B[urney]" also helped out with short pieces.[27] Johnson contributed six essays and possibly a Latin poem. He afterwards mentioned this act of charity in patronizing terms which do not suggest any great fondness for Smart: "I wrote for some months in 'The Universal Visitor,' for poor Smart while he was mad, not then knowing the terms on which he was engaged to write, and thinking I was doing him good. I hoped his wits would soon return to him. Mine returned to me, and I wrote in 'The Universal Visitor' no longer."

Smart's wits, unfortunately, did not return. Late in the spring he made a temporary recovery, which he signalized by writing the "Hymn to the Supreme Being" (*q.v.*), a poem dedicated to Dr. James in the pathetic belief that the fever pills prescribed by that worthy had cured him completely. Soon the cloud descended again, and the long seven-year period of chaos in all his affairs had begun.

The whole question of the date and degree of Smart's madness has long been a very perplexing one. Christopher Hunter says merely: "Though the fortune as well as the constitution of Mr. Smart required the utmost care, he was equally negligent in the management of both, and his various and repeated embarrassments acting upon an imagination uncommonly fervid, produced temporary alienations of mind; which were at last attended with paroxysms so violent as to render confinement necessary. . . ." Fanny Burney speaks of his having been "twice confined," and Mrs. Piozzi mentions a time when he was "first obliged to be put in private lodgings." The only definite fact we have concerning any confinement is supplied by the records of St. Luke's Hospital,

---

[27] Ann Gardner's attributions; see Walter Graham, *English Literary Periodicals*, p. 174 (same material restated and expanded by Botting, "Johnson, Smart, and the Universal Visiter," *Modern Philology*, xxxvi, 293 ff.).

where the following entry was recently discovered by Mr. William Force Stead: "Christopher Smart, of the Parish of St. Gregory's, Middlesex. Recommended by Francis Gosling. Admitted 6 May, 1757. Discharged 11 May, 1758, uncured."[28]

Smart was never finally set at liberty until 1763, but we have no other information than this as to the place or places of his confinement or the nature of the limitations placed on him. For some part of the time he may have been kept at home, possibly before and after his sojourn at St. Luke's. This was not true after January, 1759, however, for reasons which will be shown below; during the following years he must have been in some institution, possibly a private asylum.

During the first few years of Smart's illness, his family apparently hoped he would recover. Newbery continued to issue reprints, and in December, 1757, Thomas Carnan, Mrs. Smart's brother, and a member of Newbery's firm, published a collection of pieces retrieved from the defunct *Midwife* under the title *The Nonpareil*. But by the beginning of 1759 Mrs. Smart decided to remain no longer on a sinking ship. She took her two daughters and departed for Dublin, where she opened a shop. In the *Gazetteer and London Daily Advertizer* for January 3, there is an advertisement of Dr. James' powders "sold by J. Newbery at the *Bible and Sun* . . . , and by Mrs. Smart at Mr. McMahon's in Caple Street, Dublin," a notice which was repeated as late as June 27. It is not easy to understand sympathetically an action which looks, on the surface, like an attempt to get as far away from her husband as she could. Smart's sister, Marianne, had married a Mr. Falkiner of Dublin, and it is of course possible that Mrs. Smart went to them and that she remained for a time concerned about her unfortunate husband. We have no information at all about her stay in Dublin beyond the advertisement I have quoted and a letter of good wishes from Johnson which she received there. Smart's Seaton poems were reprinted in Dublin in 1761, but whether she had anything to do with this edition is not known. By 1762 she was back in England. She settled in Reading and took over the publication of her father's newspaper: the *Oxford Gazette and Reading Mercury* for January 25 of that year

[28] *Rejoice in the Lamb*, p. 225.

has the note, "printed for Anna Maria Smart & Co." Here she established herself as a well-to-do citizen and successful business woman, but although she outlived her husband by thirty-eight years she made no effort whatever to assist him or even to see him during the last ten years of his unhappy existence. In the eyes of Reading, however, she lived a blameless life. She had become a Roman Catholic, and when she found there was no Roman church in Reading she made herself instrumental in establishing one. When the daughters were old enough, she sent them to be educated at a convent in France. The elder, Mary Ann, returned to Reading to marry a Mr. Cowslade, and her descendants continued to own and publish the *Mercury* until very recent years; after the French Revolution, Elizabeth married an emigré, one Captain LeNoir. She it was who in the early nineteenth century made a small reputation with novels and poems. She seems to have been more kindly disposed towards her father's memory than were the other members of the family, but even she felt obliged to "improve" his beautiful *Hymns* and to explain that *A Song to David* was greatly overestimated!

Perhaps one should not censure Mrs. Smart and her relatives too severely for their treatment of the poet. He, after all, was a genius, and during much of the time they were intimate with him he was an overworked and frustrated genius. Such people are not easy to live with. Furthermore, he was abnormally sensitive. Hunter, calling attention to Smart's uncommon shyness, tells a revealing and pathetic little story: "Having undertaken to introduce his wife to my Lord Darlington, with whom he was well acquainted; he had no sooner mentioned her name to his Lordship, than he retreated suddenly, as if stricken with a panic, from the room, and from the house, leaving her to follow overwhelmed with confusion." The Carnans and the Newberys, and indeed Smart's own blood kin, were not the sort of people who could get out of such a situation gracefully. They were "good," respectable middle-class souls, with a certain amount of commercial shrewdness, but without imagination or intellectual depth. With the brilliant, nervous, scholarly poet they had virtually nothing in common; so long as he accepted their mode of life and by sheer dint of labor managed to keep himself and his family solvent, they got along with him well enough, but when the strain of trying to accommodate himself and his talent to their bourgeois ideals broke his health and drove him mad, they gave him up as a bad job. Thereafter, they troubled themselves no more about him.

To return to Smart: At about the time Mrs. Smart left him, his misfortunes were brought to the attention of the literary world by an act of singular kindness on the part of David Garrick, who had long been friendly towards him. On January 26, 1759, Garrick presented the "double bill" of *Merope* and *The Guardian* for his benefit. This benefit performance, coming just when it did, suggests very strongly that Smart's family had given up the attempt to keep him at home, and that he was being placed in some asylum where money would be needed for his support. Again various friends rallied round him. When the benefit was announced, Richard Rolt, Arthur Murphy, William Woty, and John Lockman all published poems on the occasion, hoping, no doubt, to increase by this means the sale of tickets.[29] Gray, who

[29] Woty's and those of Rolt are quoted by Ainsworth and Noyes, *op.cit.*, p. 93. Lockman, in the *Public Advertiser* on January 30, 1759, wrote as follows:

> Amazing change in that capacious mind
> Where piercing wit with Wisdom's Charm was join'd!
> Wrapt in a Vision, he presum'd to sing
> The Attributes of Heav'ns eternal King:
> But O! approaching tow'rds the Throne of Light,
> Its flashing splendors over pow'r'd his Sight.
> Hence blind on Earth, behold him sadly stray;
> 'Tis We must chear the Horrors of his way.

A much clearer indication of the opinion Smart's friends had of both his poetry and his character is given by Arthur Murphy's lines in the *Public Advertiser* of February 3:

> Mourn not, my *Smart*, that now no more the Muse
> Brings to the hallow'd Lip Castalian Dews;
> That with thy Horace thou no more can'st sing,
> Or with bold hand awake the sounding String.
> What tho' thy Pow'rs have felt th' envious Blast?
> Still to late Time thy Deathless Fame shall last.
> Caecilia's Praise Pope, taught by thee, shall tell
> In numbers worthy of the Latian Shell.
> Tho' mute thy Tongue, thy Lines melodious flow,
> And in thy Hop-Land thy own Laurels grow.
> Still mounting hence, on the rapt Seraph's Ray,
> To the All Good thy Muse attunes her Lay.
> To hear thee, Angels from their Golden Beds
> Willing bend down their Star-encircled Heads.
> A Soul congenial the whole Host admire,
> The Hallelujahs kindling Heav'nly Fire.

was in London at the time, wrote of the performance to William Mason, who had also known Smart at Cambridge, and Mason answered: "this resuscitation of Poor Smart pains me, I was in hopes he was safe in that state where the best of us will be better than we are & the worst I hope as little worse as infinite Justice can permit. But is he returned to his senses? if so I fear that will be more terrible still, pray, if you can dispose of a Guinea so as it will in any sort benefit him (for tis too late for a ticket) give it for me."

The nature of Smart's malady has been discussed by several contemporaries, and their comments may be considered at this point. Hunter, as has been noticed (see above, p. 35), attributed the illness to a combination of ill health and worry over financial matters, and when all is considered this seems the likeliest explanation. The madness manifested itself, however, as a definite religious mania. Dr. Johnson's description is well known: "My poor friend Smart showed the disturbance of his mind, by falling upon his knees, and saying his prayers in the street, or in any other unusual place. Now although, rationally speaking, it is greater madness not to pray at all, than to pray as Smart did, I am afraid there are so many who do not pray, that their understanding is not called in question." On another occasion Johnson remarked: "I did not think he ought to be shut up. His infirmities were not noxious to society. He insisted on people praying with him; and I'd as lief pray with Kit Smart as any one else. Another charge was that he did not love clean linen; and I have no passion for it."

Much less familiar are the comments of Mrs. Piozzi, derived doubtless from Johnson but with interesting additions: "The famous Christopher Smart, who was both a wit and a scholar

This Praise, my Friend, nor this thy Praise alone;
A higher Claim, and nobler Wreaths you own,
Thy wide Benevolence, thy Soul sincere,
Thy gen'rous Friendship, and thy social Tear,
Thy Public Spirit that disdain'd a Slave;
Thy honest Pride that still despis'd a Knave,
Thy manly Warmth each Rival to Commend;
Thy Rapture to the Merit of a Friend,
Thy steady Morals that ne'er lost their Sway,
Nor, like thy vernal Genius, felt Decay,
All this was thine; this it's Reversion brings
When Wit and Poetry are idle Things.

and visited as such while under confinement for madness, would never have had a commission of lunacy taken out against him, had he managed with equal ingenuity [*i.e.*, kept his peculiarities to himself]—for Smart's melancholy shewed itself only in a preternatural excitement to prayer, which he held it as a duty not to controul or repress—taking *au pied de la lettre* our blessed Saviour's injunction to *pray without ceasing.*—So that beginning by regular addresses to the Almighty, he went on to call his friends from their dinners, or beds, or places of recreation, whenever that impulse towards prayer pressed upon his mind. In every other transaction of life no man's wits could be more regular than those of Smart; for this prevalence of one idea pertinaciously keeping the first place in his head, had in no sense except what immediately related to itself, perverted his judgment at all: his opinions were unchanged as before, nor did he seem more likely to fall into a state of distraction than another man; less so, perhaps, as he calmed every start of violent passion by prayer. Now, had this eminently unhappy patient been equally seized by the precept of *praying in secret*; as no one would then have been disturbed by his irregularities, it would have been to no one's interest to watch over or cure them; and the absurdity would possibly have consumed itself in private, . . . I well remember how after the commission was put in force, poor fellow! he got money from the keeper of the mad-house for teaching his little boys Latin—a proof, as vulgar people would imagine, that his intellects were sound; for mean observers suppose all madness to be phrenzy, and think a person insane in proportion as he is wild, and disposed to throw things about—whereas experience shows that such temporary suspensions of the mental faculties are oftener connected with delirium than with *mania*, and, if not encouraged and stimulated by drunkenness, are seldom of long duration."[30]

That Smart's madness should have shown itself as religious mania is not surprising. His was a deeply religious nature, and since he was a poet it would seem a necessity of his existence that some of his religious emotion should have found expression in his work. But there was no place for it in *The Midwife* or "Mother Midnight's Entertainments," or in the other undertakings by which he tried to make a living. Even the Seaton poems were

[30] Hester Lynch Piozzi, *The British Synonymy*, London, 1794, ii, 3-6.

"set pieces," written specifically for the prize. When the inhibitions were broken down by insanity, it is natural that his latent religious enthusiasm should find release.

Until very recently we have had no inkling that any of the wanderings of his disordered mind were ever committed to paper, and in the absence of such evidence some thoughtless critics have assumed that *A Song to David* was such a composition, forgetting that the masterpiece was not published until several months after he had been released. In 1939, however, Mr. William Force Stead edited and published a manuscript in which Smart had written fairly consistently a line or two a day during several years of his confinement. This fascinating document, published under the title, *Rejoice in the Lamb*, enables us to follow the tortured road by which Smart fought his way back to sanity and health and to renewed command over his literary medium. (See the selections printed within, pp. 106 ff., and Notes, pp. 274 ff.) From it certain facts can be drawn: we do not yet know where he was confined except for the one year in St. Luke's, but it is evident that he was allowed to have company, as Mrs. Piozzi says, and that he was supplied with newspapers, books, and writing materials. In the spring of 1760 he received another benefit, this time from his former associates in "Mrs. Midnight's Oratory"; the following single-sheet advertisement has survived among the Douce prints: "For the last time this season, for the benefit of Mr. Gaudry[31] and Mrs. Midnight, at the Theatre in the Haymarket, on Thursday the 6th of March, 1760, will be performed Mrs. Midnight's Concert and Oratory, as it was originally in the year 1754."

Gradually the attacks of insanity became less violent and less frequent, and during lucid intervals Smart began to try his hand again. Characteristically, he tried religious verse. He had long thought of making a verse translation of the Psalms, and had, I believe, occasionally done a few in earlier years (see Notes, p. 278). He turned to this task again, and in the June supplement (1761) of the *Christian's Magazine* (a paper edited by Dr. William Dodd of sad memory) appeared a version of Psalm 100, "to a

[31] When *Mrs. Midnight's Orations* was published in 1763 (see below, p. 43), one part of the contents was "The Gifts, a Dramatic Interlude, as it was intended to be performed at the theatre in the Hay-Market, London. Set to Music by Mr. Joseph Gaudry."

Scotch tune" and written in what he imagined was Scottish dialect. This was followed in August by an "Epitaph on a Young Clergyman" in the same magazine. It is evident that although he was to remain under confinement for nearly two more years he was able to write occasionally and also to maintain communication with the outside world. In March of the following year Newbery published an *Art of Poetry, on a New Plan* in which a number of Smart's early pieces were reprinted. Perhaps this indicates that Newbery's violent antipathy to Smart had not yet developed; on the other hand the poems may have been included because they were already in other Newbery publications or simply because the editor considered them worth inclusion. There is a story, however, that Newbery set aside for Smart the profits from the *Martial Review or General History of the Late War*, which he published about this time (see Forster's *Goldsmith*, 1854, i, 324), and the story may be true.

Smart's recovery came slowly, but during the last two years there were many intervals in which he was able to work. He set about the enormous task of versifying the Psalms, and I think that he also began work on the *Hymns and Spiritual Songs* (see Notes, p. 277). Friends old and new visited him, and he was allowed to make a garden. When Burney returned to London in 1760 after an absence of nine years, he inquired of Johnson, "How does poor Smart do, Sir; is he likely to recover?"

JOHNSON: "It seems as if his mind had ceased to struggle with the disease; for he grows fat upon it." BURNEY. "Perhaps, Sir, that may be from want of exercise." JOHNSON. "No, Sir; he has partly as much as he used to have, for he digs in the garden."

If we may judge from the strangely beautiful passages on flowers in *Rejoice in the Lamb* (*q.v.*) and his little prayer, "The Lord succeed my pink borders," the garden must have been one of his chief consolations. From the evidence of the manuscript also it is clear that for several years he lived the life of "prayer and praise" which he was to glorify after his recovery in so many glowing passages.

At length, in the winter of 1762-1763 he was well enough to permit his friends to obtain his release. As he has told us in the "Epistle to John Sherratt, Esq.," it was the ever-faithful Richard Rolt, together with Sherratt and a family named Sheeles, who brought this about. The last date in *Rejoice in the Lamb* is January 13, 1763, and Smart ceased to write in it about the end of that month. In that month had appeared *Mrs. Midnight's Orations,* a collection of pieces that had been used in the performances; very likely Rolt had this published as a means of providing the poet with a little money upon his return to the world.

After his release, Smart entered the most productive period of his literary life. During the long period of rest and care, freed from economic pressures and with liberty to meditate the religious themes that were most congenial to him, he had achieved at last the preparation for his real lifework. He had arrived at this stage by the hardest possible route, and it must be admitted that insanity had left traces which were never completely eliminated. This does not mean that any of his later poems are "crazy" nor that they contain meaningless and incomprehensible passages; it simply means that he was not able always to undergo the severe mental discipline which produced *A Song to David* and the best of his other pieces. Furthermore, once he was free he had to accept the responsibility of his own support, and once again he found himself having to write too much too hastily. Some of his later work suffers because he had to publish it before he had time for critical revision. Nevertheless, the eight years that were left to him were, in spite of handicaps, his richest creative period, not only in the quantity of his production but in the quality as well. During his confinement he had found himself, so to speak, and from this point onward he wrote in his own idiom, discarding all the tricks of fashionable mediocrity which had enabled him to sell his hack work. Sometimes his later work is bad, but whether good or bad it is distinctly his own.

Some three months after his release, he published the poem which is, of all his work, the most characteristic and the finest. There are passages in other poems that are equal to its best stanzas, but nowhere else is there the sustained perfection of *A Song to David* (*q.v.*, and see Notes, pp. 292 ff.). This masterpiece, however, fell upon deaf ears. Many things militated against a favorable reception. Possibly the literary world was so excited over John Wilkes' notorious "No. 45" (published April 30) that it had no time for poetry. More probably, Smart's history being known to all in the small world of literary London, people simply concluded that a recently mad poet would write mad poetry, and let it go at that. If they read the poem, its daring imagery and extraordinary complexity of thought must have seemed to confirm the prejudice. The reviewers were worse than patronizing, the *Critical Review* making the following sneering comments: "Without venturing to criticize upon the propriety of a Protestant's offering up either hymns or prayers to the dead, we must be of opinion that great rapture and devotion is discernable in this extatic song. It is a fine piece of ruins, and must at once please and affect a sensible mind."

Such a reception of his returned genius must have cut Smart to the quick, and he did not improve matters by his reaction, as we shall see (see below, p. 45). Meantime, he went ahead with his plans. When the *Song* was published, he advertised his new *Translation of the Psalms of David*, with the statement that the copy was then in the possession of C. Say, Printer. It was to be a subscription volume and, as with his 1752 collection, two years were to elapse before his list was large enough to permit publication.

The letters of Mason and Gray tell of another disturbing element. Mason wrote from York on June 28: "I have got about 10 Subscribers to Smart & dont know how to transmit him the money. Stonehewer advises me to keep it, as he hears he is in somebodys hands who may cheat him. I have seen his Song to David & from thence conclude him as mad as ever. But this I mention only that one should endeavour to assist him as affectually as possible wch one cannot do without the mediation of a third person. . . . Tis said in the papers he is prosecuting the people who confined him. if so, assisting him at present is only throwing ones money to the Lawyers." Gray answered that it would be better to keep the money until Smart had dropped his lawsuit, "wch I dont doubt will go against him, if he pursues it." This is the only contemporary reference to a lawsuit. It is quite possible that Smart did threaten to sue Newbery, and possibly the rest of the family. If he did, this may account for Newbery's antagonism towards him. It may also help to explain Smart's later indifference towards his own mother and sister, although we have no way of knowing whether they were instrumental in having him confined.

Such troubles did not interfere seriously with his literary production, which during the next few years was very large. In July, 1763, he issued a pamphlet collection of *Poems . . . by Mr. Smart.* In an advertisement in this pamphlet, he printed a scathing retort to the *Critical Review's* remarks on the *Song to David.* The *Monthly Review* now took up the cudgels, making their review of *Poems . . . by Mr. Smart* nothing but an open insult. For this they were roundly cursed in an advertisement printed in *Poems on Several Occasions,* another pamphlet collection issued by Smart in November, 1763 (see Notes, p. 311). Thereafter one may look in vain for any real criticism of Smart's books in either magazine. Each publication brought the poet only fresh abuse until after the appearance of the *Psalms* late in 1765. His succeeding volumes were simply ignored, except for brief contemptuous notices of the *Parables.* It is quite possible that without this antagonism on the part of the reviewers, Smart might have been able to regain something of the reputation he had won with the Seaton poems, though it is clear that even his well-wishers were too startled by much of his religious poetry to pass a reasonable judgment upon it. Boswell's remarks, in a letter of July 30, 1763, to Sir David Dalrymple, may be taken as typical: "I have sent you Smart's *Song to David,* which is a very curious composition, being a strange mixture of *dun obscure* and glowing genius at times. I have also sent some poems which he has lately published. His Genius and Imagination [*sic*] is very pretty. The other pieces have shivers of genius here and there, but are often ludicrously low. Poor man, he has been relieved from his confinement, but not from his unhappy disorder. However, he has it not in any great height. He is not a poet of the first rank."

In the spring of 1764 Smart returned again to the composition of material for performance to music, but in keeping with the strongly religious cast of his thought his production was not a sprightly piece for Vauxhall Gardens. It was the oratorio, *Hannah,* and it was produced at the King's Theatre in the Haymarket on April 3. The music was by John Worgan, who had set Smart's *Solemn Dirge* thirteen years before. We do not know what success the piece may have had, but the printed text was mentioned as having "some poetical merit" in the *St. James Magazine* for May. Smart's only other publication of that year was the *Ode to the . . . Earl of Northumberland . . . etc.,* another pamphlet collection which contained, among several other pieces, three of his finest short lyrics.

That he was well and reasonably comfortably situated is evident from one of the most interesting passages written about him by one of his contemporaries. Dr. John Hawkesworth, the essayist of *Adventurer* fame, had been with his wife to visit Smart's mother and sister Margaret (Mrs. Hunter) in Kent, and they had asked him to try, when he returned to London, to see the poet. Apparently, they were eager to learn whether he was really insane and whether his former associates were ashamed to be seen with him. This is Hawkesworth's answer: "I have, since my being in town, called on my old friend, and seen him. He received me with an ardour of kindness natural to the sensibility of his temper; and we were soon seated together by his fire-side. I perceived upon his table a quarto book, in which he had been writing, a prayer-book, and a Horace. After the first compliments, I said I had been at Margate, had seen his mother and sister, who expressed great kindness for him, and made me promise to come and see him. To this he made no reply; nor did he make any inquiry after those I mentioned. He did not even mention the place, nor ask me any question about it, or what carried me thither. After some pause, and some indifferent chat, I returned to the subject, and said that Mr. Hunter and you would be very glad to see him in Kent. To this he replied very quick, 'I cannot afford to be idle.' I said he might employ his mind as well in the country as in town; at which he only shook his head, and I entirely changed the subject. Upon my asking him when we should see the *Psalms*, he said they were going to press immediately: as to his other undertakings, I found he had completed a translation of *Phædrus* in verse, for Dodsley, at a certain price,[32] and that he is now busy in translating all *Horace* into verse; which he sometimes thinks of publishing on his own account, and sometimes of contracting for it with a bookseller. I advised him to the latter; and he then told me he was in treaty about it, and believed it would be a bargain.

[32] Smart had renewed relations with Robert Dodsley when the *Ode to . . . Northumberland* was published at "Tully's Head." The old publisher died in 1764 and the *Phaedrus* was published in January of the following year by his successor. It was dedicated to Master J. H. Delaval, the small son of Smart's one-time pupil and patron.

He told me, his principal motive for translating *Horace* into verse, was to supersede the prose translation, which he did for Newbery; which, he said, would hurt his memory. He intends, however, to review that translation, and print it at the foot of the page in his poetical version; which he proposes to print in quarto, with the Latin, both in verse and prose, on the opposite page. He told me he once had thoughts of publishing it by subscription; but as he had troubled his friends already, he was unwilling to do it again; and had been pursuaded to publish it in numbers; which, though I rather dissuaded him, seemed at last to be the prevailing bent of his mind. He read me some of it: it is very clever; and his own poetical fire sparkles in it very frequently; yet, upon the whole, it will scarcely take place of Francis's; and therefore, if it is not adopted as a school book, which, perhaps, may be the case, it will turn to little account. Upon mentioning his prose translation, I saw his countenance kindle; and snatching up the book, 'what,' says he, 'do you think I had for this?' I said I could not tell. 'Why,' says he with great indignation, 'thirteen pounds.' I expressed very great astonishment, which he seemed to think he should increase by adding—'but I gave a receipt for a hundred.' My astonishment was now over; and I found that he received only thirteen pounds because the rest had been advanced for his family. This was a tender point; and I found means immediately to divert him from it. He is with very decent people, in a house most delightfully situated, with a terras that overlooks St. James's Park, and a door into it. He was going to dine with an old friend of my own, Mr. Richard Dalton, who has an appointment in the King's Library; and if I had not been particularly engaged, I would have dined with him. He had lately received a very genteel letter from Dr. Lowth, and is by no means considered in any light, that his company as a gentleman, a scholar, and a genius, is less desirable."[33]

On the whole, it would seem that these years immediately after his release from confinement were happy ones. Certainly he was industrious, for these are the years of his greatest productivity. Although a few of his former friends (notably Dr. Johnson) had dropped their acquaintance, there were many, both old and new,

---

[33] The letter is dated "London, October, 1764"; printed by Hunter, *op.cit.*, vol. I, pp. xxiii ff.

with whom he could enjoy his favorite diversions of good food,
good talk, and good music. The charming little verse "Invitation
to Dr. Nares" (*q.v.*) and the "verses from Catullus, after Dining
with Mr. Murray" add their evidence to that supplied by Hawkesworth. A hitherto unnoticed account of one John Kempe (died
June 1, 1823, aged 75) tells of an even wider circle of acquaintance: "Mr. John Kempe for some years resided at the house of his
father, who lived according to the true style of old English hos-
pitality . . . many eminent persons of the day were the frequent
guests of his table. Among these were Romney the portrait painter,
and Stubbs the animal painter, Dixon the celebrated mezzotinto
engraver, Mr. N. Kempe's sister the lovely Lady Hamer, Sir
Thomas Robinson, the unhappy poet Smart, and the Rev. Mr.
Inkson."[34]

Later in the same article John Kempe is quoted as follows:
"Smart loved to hear me play upon my flute, and I have often
soothed the wanderings of his melancholy by some favorite air;
he would shed tears when I played, and generally wrote some
lines afterwards." The writer of the article adds that Kempe "had
a great natural talent for music. He drew the sweetest tones from
his flute, could play almost any air by ear, and was so sensibly
alive to the charms of harmony, that the sublime compositions of
Handel and Mozart produced on him an effect, at times, altogether overpowering." The young flute player makes a charming
addition to the circle of Smart's friends.

That it was a large group is evidenced by the list of subscribers
to the *Psalms* which appeared in a handsome volume late in 1765.
It is a rather astonishing list, as interesting for its omissions as for
the host of familiar names included. Conspicuous by their absence
are Mrs. Smart, the Newbery-Carnan family, and Dr. Johnson.
Aside from these, and such friends as Fielding who had died, and
Rolt who was living in poverty, the list recalls virtually every
association the poet had formed in forty-three years of his life.
There is first his family: his mother, his sister Margaret and her
husband, and Mr. and Mrs. Falkiner (Marianne Smart), the
latter couple taking ten books. His early patrons, the Vane family, are represented by seven members headed by the Earl of

---

[34] "Memoir of John Kempe, Esq.," *Gentleman's Magazine*, 1823, vol. 1, pp. 603-
605.

Darlington. Then come the Cambridge friends: Gray, Mason, Stonehewer, Randall, Addison, Francis Fawkes, Dr. Long, and nearly the whole company of fellows of Pembroke College. The Rev. Jermyn Pratt, brother of the lovely Harriet, is there, and it may be the lady herself is concealed by a married name. Seeing the names of Colman and Thornton one remembers the *Student*, and Smart's early connections with Vauxhall are brought to mind by a number of names: Jonathan and Thomas Tyers, Boyce, Arne, Hogarth, Hayman, Worlidge, Beard, and Lowe. The publishers and editors who had accepted his work are represented by Dodsley, by Cave and Henry of the *Gentleman's*, by Dodd of the *Christian's*, and by Lloyd of the *St. James's*. Even literary "enemies" came to his assistance, for among the names are those of Smollett and of William Kenrick, who generously took six books. Even in the depths of his misery, Smart seems to have had the rare power of making permanent friends; one of the subscribers was "Rev. Mr. Maxwell, Chaplain to the Asylum," and there are also John Sherratt and the Sheeles family, including Miss A. F. Sheeles, the "sublime, transcendant maid" who had helped to bring about his release. Faithful friends like Burney, Dalton, Arthur Murphy, and Garrick are of course represented; and kindly unimpressive names like "Rev. Mr. Tyler" and "Rev. Mr. Morgan Powell" show that their owners had not forgotten the little occasional verses Smart had written for them years before. Poets and poetasters included Whitehead, the Wartons, Cumberland, Churchill, Woty, Grainger, John Phillips, and William Cowper, the last of whom must surely have been the book's most sympathetic reader. All in all, this list of subscribers is a convincing proof that, whatever their opinion of his poetry may have been, people who knew Christopher Smart discovered in him qualities that demanded their respect and their continued friendship.

During these years Smart seems to have been fairly well off. Hunter says, "He was maintained partly by his literary occupations, and partly by the generosity of his friends; receiving among other benefactions fifty pounds a year from the Treasury." The *Psalms* should have brought in a considerable amount. There is furthermore another publication at this time which speaks eloquently for the benevolence of Smart's friends. On October 31, 1765, was published "*A Collection of Melodies for the Psalms of*

David According to the Version of Christopher Smart, A.M. By the most eminent Composers of Church Music."[35]

There were forty-five melodies, corresponding to the different verse forms used. Twelve well-known organists united to produce the book, of whom the most eminent were Boyce and Nares, each of whom provided six melodies, and Randall who did two. It seems unlikely that the book could have been meant to accompany the subscribers' copies of the text, for it was done by another publisher. A more probable conjecture is that it was undertaken as a charity, with the hope that it might stimulate sales of the text, or with the possible idea that the *Psalms* might be adopted by the Church to replace the Psalters then in use. If either of these was the motive, the plan did not succeed; Smart's *Psalms* were never used by the Church, and his book has never been reprinted.

In addition to such acts of kindness as this, it may well be that Smart's Masonic brothers aided him. At what time Smart became a member of this order is not known, but in *Rejoice in the Lamb* he had written, "For I am the Lord's builder and free & accepted MASON in CHRIST JESUS" (viii, 39). Mr. Stead has noted that "a pamphlet entitled *A Defence of Freemasonry* (1765) contains "A Song by Brother C. Smart, A.M. Tune, 'Ye frolicksome Sparks of the Game'" (*Rejoice in the Lamb*, p. 25). The only unpleasant theme in Smart's later poetry is a certain antipathy to the Roman church; it may owe its existence to his Masonic connections, and have been aggravated by the conversion of his estranged wife.

On April 22, 1766, another gesture of benevolence was made to the poet. The king promised him the next place as Poor Pensioner of St. George's, Windsor. However, it appears that no vacancy occurred before Smart's death, and he never enjoyed the privilege. Indeed, from this point onward his affairs seem to have gone from bad to worse. In 1767 the splendid verse translation of *The Works of Horace* appeared in four beautifully printed volumes, the last of his work to be given a dignified and handsome

---

[35] See E. G. Ainsworth, Jr., "An Unrecorded Work by [*sic*!] Christopher Smart," *TLS*, 15 Oct. 1938, who says there is in the Cowan collection a "manuscript of the same in Smart's hand." This indicates a much more thorough knowledge of music on his part than we have known of before. *A Collection of Melodies*, like many of Smart's own works, is now a very rare book. There is a copy in the British Museum, and I have heard of one in private hands.

publication. Despite its merit, it seems to have been a commercial failure. Only two or three pieces from it have ever been reprinted, and copies are very difficult to find today.

It is quite possible that about the time the *Horace* was completed Smart fell ill again. Certainly there is a sudden and astonishing falling-off of his creative power in his two succeeding undertakings. His second oratorio, *Abimelech*, performed in 1768 at the Theatre-Royal in Covent Garden to the music of Dr. Arnold, is a very feeble composition, only occasionally brightened by a few lyrical lines. In the same year he returned to the writing of verse for children, for whom he had earlier designed his translation of the fables of Phaedrus. The new book was *Parables of Our Lord and Saviour Jesus Christ, done into familiar verse* (see Notes, p. 314). It was dedicated to Bonnell George Thornton, the three-year-old son of the wit with whom Smart had long been friendly. By the time of its publication, Smart had completely alienated the critics; by way of review of this volume the *Monthly Review* merely snorted, "*Familiar* verse, indeed!"

Smart was, in truth, in a serious decline. He had broken so completely and violently with his wife and her relatives that when Newbery died in 1767 he arranged for his anger against Smart to be perpetuated. In his will he made provision for Mrs. Smart and the children, but emphatically repeated several times the condition that the poet was under no circumstances to be allowed to enjoy any part of the legacy. Smart had also severed relations with his own family. A hitherto unpublished letter from Mrs. Hunter to Mrs. Smart, preserved in the Reading Library, reveals the pathetically strained relationship that existed within the family:

Margate May 8th

My Dear Sister

I am very sorry that after so Long an interval, I should renew our correspondence on a melancholy occasion, but I owe it to the tender respect which I shall always bear you, for your many actions towards me of affectionate and friendly regard, to inform you that it has pleased God to take our poor Mother to his Mercy out of this scene of sorrow and disappointment, for such it has been to her on many sad accounts; she departed Last night at about a quarter past 8. There is a paper in her own handwriting giving orders about her Funeral. Six of the poorest Widows of the place are to be pall bearers to have each a stuff Gown, to be saved out of the price of the Coffin, which is to be a very mean one, besides these we are ordered to make no invitations, but this days post carrys a Letter to my Brother to tell him if he thinks of coming to the Buring he must be at Margate by next Teusday night. God Bless you, and yours, my dear sister, with every Happiness that does indeed deserve the name. I hope you and I shall see each other again in this World, if not I humbly trust we shall meet in the Blissful Regions of Love, Harmony, and everlasting Friendship,

Yours truly affectionate
M. Hunter.

So far as we know, this bitter rupture was never healed.

During the last two or three years of his life, Smart's fortunes continued to decline. The few letters of his that have survived are only brief notes and tell us nothing except that he was in constant need of money. Some of the friends continued to assist him; Burney, especially, constantly advanced small loans, which were doubtless accepted as gifts. Fanny Burney quotes a delightful phrase from one of Smart's letters to her father: "I bless God for your good nature; which please take as a receipt." Less intimate friends than Burney and those who lacked his genial kindliness were unable to endure this sort of behavior, however. There is a letter dated 1769 from a poetaster named Cuthbert Shaw which shows how Smart's habits must have annoyed many people. Shaw says in part: "I beg your pardon for having troubled you with a letter relative to Mr. Smart whose pretensions, I am since informed, are merely visionary, and indeed from that and other circumstances, I am led to believe he still retains something of his former insanity. I have withdrawn myself from him for some weeks past."[36] There can be little doubt that Smart's mind was once again affected by disease.

Records of the last two years are very meager. In the pages of Fanny Burney's *Diary* we catch glimpses of the ill and broken

---

[36] The letter is printed in Longstaffe, W. H. D.: *The History and Antiquities of the Parish of Darlington in the Bishopric of Durham*, London, 1909.

poet as he was seen by a lively girl of sixteen. On September 14, 1768, she wrote: "Mr. Smart the poet was here yesterday. . . . This ingenious writer is one of the most unfortunate of men—he has been twice confined in a madhouse—and but last year sent a most affecting epistle to papa, to entreat him to lend him half-a-guinea! —How great a pity so clever, so ingenious a man should be reduced to such shocking circumstances. He is extremely grave, and has still great wildness in his manner, looks, and voice; but 'tis impossible to *see* him, and to *think* of his works, without feeling the utmost concern for him. . . ." Just over a year later, in an undated entry between October 4 and November 13, Fanny Burney again records a visit from the poet. "Poor Mr. Smart presented me this morning with a rose, blooming and sweet as if we were in the month of June. 'It was given me,' said he, 'by a fair lady— though not so fair as *you!*'" Such charming little gallantries provided an occasional pleasure in a life that was fast becoming more and more gloomy.

Smart was aware of the road he was going, but he seems to have been powerless to help himself. The friends did what they could, but his debts mounted and his health declined. One event which particularly brightened his prospects was a movement towards reconciliation with him which was made by his brother-in-law, Thomas Carnan. With Newbery dead and buried, Carnan, who had taken over the management of the business, determined to help the poet, and Smart, hearing of his intentions, wrote a letter to him on April 16, 1769. This letter, which is preserved in the Bodleian Library, expresses a strange mixture of emotions, genuine gratitude and pleasure at the prospect of reconciliation struggling with the pride that Newbery had wounded so deeply:

Dear Sir/

Being informed first by Mr. Leach & afterwards by Messrs Mason & Stonhewer that you have determined very benevolently in my favour, I think it incumbent upon me to be thankful. Indeed if mercy be not shewn me somewhere or other I do not see how I can possibly escape a prison. I congratulate you upon your kind resolution, as you may depend upon it, that it will not only be finally a great thing for yourself, but people even now will applaud your generosity and good nature. I desire my duty to Mrs. Newbery and will wait on you or give you the meeting when and where you will please to name.

Yours most sincerely and affectionately,
Christopher Smart.

Carnan had almost certainly offered to publish something, and Smart very likely set to work upon his last production, the *Hymns for . . . Children* which Carnan later published.

In the meantime, Smart made with his work one final "public appearance." The *Public Advertiser* for October 30, 1769, had the following advertisement:

> Devil Tavern, Temple Bar.
> Tomorrow will be performed an ODE in Commemoration of the Birthday of JOHN WILKES, Esq.
>
> Written by CHRIST. SMART, A.M.

That Smart ever knew personally the brilliant firebrand whose birthday he celebrated is not definitely known, but there is every indication that he did. He was apparently one of Wilkes' supporters, for in *Rejoice in the Lamb* there is the entry "For I stood up betimes in behalf of LIBERTY, PROPERTY, and NO EXCISE" (viii, 37). Wilkes had subscribed to the *Psalms*, and probably their acquaintance was of long date. At any event, the following anecdote indicates an acquaintance during the early years of Smart's residence in London: "The late Mr. Christopher Smart, with some poetical Friends, were, one night, on a party at Vauxhall. They had not been long in the Box, before it was proposed to write some humorous descriptive Verses of a Person who squinted—we believe it was Mr. Wilkes, and, too, that he was one among them, but our authority does not positively assert this. Every Man was to write two or more lines; but not one of them, when they came to the eyes, could write anything drolly depicturative of the Party's Squinting—at last Kit Smart jumps up, darts out of the box, runs quite round the Garden, returns out of breath with 'Give me the pen, I have got it,' and immediately writes down the following truly whimsical Couplet:

His eyes are surely of the *am'rous* kind,
For to *each other* they are *still inclin'd*."[37]

When the birthday ode was performed, Wilkes was in prison and
the furious row between the government and the electors of Middlesex was at its height; Wilkes had been thrice elected to represent Middlesex, and thrice the government had refused to allow
him to be seated. Probably Smart's last appearance as "librettist,"
regardless of what merit it may or may not have possessed, met
with a warm reception from the audience of Wilkes' determined
supporters.

Shortly after this occasion, the poet was overtaken by the fate
he had fearfully anticipated in his letter to Carnan. His debts became so excessive that his friends could no longer prevent his im-
prisonment. He was accordingly confined in the King's Bench
Prison, at what exact date is uncertain. Even in prison he seems
to have kept up a good-natured kindliness towards the world. His
last volume, the charming little *Hymns for the Amusement of
Children* was completed there. The verses are touched with a
gentle melancholy, it is true, but they are filled with expressions
of forgiveness towards one's enemies, charity towards a cruel
world, and a sweet hopefulness of better things to come. Fanny
Burney remarks that in one of his last notes to her father, Smart
asked for a donation on behalf of one of his fellow-prisoners
"whom I have already aided according to my willing poverty."

Carnan and Burney obtained "the rules" for him, but his condition during his last months was miserable indeed. A note, said
to have been addressed to the Rev. Mr. Jackson and to have been
written not long before his death, provides the last glimpse of the
poor poet, still patiently hopeful even in the wretchedness to which
his troubled life had finally brought him: "Being upon the recovery of a fit of illness, and having nothing to eat, I beg you to send
me two or three shillings, which (God willing) I will return, with

[37] Printed under the title, "Anecdote of the late Mr. Christopher Smart" in a
clipping, from I know not what source, pasted in Isaac Reed's copy of the *Collected Poems* (Reading, 1791), now in my possession. That Wilkes was the person
intended is confirmed by William Cole: Add. MS. 5080, p. 146 (British Museum):
"Mr. Smart made the following Distic or Epigram upon squinting John Wilkes."
(The couplet then quoted.) Cole's notes reprinted verbatim in Nichols' *Illustrations
of the Literary History of the 18th Century*, vii, 581.

many thanks, in two or three days." On the twenty-first of May, 1771, Christopher Smart died. His remains were buried in St. Paul's Churchyard.

II

Despite the wide range of his work, Christopher Smart was fundamentally and foremost a writer of devotional lyrics. It is true that he tried his hand at virtually every form and type popular in his day, and his contemporaries conceded that he made a respectable sort of accomplishment in many of them. But it is in the religious lyric that Smart's work reaches greatness, and it is to this material that we must return after a brief summary of his other contributions.

The work of Smart's "first period" (before 1756) seldom rises above the level of contemporary versifying, but this fact alone gives it a certain value to the student of the mid-eighteenth century. Most of it is completely typical of its time, and it gives us as good an illustration of the literary fashions of the forties and fifties as that of John Gay provides for the time of Anne and the first George. The favorite epithet for the young poet at the time was "the ingenious Mr. Smart," and like many other good eighteenth-century phrases it describes with aptness what it sets out to describe, in this instance the extent of his talent. Talent he indubitably had, and it was nothing if not ingenious.

Proof of this statement is furnished very early in his career by his translations and original compositions in Latin. The taste for Latin renderings of *L'Allegro* and *Hudibras* and the *Ode for St. Cecilia's Day* has long since declined and will almost certainly never revive, but Pope's gracious note upon receiving the *Ode* is enough to establish its merit. We have also ceased to write or to read original compositions in Latin, but if this were not so we should discover in the Tripos verses the wit and skill which prompted the writer of the article on Smart in Baker's *Biographica Dramatica* to call them "the performance that exhibits the highest flight of his genius," although we should hardly concur in the opinion. Nowadays only one line from these productions is ever repeated, the witty extempore hexameter on the fat beadles of the university: *Pinguia tergeminorum abdomina bedellorum.*

Of the mass of his "magazine verse" (occasional pieces, fables, "ballads," epigrams, and the like), selections are printed in the present volume which will be sufficient, it is hoped, to indicate Smart's abilities along this line. It is only necessary here to remark on them in general that although they show a certain facility in verse-making and are frequently graceful and witty there is in them no evidence of great imagination or daring invention. At times, as in "To the Memory of Master Newbery," there is dignity and strength, and frequently there is real gaiety. But there is nothing to indicate the productions of Smart's later work.

In connection with his magazine work, mention might be made of his prose. He had a gift for the humorous, often ribald, brief essay which is demonstrated in many pages of the *Midwife*. What else he may have written during the association with Newbery is an open question. There is some evidence for believing that he at least had a hand in the composition of one of the famous books for children, *The History of Jack the Giant Killer* (see Mr. Botting's "Christopher Smart in London," *Research Studies of the State College of Washington*, vii, 9) but we have no way of knowing what other hack work Newbery found for him to do. Since in the later part of his life he did three volumes of verse for children (not to mention the prose version of Horace which he had done for Newbery), it does not seem unlikely that he had previously gained some experience in writing for the juvenile market.

Of his "dramatic" efforts, only a few fragments have survived from his one play and from "Mother Midnight's Entertainments," and they do not indicate any particular talent. We possess the texts of his two oratorios, but there is likewise no trace of dramatic ability in them: a few graceful lyrics are all that is worth reading. In the same way, his two extended satires serve only to show that in his early days in London he could turn his verse-making to whatever job was offered. They served their purpose, but are of little interest today.

Something should be said of *The Hop-Garden*, however, which is the longest of all Smart's poems and was the featured work in his 1752 volume. The tradition of the English georgic, in which versified directions for performing some agricultural task provide a framework for descriptive or topographical poetry, had been given its permanent form by John Phillips in his famous poem, *Cyder*. Gay's *Wine*, Grainger's *The Sugar Cane*, and Dyer's *The*

Fleece are among the best-known examples. Whether these versi-fied manuals of husbandry were of any assistance to farmers (if indeed they ever troubled to read them) may well be doubted; but that they pleased the taste of men who knew more of books than of the land is beyond question. The fact that they were modeled upon the lesser work of Virgil made them seem to the literary truly "Augustan." Furthermore, Phillips had adopted for his poem a pseudo-Miltonic versification which to his audience seemed to dignify and ennoble his subject. All his imitators, Smart included, strove to reproduce this bloated and outlandish jargon, with the result that the curse of Miltonism lies like a blight on *The Hop-Garden*, as well as on much other verse of the period.

Smart's poem, ironically, fails to interest the modern reader in inverse proportion to the degree with which it succeeds at what Smart was trying to do. The worst things about it are the two features of the georgic tradition which his first audience expected and admired, namely: the rules for growing hops, and the "Mil-tonic" versification. If we could ignore these, the poem would become not only readable but interesting. Even as it is, one catches behind the heavy draperies of Thomsonian language delightful glimpses of the Kentish countryside, with the silver Medway flow-ing between the hop-fields and the woods. The chief value of the poem is here, in the vivid recollections of the scenes of Smart's childhood at Fairlawn. If he had forgotten about the georgic tradition and written a poem simply describing his boyhood in Kent, our literature would have been enriched far more than it is by *The Hop-Garden*. Unfortunately, he did not write such a poem. But much of the material he did remember and use later for some of his most brilliant descriptions. His religious lyrics are filled with pictures drawn from his observation in Kent. It is these pictures, obscured though they are by the language, that constitute the real value of *The Hop-Garden*.

It remains to speak only of the translations before returning to the religious lyrics. If we except the occasional epigram, Smart's first translation into English was a prose version of the com-plete works of Horace, done in the last years before his complete breakdown and published by Newbery in the spring of 1756. Within its own limitations, it is a masterful job. It attempts to give simply a nearly literal translation; its success may be judged

by the numerous reprintings which have appeared steadily since
its first publication, and by the fact that it is still one of the standard ponies for cribbing schoolboys. Some ten years later, Smart
returned to Horace, and this time translated the entire works into
verse, because, as he told Hawkesworth, he feared the prose version would hurt his memory. It is ironic, considering the popu-
larity of the prose, that this really splendid work never got beyond
its first printing. It was published in four handsome volumes, with
the Latin and English poems on opposite pages and the prose
version as a sort of commentary at the bottom, but few readers
have apparently looked into it, and today copies are virtually unobtainable. A representative selection from it is printed in the following pages. Smart's final attempt at translation was a verse
rendering of the fables of Phaedrus. Since the volume was intended for children, the verse was designed to be simple and plain,
and simple and plain it is.

Of all Smart's non-religious poetry, in spite of a good bit of
cleverness, only the verse translations of Horace and an occasional
lyric such as "On a Bed of Guernsey Lilies" reach heights that
are comparable with those scaled by his religious lyrics. In scope,
in intensity, in the precision and grace of their versification, his
collection of religious poems is worthy to be set beside the work
of our finest devotional lyricists. Since it is upon this poetry that
Smart's reputation must finally rest, the following pages will be
devoted to an analysis of Smart's religious experience and of the
peculiar qualities of his poetry which make it at once so difficult
and so rewarding.

The religion of Christopher Smart is rooted in his response to
the great injunction, "O all ye works of the Lord, bless ye the
Lord: praise Him and magnify Him forever." This is the theme
of all his song, from the Seaton poems to *A Song to David*, from
the *Hymns for Children* to the *Hymns and Spiritual Songs*. He
never tired of it, and upon it he lavished the finest resources of his
art. And in a way it expresses the sum and substance of his religious experience. Religion, for him, was a thing of joy.

There is therefore in his poetry none of the morbid concern
with "sin," none of the groanings and self-lacerations which dis-
figure so much religious verse. In fact, this sort of thing is totally
absent from the character of the man, and finds no expression

whatever in his work. Aside from a momentary shudder over his past "follies" in the *Hymn to the Supreme Being*, there is not a mention of it except when he is paraphrasing the Psalmists. Smart is far more concerned with eulogizing human virtues than in castigating human sins. His moral system is a simple one: the cardinal virtues are sincerity, good-will, and gratitude, and of these he repeatedly sings. They are glorified in the poetry of his youth, maturity, and decline. As early as 1752 we find him referring to "the phenix, fair Sincerity" (*The Hop-Garden*, ii, 12) and his finest eulogy of this virtue is in the lovely poem on St. Bartholomew (Hymn xxii).

The virtue of good-will, which combines both charity and good-nature, Smart early personified as a cherub. He himself was always charitably disposed towards his fellow men, so far as what he called his "willing poverty" would permit him to be, and it is not surprising that in all his religious verse "the poor" make one of the most important themes. It is chiefly by the "preaching of the poor" that all the Christian virtues are instilled:

> Lo! the poor, alive and likely
>   Midst desertion and distress,
> Teach the folk that deal obliquely
>   They had better bear and bless.
>
> Sick and weakly, pris'ners, strangers,
>   Cold in nakedness we lie;
> Train'd in hunger, thirst, and dangers,
>   As in exercise to die.
>
> All avail not to dispirit
>   Toil, determin'd to succeed;
> And we trust in Christ his merit
>   As we have his woes to plead.
>   (*Hymns for . . . Children*, HYMN viii, stanzas 2, 6, & 7)

Towards these poor preachers the rest of the world is frequently exhorted, in Smart's poems, to show charity. The background of Smart's own life is of course an explanation for his interest in and sympathy with the poor. One must remember that he lived in a world that was eventually to let him die in prison for his debts. He was almost constantly the recipient of charity, and his grateful nature responded with the praise of that virtue. There is more in his eulogies of benevolence than the convention of the day.

From this natural thankfulness arises the principal theme of Smart's poetry, the theme of gratitude. This was the deepest emotion of which his nature was capable, and the expression of it runs like Medea's thread through all the mazes of his work. There is first his grateful acknowledgment of kindnesses done him by men and women, of which his writings are a continuous record. It is doubtful that anyone ever assisted him without receiving some expression of his appreciation. It must have been this trait in the man, more than anything else, that kept such sober friends as Dr. Burney faithful to the end.

But in the purely religious verse this emotion is refined into an almost rapturous sense of gratitude to God. "Praise ye the Lord, for He is good, and His mercy endureth forever" is Smart's favorite theme. It was the element that appealed most strongly to him in the Psalms, which he called "the great book of Gratitude," and it is the center and core of *A Song to David*. A lively sense of gratitude was, for Smart, an instinctive reaction to God's goodness, and it seemed to him that all the created universe shared it. He had early begun to attribute this sense of thankfulness to the animals, birds, and fishes (in the Seaton poems, especially), and at last he perceived in the very stones a grateful acknowledgment of the Deity. In translating Ps. xcviii, 9, he gratuitously adds to his original

> . . . the mountain and the rock
> Which also have their ways
> In spirit God to praise.

In the word "praise" lies the complement of "gratitude." All created things, responding "in the spirit" to the infinite goodness of the Creator with a sense of devout gratitude, spontaneously burst forth in hymns of adoration. "To glorify God and to enjoy him forever"—this is not merely the "whole duty of man," as the Catechism assures us; it is the whole purpose and meaning of life, both of man and of all things besides. "Music exists," said Bach, "for the glory of God, and to give pleasure"; Smart substitutes for the word "music," the word "life," and accepts the whole not as an injunction to action but as the statement of a condition.

From the apperception of a validity in this thesis comes the substance of most of those passages upon which his reputation must finally rest.

Religion, for him, consisted primarily in a whole-hearted participation in this universal chorus of praise to the Deity, in which all living things unite, being prompted by a sense of gratitude for the inestimable gift of life. He perceived "the Spirit" present in non-human forms of life as well as in the hearts and minds of his fellows. The song of birds, the varied coloring of flowers, fish in their swift and nervous movements, the perfect muscular coordination of animals, even stones and clouds and rippling waters—all seemed to him expressions of the universal theme. In passage after passage of his poetry this grand chorus breaks upon the ear. It reaches its most rapturous expression in stanzas 50 to 86 of *A Song to David*. "For by the grace of God I am the Reviver of ADORATION amongst ENGLISH MEN," Smart wrote in *Rejoice in the Lamb* (xi, 37), and one who knows his religious poetry must admit that this is no idle boast.

Of the more conventional aspects of his religion, little need be said. He was an orthodox Church of England man, and the linking of the state religion with the state's power is common in his poems. He took a special pride in the English navy, mentioning its exploits on many occasions. It is natural that his nationalism should be reflected also in denunciations of the enemies of England, and we need not be surprised to find religious and political opponents grouped together. His conception of his country as a kind of modern Israel, a chosen people, makes quite natural his inevitable reference to France as "vain Moab." Catholic France is also "idolatrous Moab," for Smart, being a Protestant, sees nothing but idolatry in the veneration of holy images. His distrust of Rome goes further than this, however, and in various of his *Hymns* he inveighs against "Roman frauds and fees." It seems to me not at all unlikely that this bitterness against the Roman Church may have been one of the causes of the rupture between Smart and his wife. Certainly he would have been appalled at the idea of his daughters being educated in convents.

There are a few minor elements in Smart's personal religion, which, although quite orthodox, have an importance out of all proportion to their place in the teaching of the Church. He was fascinated, for example, by the theories concerning angels, and utilized virtually all the material that can be found about them in the accepted Scriptures and in the Apocryphal books. He also worked out a rather complete demonology, personifying through it the various evils which beset him. They were numerous: ill-health, debt, love of liquor, vanity, alienation from his family and from some of his friends; but the two that seemed to hinder his poetic accomplishment most were on the one hand the specter of remembered madness and on the other the smug, prosaic rationality of his critics. Against these two he found one sure defense: his faith in Christ, who

> . . . to the lunatic restor'd
> Serenity of soul.

"Serenity of soul": that after all is the key to Christopher Smart's secret. It is the thing he sought through all his confused and unhappy life, the peace he found upon occasions, the almost magical calm that pervades all his best work. *A Song to David*, itself, is caught and held in the serene suspense of absolute music.

In addition to the purely religious matter of Smart's poems, one other feature is so pronounced that it deserves consideration here. This is his reference to and treatment of "the catalogue of lovely things in earth, and sea, and sky." His poetry is richer in vivid description of the multitudinous life of this planet than that of any other poet of his century, even Thomson not excepted. He does not often indulge in long and minute analyses, it is true, but his pages are crowded with a succession of brilliant images which flash upon the mind's eye with startling realism. Even in the early poetry, birds and flowers, the Kentish fields, woods and clear streams are described again and again. He was particularly fascinated by fish, and it is easy to picture him as a boy lying silently beside his favorite stream watching them come and go; like the nymphs in *The Hop-Garden* who

> From yon bent oaks, in Medway's bosom fair,
> Wonder at silver bleak, and prickly pearch,
> That swiftly through their floating forests glide.
>
> i, 113-115.

When he says in *A Song to David,*

> And by the coasting reader spied,
> The silverlings and crusions glide
> For ADORATION gilt,

one remembers a boy in a boat on the Medway. It is interesting
that Smart never talks of catching fish: he seems always content
to watch them and let them be. One of the most charming aspects
of his treatment of nature is his willingness to refrain from tam-
pering. His flowers are rarely in vases, his animals never caged,
and the jewels he most admires are those in the earth. It is not
strange that his verse should be more appealing today than it was
when it was written.

The most important characteristic of Smart's nature material
seems to me to be found in what one might call an essential happiness. In the period in which he wrote, such nature material as
appears is almost universally handled in a mood of gentle melancholy or in a way which reveals a basic distrust. The great exception to this statement is of course Thomson, but even his work
reveals these qualities at times. There are traces of them in Smart's
early work, along with all the other literary conventions of the
day, but they are entirely lacking from his mature poems. Nowhere does that work show the slightest sense of nature as an
alien and hostile power. On the contrary,

> Gentle nature seems to love us
>   In each fair and finished scene,
> All is beauteous blue above us,
>   All beneath is cheerful green.
>   (HYMN xix, 4)

"Romantic shade," beloved of the late eighteenth century, is
completely absent from the landscapes of Smart's mature work.
There is never any gloom; there are no mists on the hills, no dark
and threatening clouds in the sky. Not for him the "dim religious
light" of the graveyard school, nor the sentimental gloom of such
a poem as Collins' *Ode to Evening.* On the contrary, there is a
quality in Smart's scenes akin to that of Shelley's, whose landscapes often have the wonderful luminous clarity that seems to be
peculiar to countries lying near the forty-fifth parallel. But Shel-

ley had been in Italy; Smart was never out of England. Yet his scenes are flooded with brilliant, revealing sunlight. Even in the brief and occasional night scenes, as in "The Nativity of Our Lord," there is a frosty clearness in the atmosphere and one has the impression of a cloudless sky dotted with stars.

We have had among English poets a host who have described the beauty of nature in vivid images; we have had many deeply religious poets; and we have had expert lyricists in abundance. But I do not know of any poet who has combined these three elements with quite the joy and melody of Christopher Smart.

Smart's verse, however, is of a peculiar kind. In much of his best writing there is a "queerness," an oddness of phrasing and syntax, a grouping of highly unusual elements which at first sight is puzzling. Critics, attempting to account for his very original methods of composition, have generally adopted some variant of Hunter's notion that these methods were, in themselves, "melancholy proofs of the recent estrangement of his mind." When we examine the whole of his work, however, we find that his methods were developed over the whole period of his career and that they were present, at least in embryonic form, in the work done years before there was any question of his being sane. Furthermore, Hunter altered much of the poetry he reprinted to suit himself, and thus obscured many evidences of Smart's early attempts to work out his own peculiar idiom. To take a slight example, Smart's fondness for the unusual word "grutch" is evident in *The Hop-Garden* of 1752, but Hunter blunted Smart's effect by consistently altering it to "grudge." When we find in *A Song to David*, therefore, the unusual phrase, "Grutch not of Mammon and his leaven," there is no reason to assume that Smart's recent insanity prevented him from writing what he meant.

Smart's very original idiom does not result in any way from his illness. It is accounted for principally by a combination of three elements, each perfectly rational in itself but not elsewhere found combined with the others. These elements are derived from the three forms of art which Smart apparently admired above all others; Hebrew poetry, the poetry of Horace, and eighteenth-century music. Christopher Smart's greatest "hero," whom he admired both as man and as poet, is a composite figure made up of the various Psalmists and other Biblical writers and called by him,

David. His imagination had been fired at least as early as 1746, when a friend had suggested that he take David as the subject for his "Ode on St. Cecilia's Day," but he had refused on the ground that "the chusing too high subjects hath been the ruin of many a tolerable genius." Nevertheless, the figure of David was already before his eyes; he had heard far off the echoes of that "harp of high, majestic tone" which were destined to ring in his ears for the rest of his mortal life. The Psalmist was later to become his patron saint, one of his chief poetic masters, and the source of his greatest inspiration, but the Ode does not concern itself with "the shepherd king upon his knees." Instead of that great and simple figure, the reader is asked to

> Behold Arion—on the stern he stands
> Pall'd in theatrical attire.

It took Smart seven years to divest his Muse of these unattractive garments, and when at length she appeared in her native beauty, innocent of frivolous adornment, the public was as shocked as it was later to be by the tremendous naked figures of Blake's visions.

What Smart's poetry owes to the poetry of "David" is a certain sublimity, the quality that Coleridge declared was always Hebraic in origin. It is partly accounted for by the subject matter, and is increased by such typically Hebraic material as the concern with angels, demons, and the chosen people ideology. Smart's imagery also owes much to his devoted reading of the sacred poetry. Patient editors like J. R. Tutin have discovered Biblical echoes in almost every stanza of *A Song to David*, for example, and the feat could be repeated with most of his religious poems. His images frequently seem exotic if not bizarre, for they are in the tradition of Hebraic poetry rather than English. Furthermore, he caught the trick of compressing an idea into a naked shining image which accounts for much of the brilliance of Biblical poetry. In *Rejoice in the Lamb* he noted, "For my talent is to give an impression upon words by punching, that when the reader casts his eye upon 'em, he takes up the image from the mould wᶜʰ I have made" (xii, 42). A better description of this feature of his work could hardly be devised. This matter of "impression" was an essential feature of his art, and we shall return to discuss it when we consider the Horatian elements in his work, for he professed to find it in Horace as well as in the sacred poets.

Parallelism is another device he learned from the Bible, and utilized with great effect in his own poetry. But the feature of Hebraic poetry that contributes most, perhaps, to the effect of "sublimity" in Smart is the sweeping catalogue. This naming over of all the ranks of creation appears repeatedly in the Seaton poems; it accounts for the best stanzas of the "Hymn to the Supreme Being" and of many of the *Hymns and Spiritual Songs*; and it, like many other characteristic features of Smart's work, appears at its finest in the "Adoration" stanzas of *A Song to David*. Smart's favorite sequence includes the main groups of birds, fish, trees or flowers, precious stones, animals, and man, and he achieves some of his grandest effects by combining this catalogue with the repeated word or phrase, as in the stanzas from the *Song* mentioned above, and in the "Praise Him" stanzas of Hymn vi, "The Presentation of Christ in the Temple." David's finest use of this device is probably in the great Psalm civ.

The second great master whose work Smart studied is strangely dissimilar to David; he is that urbane and impeccable pagan, Quintus Horatius Flaccus. A more unusual combination is hard to imagine, yet elements from the work of both writers are consciously and very often successfully united in the poetry of Smart. The poetry and the critical theories of Horace had much to do with Smart's production, but it might be noted at first that Smart is not Horatian in any complete sense. In the first place, he is far too direct. He can never manage the gentle aloofness of the Latin. Such a delicate mingling of poignancy and humor as Horace evokes in the "Eheu, fugaces, Posthume, Posthume" is impossible to a man of Smart's forthright nature. It is a question of difference of temperament. A second pronounced distinction is observable in the musical qualities of the two. There is a full, flowing melody in the lyrics of Horace, moving calmly and with dignity through line after line. His "phrase," to borrow a term from music, is almost always a long phrase, as serene and controlled, yet quite as full, as many of Beethoven's. Smart's phrase, on the contrary, is short and abrupt. It seldom fills more than two lines (and his lines themselves are not long), and almost never carries

over into a succeeding stanza.[38] The rhymes, the accentual nature
of the English language, and the fact that Smart's *Psalms, Hymns*,
and many of the shorter lyrics were designed to be sung probably
account for this quality.

For an understanding of what Smart did learn and utilize from
the Latin poet we have fortunately three excellent guides: the
literal prose translation of the complete works, which first appeared in 1756; the verse translation of 1767; and the critical
preface to the latter. In this preface Smart speaks enthusiastically
of "the lucky risk of the Horatian boldness" and asserts his belief
that he can preserve this feature in English. By way of explanation
he writes: "Horace is not so much an original in respect to his
matter and sentiments (which are rather too frequently bor-
rowed) as with regard to that unrivalled peculiarity of expression,
which has excited the admiration of all succeeding ages." He goes
on to point out those features of Horace's poetry which seem to
him to account for this "peculiarity of expression" and to explain
them. "In the first place I have especially attended to, what the
critics call his *curiosa felicitas*, of which many of my predecessors
seem not to have entertained the most remote idea. Mr. *Pope*
himself, however happy in taking off the spirit and music of
Horace, has left us no remarkable instance, to the best of my
memory, of this kind. In truth this is a beauty, that occurs rather
in the Odes, than the other parts of Horace's works; where the
aiming at familiarity of style excluded the curiosity of choice
diction." He then refers the reader to various places in his translation where he feels he has succeeded in bringing this stylistic
quality over into English.

In the *Ars Poetica*, Smart found certain aspects of technique
reduced to a critical theory, and an examination of his reading of
passages which concern the "curiosity of choice diction" may
throw some light on his practice. Horace's dicta regarding vocabulary refer chiefly to the use of old words, the coinage of new ones,
and the use of an unusual word or of a word in an unusual sense.
Of old words he says, *Multa* [vocabula] *renascentur, quae jam
cecidere*, or, as Smart has it in his prose translation, "Sundry words

[38] This observation applies of course only to the lyric poetry. In the Seaton
poems the Miltonic model imposed a length of phrase, fulsome rather than full.
After 1757 Smart never returned to this manner.

shall revive which now have receded." The idea appealed to Smart, and his later poetry is filled with archaic and obsolete words. I think Horace's remark encouraged him to revive such words as the following (after each I have given the latest date cited by the *N.E.D.*): "estrange" ("change," Ps. cvi, 20), 1622; "consist" ("remain," Ps. cxix, Lamed, 2), 1556; "disgust" ("loathe"), 1716; "lowth" ("My soul adheres to lowth and dust"), 1535; "meed" ("merit, worth, fame," *Song*), 1714.

Horace also gave permission for the coinage of new words, in a passage which Smart renders in prose as: "If it happens to be expedient to illustrate some abstruse subjects by new invented terms; it will follow that you must coin words never heard of by the old-fashioned Cethegi: and a dispensation will be granted if used with moderation: and new and lately coined words will have more credit if they descend from a Greek fountain sparingly deduced." In practice, Smart took the warnings about moderation more seriously than the grant of permission, but he did occasionally coin a word. When we encounter such a strange adjective as "assentatious," for example, we should remember that it is justified by Horatian authority.

As to the third aspect of his "unrivalled peculiarity of expression," Horace gives ample authority, by precept and example, for the use of an unusual word, or of a common word in an unusual sense, and this is the feature of the *curiosa felicitas* (according to Smart's definition of it) which appealed most strongly to the English poet. Horace had warned *Difficile est proprie communia dicere*, which Smart renders

> 'Tis arduous common things to say
> In such a clean peculiar way
> Until they fairly seem your own.

Smart was, I believe, quite conscious of this difficulty, but it seems to me that much of the strangeness of his verse is due to his sincere effort to find a "clean peculiar way" of giving expression to his material. A few examples out of hundreds will have to suffice for illustration. In Ps. xxxv he translates "they gaped upon me" by the phrase "with distended mows censorious," making the word *mow*, which literally means "grimace," carry a double force by its analogy with *mouth*. In *A Song to David* he uses "renown"

in the obsolete sense of "commendation of a person," and "con-
dole" with the meaning "to sorrow greatly, grieve, or lament."
The unusual word is aptly illustrated when Smart speaks in Ps.
lxxiv of "the stupendous roar/ Of billows breaking to *refund*/
The fishes on the shore." Often the peculiarity of choice diction is
attained by the old device of using a common word, usually Latin
in origin, in a strictly literal sense, as "idly *vague* from his indulgent yoke" (Ps. cvi, 29), or "*supplicate* the knee" (Ps. xlv, 13).
Again, in his desire for concrete verbs, he repeatedly makes other
parts of speech serve that purpose:

> But we to great Jehova trust
> And *prostrate* to the Lord our dust.
>
> Ps. xx

In many of his verse translations from Horace, especially in the
Odes, Smart succeeds rather brilliantly in preserving the verbal
felicity of the original, and his success often depends upon his
using the English language as audaciously as Horace had used
Latin. An obvious example is his rendering of the phrase *crinibus
ambiguoque vultu* (Bk. ii, Ode 5) as "And smooth ambiguous
face." Here the perfection of the translation does not arise from
the literalness, but from the fact that Smart's phrase is as daringly
unusual as the original. It is not to be supposed that Smart's
efforts in this direction are always so successful. Sometimes when
aiming at the *curiosa felicitas* he manages to get only a specious
sort of glamour, but in general it is fair to say that the more
strictly Horatian his verse is, the better.

A very interesting note to a line in the verse translation (Bk. i,
Ode 12) seems to put beyond reasonable doubt the contention
that Smart's practice was deliberate and calculated. He is translating the lines:

> Gentis humanae pater atque custos,
> Orte Saturno, tibi cura magni
> Caesaris fatis data: tu secundo
> Caesare regnes.

The English version runs:

> Sire and preserver of our race,
> From Saturn sprung, do thou convey

> That Caesar hold the second place
> In thine eternal sway.

Smart has placed an asterisk beside the word "convey," and in a footnote has explained: "A word attempted *in the peculiarity of Horace*—grant by delegation, make over your right." (Italics my own.)

Smart was aware, however, that the "unrivalled peculiarity of expression" was not accomplished solely by means of care in the matter of diction. He adds, and discusses at length, a further element of the Horatian technique. His definition of it is inconclusive, but the examples he cites illustrate what he understood by it. "Besides the *curiosa felicitas*, so much of Horace by himself, there is another poetical excellence, which tho' possessed in a degree by every great genius, is exceeding in our Lyric to surpass; I mean the beauty, force and vehemence of *Impression*: which leads me to a rare and entertaining subject, not (I think) any where much insisted on by others. *Impression* then, is a talent or gift of Almighty God, by which a Genius is impowered to throw an emphasis upon a word or sentence in such wise, that it cannot escape any reader of sheer good sense or true critical sagacity. This power will sometimes keep it up thro' the medium of a prose translation; especially in scripture, for in justice to truth and everlasting pre-eminence, we must confess this virtue to be far more powerful and abundant in the sacred writings." Here Smart quotes, in Hebrew and English, the following passages: "O well is thee, and happy thou shalt be!" "Her ways are ways of pleasantness, and all her paths are peace," and "How great is his goodness; and how great is his beauty!" He then gives examples of "impression" in various quotations from classic writers, ending with a number from the Odes of Horace.

By what technical devices this *impression* is accomplished, Smart does not say here, but an answer may be found, I think, in one of the rules laid down in the *Ars Poetica*:

> In verbis etiam tenuis, cautusque serendis.
> Dixeris egregie, notum si callida verbum
> Reddiderit junctura novum.

His early prose translation of this passage indicates clearly that this is what he had in mind when he later considered the device of "impression": "In the interspersing of his words too he must be nice and wary. You will express yourself admirably well, if a clever connection should impress an air of novelty to a common word."

A distinct feature of Smart's best work is the artful grouping of words within the phrase, the use of unfamiliar grammatical constructions, the alteration of normal arrangement—in short, the use of various technical devices all designed to "throw an emphasis upon a word or sentence." It would be tedious to attempt an exact classification of all Smart's devices, or indeed to list any considerable number of examples. Neither can one take individual phrases and cite exact parallels in Horace. The point to be made is that no reader can study any single page in the translation of the *Psalms*, the *Hymns and Spiritual Songs*, the verse Horace, *A Song to David*, or any of the better work in his smaller collections of the later period, without being made aware of the unusual phrase as the most distinguishing feature of the expression. "O train me in the track Of thine eternal way" (Ps. xxvii), "Death and the shades anon will press thee home" (Horace, Bk. i, Ode 4), "The nectarine his strong tint imbibes, And apples of ten thousand tribes, And quick peculiar quince" (*Song*), "Ye that skill the flowers to fancy" (Hymn iii):—the "impression" of phrases like these, as Smart sagely remarked, "cannot escape any reader of sheer good sense and true critical sagacity." There are many places in the poems of Smart's finest period where the expression is awkward, and these are without exception, I believe, places where the poet has made an attempt at an unusual grouping which does not quite come off. In contrast to these stand such felicitous instances of his success as "the blaze and rapture of the sun" (Ps. xix, 5), or "Lo, through her works gay Nature grieves/ How brief she is and frail" (Guernsey Lilies).

Something of the total effect of Horace upon Smart may be judged from the verse rendering of the Ode, *Persicos odi, puer, apparatus* (see p. 245) which is also worth noting as one of the very few eighteenth-century examples of pure Sapphics in English, and because its strikingly Browningesque quality may suggest a more pronounced influence on the great Victorian's style than Smart has hitherto been credited with.

The mingling of Hebraic splendor and license with the "un-

rivalled peculiarity of expression" which Smart admired so much
in Horace accounts for those awkward and difficult passages in
Smart's verse that Hunter, and others after him, attributed to the
poet's insanity. But it also accounts for the rare beauty of several
hundred stanzas that are unique in eighteenth-century poetry, if
not in the whole range of English lyric verse.

The third element which seems to have been combined with
the Hebraic and the Horatian to produce Smart's unusual technique is one for which it is easier to find a parallel in music, and
especially eighteenth-century music. It can best be described, perhaps, as a sense of arrangement of material which produces an
effect like that of a very complicated counterpoint in music. This
method is set forth and illustrated at length in the notes on the
Hymns and Spiritual Songs, and those on *A Song to David* in the
present volume, and it needs illustration for full comprehension.
It must suffice here to say that Smart carefully selects and ar-
ranges his words in such a manner that the extent of their reference is doubled and tripled. To state the matter in another way,
a specific word, phrase, or image, is chosen and it is placed in a
certain position because only by such selection and such placing
can it be made to refer to one or more minor themes without los-
ing any of the force of its statement of the theme which happens
at the moment to be dominant. The unwary reader is frequently
surprised to discover that Smart, instead of talking about one
thing at a time, as is the usual habit of lyricists, may at a given
moment be carrying along as many as six different themes at
once. Thus it is that a particular word or phrase or image, considered in isolation, may seem extremely odd until one notices
the subtle connections between it and the surrounding material.
While the reader is never allowed to lose sight of the immediate
meaning, he is constantly reminded of other ideas. It is this complicated arrangement of material, more than anything else, which
accounts for the richness, and at times the difficulty, of Smart's
poetry. We are not accustomed to much complexity of thought in
lyric poetry, and some readers may resent it. But if they do, they
will miss the intellectual excitement which Smart's best poetry is
capable of giving.

This third element in his technique should lay at rest finally
the notion that Smart's highly original poetry results from his

having been insane. If *A Song to David* and some of his astonishing *Hymns* are anything, they are triumphs of the artistic intellect under perfect control. Of course Smart often failed, and he was either incapable of very severe self-criticism or in too urgent need of money to hold his pieces by him for perfecting. But that one whose brain was not working with almost mathematical precision could produce Smart's best work is inconceivable. The importance of careful arrangement in his work should also dispel any ideas that Smart was in any sense a "pre-Romantic." He was a lover of nature, of course, but so was Pope. He was not working towards a new simplification and naturalness. On the contrary, he was developing to a new peak the neo-classic regard for order and regularity, for rich elaboration upon a structurally solid framework. His art is the art of baroque; it is more like that of Handel and his English successors such as Arne and Boyce than like that of any other artists I can call to mind.

Christopher Smart was neither a perfect man nor a perfect poet. The record of his life and character is marred by many flaws, and of the total mass of his writing only a portion is permanently valuable. But just as, in spite of his shortcomings, he remains a lovable and in some ways an admirable man, so that part of his work that is worth serious reading is poetry which we should be much poorer without. His art is very rare, and in his own century it is unique. The blemishes in his work, like those in his character, are obvious even to the undiscerning. Yet his admirers need offer no apologies for him, for his genuine virtues should be as obvious as his faults. It is no small accomplishment to have produced the greatest poem of its kind in our language. *A Song to David* seems to receive wider recognition year by year; in time, perhaps, the best of his other pieces will become as well known as his masterpiece, and their author will be given his rightful place in the front rank of English devotional lyricists.

Christopher Smart, from an anonymous portrait

The Midwife;

OR THE

OLD WOMAN'S MAGAZINE.

Containing all *the* WIT, *and* all *the* HUMOUR, *and* all *the* LEARNING, *and* all *the* JUDGEMENT, *that has* ever been, *or* ever will be *inserted in* all *the other* Magazines, *or the* Magazine of Magazines, *or the* Grand Magazine of Magazines, *or any other Book whatsoever. So that those who buy this Book will need no other.*

Publish'd pursuant to several Acts of Parliament, *and by the Permission of their* most Christian *and* most Catholic MAJESTIES, *the* GREAT MOGUL *and the* STATES GENERAL.

Embellish'd with CUTS *according to* CUSTOM.

LONDON.

Printed for MARY MIDNIGHT *and Sold by* T. CARNAN *in* St Pauls Church Yard.

Price Three Pence.

Title page of *The Midwife*

Minor Poems, 1735-1756

To Ethelinda

ON HER DOING MY VERSES THE HONOUR OF WEARING THEM
IN HER BOSOM.—WRITTEN AT THIRTEEN.

Happy verses! that were prest
In fair Ethelinda's breast!
Happy Muse, that didst embrace
The sweet, the heav'nly-fragrant place!
Tell me, is the omen true,
Shall the bard arrive there too?

Oft thro' my eyes my soul has flown,
And wanton'd on that ivory throne:
There with extatic transport burn'd,
And thought it was to heav'n return'd.
Tell me, is the omen true,
Shall the body follow too?

When first at nature's early birth,
Heav'n sent a man upon the earth,
Ev'n Eden was more fruitful found,
When Adam came to till the ground:
Shall then those breasts be fair in vain,
And only rise to fall again?

No, no, fair nymph—for no such end
Did heav'n to thee its bounty lend;
That breast was ne'er design'd by fate,
For verse, or things inanimate;
Then throw them from that downy bed,
And take the poet in their stead.

EDITIONS

Poems, 1752. (Text.)   *Poems*, 1791.

Ode on taking a Bachelor's Degree

IN ALLUSION TO HORACE. BOOK III, ODE 30.
EXEGI MONUMENTUM AERE PERENNIUS, &C.

'Tis done:—I tow'r to that degree,
    And catch such heav'nly fire,
That Horace ne'er could rant like me,
[1] Regali situ pyramidum altius.—   Nor is [1]King's-chapel higher.
My name in sure recording page
[2] Quod non innumerabilis Anorum feries, &c.   [2]Shall time itself o'erpow'r
If no rude mice with envious rage
    The buttery books devour.
A *title too with added grace,
    My name shall now attend,
[3] —Dum Capitolium Scandet cum tacitê virgine pontifex.   [3]Till to the church with silent pace
    A nymph and priest ascend.
Ev'n in the schools I now rejoice,
    Where late I shook with fear,
[4] —Quà violens Obstrepit Aufidus.—   Nor heed the [4]Moderator's voice
    Loud thund'ring in my ear.
[5] —Aeolium carmen ad Italos Deduxisse modos.   Then with [5]Æolian flute I blow
    A soft Italian lay,
[6] —Qua pauper aquae Daunus, &c.   Or where [6]Cam's scanty waters flow,
    Released from lectures, stray.
Meanwhile, friend Banks†, my merits claim
    Their just reward from you,
[7] —Sume superbiam Quaesitam meritis.—   For Horace bids [7]us challenge fame,
    When once that fame's our due,
Invest me with a graduate's gown,
    Midst shouts of all beholders,
[8] —Mihi Delphicâ Lauro cinge volens— comam.   [8]My head with ample square-cap crown,
    And deck with hood my shoulders.

* Bachellor.   † A celebrated Taylor.

EDITIONS

The Student, i, 348 (16 Sept., 1750).
Poems, 1791. (Text.)   *Cambridge Tart*, 1823, p. 7.
A Book of Cambridge Verse, ed. E. E. Kellett, Cambridge, 1911.

Prologue to *A Trip to Cambridge,* or *The Grateful Fair*

In ancient days, as jovial Horace sings,
When laurell'd Bards were lawgivers, and kings,
Bold was the Comic Muse, without restraint
To name the vicious, and the vice to paint;
Th'enliven'd picture from the canvas flew,
And the strong likeness crouded on the view.
Our Author practices more general rules,
He is no niggard of his knaves and fools;
Both small and great, both pert and dull his Muse
Displays, that every one may pick and chuse:
The rules dramatic though he scarcely knows
Of time and place, and all the piteous prose
That pedant Frenchmen snuffle through the nose.
Fools; who prescribe what Homer shou'd have done,
Like tattling watches, they correct the sun.
Critics, like posts, undoubtedly may show
The way to Pindus, but they cannot go.
Whene'er immortal Shakespeare's works are read,
He wins the heart before he strikes the head;
Swift to the soul the piercing image flies
Swifter than Harriot's wit, or Harriot's eyes:
Swifter than some romantic trav'llers thought,
Swifter than British fire when William fought.
Fancy precedes, and conquers all the mind,
Deliberating Judgment slowly comes behind;
Comes to the field with blunderbuss and gun,
Like heavy Falstaff, when the work is done;
Fights when the battle's o'er, with wond'rous pain,
By Shrewsbury's clock, and nobly slays the slain.
The Critic's censures are beneath our care,
We strive to please the generous and the fair:
To their decision we submit our claim,
We write not, speak not, breathe not, but for them.

EDITIONS

Cambridge Journal and Weekly Flying Post, no. 157 (Sept. 19, 1747).
Poems, 1791. (Text.)

Ode

THE AUTHOR APOLOGIZES TO A LADY, FOR HIS BEING A LITTLE MAN.

Natura nusquam magis, quam
in minimis tota est.—*Plin.*

Yes, contumelious fair, you scorn
  The amorous dwarf, that courts you to his arms,
But ere you leave him quite forlorn,
  And to some youth gigantic yield your charms,
Hear him—oh hear him, if you will not try,
And let your judgment check th' ambition of your eye.

Say, is it carnage makes the man?
  Is to be monstrous really to be great?
Say, is it wise or just to scan
  Your lover's worth by quantity, or weight?
Ask your mamma and nurse, if it be so;
Nurse and mamma, I ween, shall jointly answer, no.

The less the body to the view,
  The soul (like springs in closer durance pent)
Is all exertion, ever new,
  Unceasing, unextinguish'd, and unspent;
Still pouring forth executive desire,
As bright, as brisk, and lasting, as the vestal fire.

Does thy young bosom pant for fame;
  Would'st thou be of posterity the toast?
The poets shall ensure thy name,
  Who magnitude of *mind* not *body* boast.
Laurels on bulky bards as rarely grow,
As on the sturdy oak the virtuous mistletoe.

Look in the glass, survey that cheek—
  Where Flora has with all her roses blush'd;
The shape so tender—looks so meek—
  The breasts made to be press'd, not to be crush'd—
Then turn to me—turn with obliging eyes,
Nor longer Nature's works, in miniature, despise.

Young Ammon did the world subdue,
Yet had not more external man than I;
Ah! charmer, should I conquer you,
With him in fame, as well as size, I'll vie.
Then, scornful nymph, come forth to yonder grove,
Where I defy, and challenge, all thy utmost love.

EDITIONS
The Student, ii, 26 (Oct. [?], 1750).
Poems, 1752. (Text.)   *Poems*, 1791.

Apollo and Daphne
AN EPIGRAM

When Phoebus was amorous and long'd to be rude,
Miss Daphne cry'd, pish! and ran swift to the Wood;
And rather than do such a naughty Affair,
She became a fine Laurel to deck the God's Hair.
The Nymph was (no Doubt[1]) of a cold Constitution,
For sure to turn Tree[2] was an odd Resolution:
Yet in this she behav'd like[3] a true modern Spouse,
For she fled from his Arms to distinguish his Brows.

[1] "be sure" for "no Doubt" (1791).
[2] "To be turned to a tree" for "For sure to turn tree" (1791).
[3] "resembled" for "behav'd like" (1791).

EDITIONS
The Midwife, i, 137 (Dec., 1750).
Poems, 1752. (Text. The same as that of *The Midwife*.)
Nonpareil.   Newbery's *Art of Poetry*, 1762.
Poems, 1791.

An Epigram

ON A WOMAN WHO WAS SINGING BALLADS FOR MONEY
TO BURY HER HUSBAND.

For her Husband deceas'd, Sally chants the sweet lay,
Why, faith, this is singular sorrow;

But (I doubt) since she sings for a dead man to-day,
She'll cry for a live one to-morrow.

EDITIONS

Midwife, i, 229 (Feb., 1751). (Text.)
Nonpareil, p. 105.   *Poems*, 1791.

Care and Generosity

A FABLE

Old Care with Industry and Art,
At length so well had play'd his Part;
He heap'd up such an ample store,
That Av'rice cou'd not sigh for more:
Ten thousand flocks his shepherd told,
His coffers overflow'd with Gold;
The land all round him was his own,
With corn his crouded granaries groan.
In short so vast his charge and gain,
That to possess them was a pain;
With happiness oppress'd he lies,
And much too prudent to be wise.
Near him there liv'd a beauteous maid,
With all the charms of youth array'd;
Good, amiable, sincere and free,
Her name was Generosity.
'Twas hers the largess to bestow
On rich and poor, on friend and foe.
Her doors to all were open'd wide,
The pilgrim there might safe abide:
For th' hungry and the thirsty crew,
The bread she broke, the drink she drew;
There Sickness laid her aching head,
And there Distress cou'd find a bed.—
Each hour with an all-bounteous hand,
Diffused she blessings round the land:
Her gifts and glory lasted long,
And numerous was th' accepting throng.

At length pale Penury seiz'd the dame,
And Fortune fled, and Ruin came,
She found her riches at an end,
And that she had not made one friend.—
All cursed her for not giving more,
Nor thought on what she'd done before;
She wept, she rav'd, she tore her hair,
When lo! to comfort her came Care.—
And cry'd, my dear, if you will join,
Your hand in nuptial bonds with mine;
All will be well—you shall have store,
And I be plagu'd with Wealth no more.—
Tho' I restrain your bounteous heart,
You still shall act the generous part.—
The Bridal came—great was the feast,
And good the pudding and the priest;
The bride in nine moons brought him forth
A little maid of matchless worth:
Her face was mix'd of Care and Glee,
They christen'd her Oeconomy;
And styled her fair Discretion's Queen,
The mistress of the golden mean.
Now Generosity confin'd,
Is perfect easy in her mind:
She loves to give,[1] yet knows to spare,
Nor wishes to be free from Care.

1 "Perfectly easy in her mind; Still loves to give, . . ." (1791).

EDITIONS

Midwife, ii, 277 (Sept., 1751).   *Gentleman's Magazine,* Oct., 1751.
London Magazine, Oct., 1751.   *Poems,* 1752. (Text.)
          Universal Visiter, p. 282 (June, 1756).
Newbery's *Art of Poetry,* 1762.   *Poems,* 1791.
A Song to David and Other Poems by Christopher Smart,
     ed. Percival Serle, Melbourne, 1923.

The Tea-Pot and Scrubbing-Brush

A FABLE

A Tawdry *Tea-pot, A-la-mode,*
Where Art her utmost Skill bestow'd,
Was much esteem'd for being old,
And on its Sides with Red and Gold
Strange Beasts were drawn in Taste *Chinese,*
And frightful Fish and hump-back Trees.
  High in an elegant Beaufet
This pompous Utensil was set,
And near it, on a Marble Slab,
Forsaken by some careless Drab,
A veteran *Scrubbing-brush* was plac'd,
And the rich Furniture disgrac'd.
The *Tea-pot* soon began to flout,
And thus its Venom *spouted* out.
"Who from the Scullery or Yard,
Brought in this low, this vile Black-guard,
And laid in insolent Position,
Amongst us People of Condition?
Back to the Helper in the Stable,
Scour the close-stool, or wash-house table,
Or cleanse some horsing-block, or Plank,
Nor dare approach us Folk of Rank.
Turn—Brother Coffee-pot, your Spout,
Observe the nasty stinking lout,
Who seems to scorn my Indignation,
Nor pays due Homage to my Fashion:
Take, Sister[1] Sugar-dish, a View,
And Cousin Cream-pot, pray do you."
"Pox on you all," replies old *Scrub*—
"Of Coxcombs ye confederate Club.
Full of Impertinence, and Prate,
Ye hate all Things that are sedate.
None but such ignorant Infernals,

[1] "silver" for "sister" (1791).

Judge, by Appearance, and Externals.
Train'd up in Toil and useful Knowledge,
I'm Fellow of the Kitchen College,
And with the Mop, my old Associate,
The Family Affairs negociate—
Am Foe to Filth, and Things obscene,
Dirty by making others clean—
Not shining, yet I cause to shine,
My Roughness makes my Neighbours fine;
You're fair without, but foul within,
With Shame impregnated, and Sin;
To *you* each impious Scandal's owing,
You set each Gossip's Clack a-going.—
How Parson *Tythe* in secret Sins,
And how Miss *Dainty* brought forth Twins:
How dear delicious *Polly Bloom,*
Owes all her Sweetness to Perfume;
Tho' grave at Church, at Cards can bet,
At once a Prude and a Coquette.
'Twas better for each *British* Virgin,
When on roast Beef, strong Beer, and Sturgeon,
Joyous to Breakfast they sat² round,
Nor was³ asham'd to eat a Pound,
These were the Manners, these the Ways,
In good Queen Bess's golden Days,
Each Damsel ow'd her Bloom and Glee,
To wholesome Elbow-grease, and me.
But now they center all their Joys
In empty Rattle traps and Noise.
Thus where the Fates send *you,* they send
Flagitious Times, which ne'er will mend,
Till some Philosopher can find
A *Scrubbing-brush* to scour the Mind."

² "set" for "sat" (1791).   ³ "were" for "was" (1791).

EDITIONS

Midwife, iii, 134 (April [?], 1753). (Text.)
Universal Visiter, No. IV, p. 190 (April, 1756).
Mrs. Midnight's Orations, 1763.
St. James Magazine, iii, 365 (Feb., 1764).
A Collection of Modern Fables, London, 1771.   *Poems,* 1791.

On an Eagle
Confined in a College-Court

Imperial bird, who wont to soar
 High o'er the rolling cloud,
Where Hyperborean mountains hoar
 Their heads in Ether shroud;—
Thou servant of almighty Jove,
Who, free and swift as thought, could'st rove
 To the bleak north's extremest goal;—
Thou, who magnanimous could'st bear
The sovereign thund'rer's arms in air,
 And shake thy native pole!—

Oh cruel fate! what barbarous hand,
 What more than Gothic ire,
At some fierce tyrant's dread command,
 To check thy daring fire,
Has plac'd thee in this servile cell,
Where Discipline and Dullness dwell,
 Where Genius ne'er was seen to roam;
Where ev'ry selfish soul's at rest,
Nor ever quits the carnal breast,
 But lurks and sneaks at home!

Tho' dim'd thine eye, and clipt thy wing,
 So grov'ling! once so great!
The grief-inspired Muse shall sing
 In tend'rest lays thy fate.
What time by thee scholastic Pride
Takes his precise, pedantic stride,
 Nor on thy mis'ry casts a care,
The stream of love ne'er from his heart
Flows out, to act fair pity's part;
 But stinks, and stagnates there.

Yet useful still, hold to the throng—
 Hold the reflecting glass,—
That not untutor'd at thy wrong

The passenger may pass:
Thou type of wit and sense confin'd,
Cramp'd by the oppressors of the mind,
  Who study downward[1] on the ground;
Type of the fall of Greece and Rome;
While more than mathematic gloom,
  Envelopes all around.

[1] "Born to look downward" for "Who study downward" (*Student*).

EDITIONS

The Student, ii, 356 (June [?], 1751)—here dated "5 May, 1751."
Royal Magazine, or Quarterly Review, vol. III, April-June, 1751.
Poems, 1752. (Text.)   *Oxford Sausage*, 1764.   *Poems*, 1791.
Southey's *Specimens of the Later English Poets*, ii, 443 (London, 1807).
Cambridge Tart, 1823 (p. 172).
Campbell's *Specimens of the British Poets*, London, 1841.
A Book of Cambridge Verse, ed. Kellett, Cambridge, 1911.
A Song to David and Other Poems by Christopher Smart, ed. Percival Serle,
  Melbourne, 1923.

The Force of Innocence

TO MISS C———[1]

The blooming damsel, whose defence
Is adamantine innocence,
Requires no guardian to attend
Her steps, for modesty's her friend:
Tho' her fair arms are weak to wield
The glitt'ring spear, and massy shield;
Yet safe from force and fraud combin'd,
She is an Amazon in mind.

With this artillery she goes,
Not only 'mongst the harmless beaux:
But even unhurt and undismay'd,
Views the long sword and fierce cockade.
Tho' all a syren as she talks,
And all a goddess as she walks,

[1] Title "The Power of Innocence. A Song. By Mrs. Midnight."
  (*Midwife* version.)

Yet decency each action[2] guides,
And wisdom o'er her tongue presides.

Place her in Russia's showery plains,
Where a perpetual winter reigns,
The elements may rave and range,
Yet her fix'd mind will never change.
Place her, Ambition, in thy tow'rs,
'Mongst the more dang'rous golden show'rs,
E'en there she'd spurn the venal tribe,
And fold her arms against the bribe.

Leave her defenceless and alone,
A pris'ner in the torrid zone,
The sunshine there might vainly vie
With the bright lustre of her eye;
But Phoebus' self, with all his fire,
Cou'd ne'er one unchaste thought inspire.
But virtue's path she'd still pursue,
And still, my fair,[3] wou'd copy you.

[2] "each motion guides" for "each action guides" (*Midwife*).
[3] "And still ye fair," for "And still, my fair" (*Midwife*).

EDITIONS

The Midwife, ii, 111 (June, 1751).   *Poems*, 1752. (Text.)
*A Collection of Pretty Poems, for the Amusement of
    Children Six Foot High* . . . etc., c. 1758. (Here entitled
    "The Power of Innocence.")
Poems, 1791.

To the Rev. Mr. Powell,

ON THE NON-PERFORMANCE OF A PROMISE
HE MADE THE AUTHOR OF A HARE

FRIEND, with regard to this same Hare
Am I to hope, or to despair?
By punctual Post the Letter came,
With P____l's Hand, and P____l's Name;
Yet there appear'd for Love or Money,
Nor Hare, nor Leveret, nor Coney.
Say, my dear Morgan, has my Lord,

Like other great Ones kept his Word,
Or have you been deceiv'd by 'Squire;
Or has your Poacher lost his Wire,
Or in some unpropitious Hole,
Instead of Puss trepan'd a Mole?
Thou valiant Son of great Cadwallader,
Hast thou a Hare, or hast thou swallow'd her?
  But now, methinks I hear you say,
(And shake your Head, "Ah, well-a-day!
"Painful Pre-eminence to be wise,
"WE WITS have such short Memories.
Oh, that the Act was not in Force!
A Horse!—My Kingdom for a Horse!
To love—yet be denied the Sport;
Oh, for a Friend or two at Court!
God knows there's scarce a Man of Quality
In all our peerless Principality—"
  But hold—for on his Country joking
To a warm Welchman's most provoking.
As for poor Puss, upon my Honour,
I never set my Heart upon her.
But any Gift from Friend to Friend
Is pleasing in its Aim and End.
I, like the Cock, wou'd spurn a Jewel
Sent by th' unkind, th' unjust or cruel.[1]
But honest P____el!—Sure from him
A Barley-corn wou'd be a Gem.
Pleas'd therefore had I been, and proud,
And prais'd thy generous Heart aloud,
If 'stead of Hare (but do not blab it)
You'd sent me only a Welch Rabbit.

[1] "and cruel" for "or cruel" (1791).

EDITIONS

The Midwife, iii, 120 (April [?], 1753). (Text.)   *Nonpareil*, p. 220.
Arthur Murphy's "Gray's Inn Journal" in *The Craftsman*, no. 32 (with many
  variants; see Botting: "Christopher Smart's Association with Arthur Murphy,"
  JEGP, xliii, 54-55).   *Poems*, 1791.
A Song to David and Other Poems by Christopher Smart, ed. Percival Serle,
  Melbourne, 1923.

To the Memory of Master N———,

WHO DIED OF A LINGERING ILLNESS, AGED ELEVEN[1]

Henceforth be every tender Tear supprest,
Or let us weep for Joy, that he is blest;
From Grief to Bliss, from Earth to Heav'n remov'd,
His Mem'ry honour'd, as his Life belov'd.
That Heart o'er which no Evil e'er had Pow'r!
That Disposition, Sickness could not sour!
That Sense, so oft to riper Years denied!
That Patience Heroes might have own'd with Pride!
His painful Race undauntedly he ran,
And on[2] the Eleventh Winter died a MAN.

[1] Title—"On the Death of Master Newbery,
after a lingering illness" (1791).
[2] "in" for "on" (1791).

EDITIONS

The Midwife, iii, 146 (April [?], 1753). (Text.)   *Nonpareil*, p. 227.
Newbery's *Art of Poetry*, 1762.
Christian's Magazine, iii, 136 (March, 1762).   *Poems*, 1791.

An Invitation to Mrs. Tyler,

A CLERGYMAN'S LADY,
TO DINE UPON A COUPLE OF DUCKS
ON THE ANNIVERSARY OF THE AUTHOR'S WEDDING-DAY

Had I the pen of Sir John Suckling,
And could find out a rhyme for duckling,
Why dearest madam, in that case,
I would invite you to a brace.
Haste, gentle shepherdess,* away,
Tomorrow is the gaudy day,
That day, when to my longing arms,
Nancy resign'd her golden charms,
And set my am'rous inclination
Upon the bus'ness of the nation.
Industrious *Moll*,† with many a pluck,

Unwings the plumage of each duck;
And as she sits a brooding o'er,
You'd think she'd hatch a couple more.
Come, all ye Muses, come and sing—
Shall we then roast them on a string?
Or shall we make our dirty jilt run,
To beg a roast of Mrs.‡ Bilton?
But to delight you more with these,
We shall provide a dish of pease:
On ducks alone we'll not regale you,
We'll wine, we'll punch you, and we'll ale you.
To-morrow is the gaudy day,
Haste, gentle shepherdess, away.

  * As every good parson is the shepherd of his flock,
his wife is a shepherdess, of course.
  † The Maid.   ‡ The Landlady of the Public House.

EDITIONS

Gentleman's Magazine, July, 1754, p. 335.
Poems, 1791. (Text.)

The Seaton Poems

On the IMMENSITY of the
SUPREME BEING

Once more I dare to rouse the sounding string,
The Poet of my God—Awake my glory,
Awake my lute and harp—my self shall wake,
Soon as the stately night-exploding bird
In lively lay sings welcome to the dawn.

   List ye! how nature with ten thousand tongues
Begins the grand thanksgiving, Hail, all hail,
Ye tenants of the forest and the field!
My fellow subjects of th' eternal King,
I gladly join your Mattins, and with you
Confess his presence, and report his praise.

   O Thou, who or the Lambkin, or the Dove
When offer'd by the lowly, meek, and poor,
Prefer'st to Pride's whole hecatomb, accept
This mean Essay, nor from thy treasure-house
Of Glory' immense the Orphan's mite exclude.

   What tho' th' Almighty's regal throne be rais'd
High o'er yon azure Heav'n's exalted dome
By mortal eye unken'd—where East nor West
Nor South, nor blust'ring North has breath to blow;
Albeit He there with Angels, and with Saints
Hold conference, and to his radiant host
Ev'n face to face stand visibly confest:
Yet know that nor in Presence or in Pow'r
Shines He less perfect here; 'tis Man's dim eye
That makes th' obscurity. He is the same,
Alike in all his Universe the same.

   Whether the mind along the spangled Sky
Measures[1] her pathless walk, studious to view
Thy works of vaster fabrick, where the Planets
Weave their harmonious rounds, their march directing

[1] "measure" for "measures" (1791).

Still faithful, still inconstant to the Sun;
Or where the Comet thro' space infinite
(Tho' whirling worlds oppose and globes of fire)
Darts, like a javelin, to his destin'd goal;
Or where in Heav'n above the Heav'n of Heav'ns
Burn brighter Suns, and goodlier Planets roll
With Satellits more glorious—Thou art there.
  Or whether on the Ocean's boist'rous back
Thou ride triumphant, and with out-stretch'd arm
Curb the wild winds and discipline the billows,
The suppliant Sailor finds Thee there, his chief,
His only help—When Thou rebuk'st the storm—
It ceases—and the vessel gently glides
Along the glassy level of the calm.
  Oh! cou'd I search the bosom of the sea,
Down the great depth descending; there thy works
Wou'd also speak thy residence; and there
Wou'd I thy servant, like the still profound,
Astonish'd into silence muse thy praise!
Behold! behold! th' unplanted garden round
Of vegetable coral, sea-flow'rs gay,
And shrubs of[2] amber from the pearl-pav'd bottom
Rise richly varied, where the finny race
In blithe security their gambols play:
While high above their heads Leviathan,
The terror and the glory of the main,
His pastime takes with transport, proud to see
The ocean's vast dominion all his own.
  Hence thro' the genial bowels of the earth
Easy may fancy pass; till at thy mines
Gani or *Raolconda* she arrive,
And from the adamant's imperial blaze
Form weak ideas of her maker's glory.
Next to *Pegu* or *Ceylon* let me rove,
Where the rich ruby (deem'd by Sages old
Of Sovereign virtue) sparkles ev'n like *Sirius*
And blushes into flames. Thence will I go

2 "shrubs with" for "shrubs of" (1791).

To undermine the treasure-fertile womb
Of the huge *Pyrenean*, to detect
The Agat and the deep-intrenched gem
Of kindred Jasper—Nature in them both
Delights to play the Mimic on herself;
And in their veins she oft pourtrays the forms
Of leaning hills, of trees erect, and streams
Now stealing softly on, now thund'ring down
In desperate cascade, with flow'rs and beasts
And all the living landskip of the vale:
In vain thy pencil *Claudio*, or *Poussin*,
Or thine, immortal *Guido*, wou'd essay
Such skill to imitate—it is the hand
Of God himself—for God himself is there.

    Hence with the ascending springs let me advance,
Thro' beds of magnets, minerals and spar,
Up to the mountain's summit, there t'indulge
Th' ambition of the comprehensive eye,
That dares to call th' Horizon all her own.
Behold the forest, and the expansive verdure
Of yonder level lawn, whose smooth-shorn sod
No object interrupts, unless the oak
His lordly head uprears, and branching arms
Extends—Behold in regal solitude,
And pastoral magnificence he stands
So simple! and so great! the under-wood
Of meaner rank an awful distance keep.
Yet Thou art there, yet God himself is there,
Ev'n on the bush (tho' not as when to *Moses*
He shone in burning Majesty reveal'd)
Nathless conspicuous in the Linnet's throat
Is his unbounded goodness—Thee her Maker,
Thee her preserver chants she in her song;
While all the emulative vocal tribe
The grateful lesson learn—no other voice
Is heard, no other sound—for in attention
Buried, ev'n babbling *Echo* holds her peace.

    Now from the plains, where th' unbounded prospect

Gives liberty her utmost scope to range,
Turn we to yon enclosures, where appears
Chequer'd variety in all her forms,
Which the vague mind attract and still suspend
With sweet perplexity. What are yon tow'rs,
The work of lab'ring man and clumsy art,
Seen with the ring-dove's nest—on that tall beech
Her pensile house the feather'd Artist builds—
The rocking winds molest her not; for see,
With such due poize the wond'rous fabrick's hung,
That, like the compass in the bark, it keeps
True to itself and stedfast ev'n in storms.
Thou ideot that asserts, there is no God,
View and be dumb for ever—
Go bid *Vitruvius* or *Palladio* build
The bee his mansion, or the ant her cave—
Go call *Correggio,* or let *Titian* come
To paint the hawthorn's bloom, or teach the cherry
To blush with just vermilion—hence away—
Hence ye prophane! for God himself is here.
Vain were th' attempt, and impious to trace
Thro' all his works th' Artificer Divine—
And tho' nor shining sun, nor twinkling star
Bedeck'd the crimson curtains of the sky;
Tho' neither vegetable, beast, nor bird
Were extant on the surface of this ball,
Nor lurking gem beneath; tho' the great sea
Slept in profound stagnation, and the air
Had left no thunder to pronounce its maker;
Yet man at home, within himself, might find
The Deity immense, and in that frame
So fearfully, so wonderfully made,
See and adore his providence and pow'r—
I see, and I adore—O God most bounteous!
O infinite of Goodness and of Glory!
The knee, that thou hast shap'd, shall bend to Thee,
The tongue, which thou hast tun'd, shall chant thy praise,

And, thine own image, the immortal soul,
Shall consecrate herself to Thee for ever.

EDITIONS

On the Immensity of the Supreme Being, Cambridge, 1751.
On the Immensity of the Supreme Being, Cambridge, 1753.
On the Immensity of the Supreme Being, London, 1756. (Text.)
Poems on the Attributes of the Supreme Being, Dublin, 1761.
Pearch, *A Collection of Poems by Several Hands*, London, 1770.
Elegant Extracts . . . etc., London, 1790, *etc.*
Poems, 1791.
Musae Seatoniensis.

On the OMNISCIENCE of the SUPREME BEING

Arise, divine Urania, with new strains
To hymn thy God, and thou, immortal Fame,
Arise, and blow thy everlasting trump.
All glory to th' Omniscient, and praise,
And pow'r, and domination in the height!
And thou, cherubic Gratitude, whose voice
To pious ears sounds silverly so sweet,
Come with thy precious incense, bring thy gifts,
And with thy choicest stores the altar crown.
Thou too, my Heart, whom he, and he alone
Who all things knows, can know, with love replete,
Regenerate, and pure, pour all thyself
A living sacrifice before his throne:
And may th' eternal, high mysterious tree,
That in the center of the arched Heav'ns
Bears the rich fruit of Knowledge, with some branch
Stoop to my humble reach, and bless my toil!

When in my mother's womb conceal'd I lay,
A senseless embryo, then my soul thou knewst,
Knewst all her future workings, every thought,
And every faint idea yet unform'd.
When up the imperceptible ascent
Of growing years, led by thy hand, I rose,

Perception's gradual light, that ever dawns
Insensibly to day, thou didst vouchsafe,
And taught me by that reason thou inspir'dst,
That what of knowledge in my mind was low,
Imperfect, incorrect—in Thee is wondrous,
Uncircumscrib'd, unsearchably profound,
And estimable solely by itself.
    What is that secret pow'r, that guides the brutes,
Which Ignorance calls Instinct? 'Tis from Thee,
It is the operation of thine hands
Immediate, instantaneous; 'tis thy wisdom,
That glorious shines transparent thro' thy works.
Who taught the Pye, or who forwarn'd the Jay
To shun the deadly nightshade? tho' the cherry
Boasts not a glossier hue, nor does the plumb
Lure with more seeming sweets the amorous eye,
Yet will not the sagacious birds, decoy'd
By fair appearance, touch the noxious fruit.
They know to taste is fatal, whence alarm'd
Swift on the winnowing winds they work their way.
Go to, proud reas'ner, philosophic Man,
Hast thou such prudence, thou such knowledge?—No.
Full many a race has fell[1] into the snare
Of meretricious looks, of pleasing surface,
And oft in desart isles the famish'd pilgrim
By forms of fruit, and luscious taste beguil'd,
Like his forefather Adam, eats and dies.
For why? his wisdom on the leaden feet
Of slow experience, dully tedious, creeps,
And comes, like vengeance, after long delay.
    The venerable Sage, that nightly trims
The learned lamp, t'investigate the pow'rs
Of plants medicinal, the earth, the air,
And the dark regions of the fossil world,
Grows old in following, what he ne'er shall find;
Studious in vain! till haply, at the last
He spies a mist, then shapes it into mountains,
And baseless fabrics[2] from conjecture builds.

[1] "fall'n" for "fell" (1791).   [2] "fabric" for "fabrics" (1791).

While the domestic animal, that guards
At midnight hours his threshold, if oppress'd
By sudden sickness, at his master's feet
Begs not that aid his services might claim,
But is his own physician, knows the case,
And from th' emetic herbage works his cure.
Hark from afar the *feather'd matron screams,
And all her brood alarms; the docile crew
Accept the signal one and all, expert
In th' art of nature and unlearn'd deceit:
Along the sod, in counterfeited death,
Mute, motionless they lie; full well appriz'd,
That the rapacious adversary's near.
But who inform'd her of th' approaching danger,
Who taught the cautious mother, that the hawk
Was hatcht her foe, and liv'd by her destruction?
Her own prophetic soul is active in her,
And more than human providence her guard.

   When Philomela, e'er the cold domain
Of cripled winter 'gins t'advance, prepares
Her annual flight, and in some poplar shade
Takes her melodious leave, who then's her pilot?
Who points her passage thro' the pathless void
To realms from us remote, to us unknown?
Her science is the science of her God.
Not the magnetic index to the North
E'er ascertains her course, nor buoy, nor beacon.
She heav'n-taught voyager, that sails in air,
Courts nor coy West nor East, but instant knows
What †Newton, or not sought, or sought in vain.
   Illustrious name, irrefragable proof
Of man's vast genius, and the soaring soul!
Yet what wert thou to him, who knew his works,
Before creation form'd them, long before
He measur'd in the hollow of his hand
Th' exulting ocean, and the highest Heav'ns
He comprehended with a span, and weigh'd
The mighty mountains in his golden Scales:

* The Hen Turkey.   † The Longitude.

Who shone supreme, who was himself the light,
E'er yet Refraction learn'd her skill to paint,
And bend athwart the clouds her beauteous bow.
  When Knowledge at her father's dread command
Resign'd to Israel's king her golden key,
Oh to have join'd the frequent auditors
In wonder and delight, that whilom heard
Great Solomon descanting on the brutes.
Oh how sublimely glorious to apply
To God's own honour, and good will to man,
That wisdom he alone of men possess'd
In plenitude so rich, and scope so rare.
How did he rouse the pamper'd silken sons
Of bloated ease, by placing to their view
The sage industrious ant, the wisest insect,
And best oeconomist of all the field!
Tho' she presumes not by the solar orb
To measure times and seasons, nor consults
Chaldean calculations, for a guide;
Yet conscious that December's on the march
Pointing with icie hand to want and woe,
She waits his dire approach, and undismay'd
Receives him as a welcome guest, prepar'd
Against the churlish winter's fiercest blow.
For when, as yet the favourable Sun
Gives to the genial earth th'enlivening ray,
Not the poor suffering slave, that hourly toils
To rive the groaning earth for ill-sought gold,
Endures such trouble, such fatigue, as she;
While all her subterraneous avenues,
And storm-proof cells with management most meet
And unexampled housewifry she forms:
Then to the field she hies, and on her back,
Burden immense! she bears the cumbrous corn.
Then many a weary step, and many a strain,
And many a grievous groan subdued, at length
Up the huge hill she hardly heaves it home:
Nor rests she here her providence, but nips
With subtle tooth the grain, lest from her garner

In mischievous fertility it steal,
And back to day-light vegetate its way.
Go to the Ant, thou sluggard, learn to live,
And by her wary ways reform thine own.
But, if thy deaden'd sense, and listless thought
More glaring evidence demand; behold,
Where yon pellucid populous hive presents
A yet uncopied model to the world!
There Machiavel in the reflecting glass
May read himself a fool. The Chemist there
May with astonishment invidious view
His toils outdone by each plebeian Bee,
Who, at the royal mandate, on the wing
From various herbs, and from discordant flow'rs
A perfect harmony of sweets compounds.
    Avaunt Conceit, Ambition take thy flight
Back to the Prince of vanity and air!
Oh 'tis a thought of energy most piercing,
Form'd to make pride grow humble; form'd to force
Its weight on the reluctant mind, and give her
A true but irksome image of herself.
Woful vicissitude! when Man, fall'n Man,
Who first from Heav'n from gracious God himself
Learn'd knowledge of the Brutes, must know, by Brutes
Instructed and reproach'd, the scale of being;
By slow degrees from lowly steps ascend,
And trace Omniscience upwards to its spring!
Yet murmur not, but praise—for tho' we stand
Of many a Godlike privilege amerc'd
By Adam's dire transgression, tho' no more
Is paradise our home, but o'er the portal
Hangs in terrific pomp the burning blade;
Still with ten thousand beauties blooms the Earth
With pleasures populous, and with riches crown'd.
Still is there scope for wonder and for love
Ev'n to their last exertion—show'rs of blessings
Far more than human virtue can deserve,
Or hope expect, or gratitude return.
Then, O ye People, O ye Sons of men,

Whatever be the colour of your lives,
Whatever portion of itself his Wisdom
Shall deign t' allow, still patiently abide,
And praise him more and more; nor cease to chant
ALL GLORY TO TH'OMNISCIENT, AND PRAISE,
AND POW'R, AND DOMINATION IN THE HEIGHT!
And thou, cherubic Gratitude, whose voice
To pious ears sounds silvery so sweet,
Come with thy precious incense, bring thy gifts,
And with thy choicest stores the altar crown.
ΤΩ ΘΕΩ ΔΟΞΑ.

EDITIONS

On the Omniscience of the Supreme Being, Cambridge, 1752.
On the Omniscience of the Supreme Being, Cambridge, 1756. (Text.)
Poems on the Attributes of the Supreme Being, Dublin, 1761.
Elegant Extracts, or Useful and Entertaining Pieces of Poetry, London,
   1790, *etc.* 1791.
Musæ Seatoniensis.

Hymn to the Supreme Being

on Recovery
from a Dangerous Fit of Illness
To Doctor James

Dear Sir,

Having made an humble offering to HIM, without whose
blessing your skill, admirable as it is, would have been to no purpose, I think myself bound by all the ties of gratitude, to render
my next acknowledgments to you, who, under God, restored me
to health from as violent and dangerous a disorder, as perhaps
ever man survived. And my thanks become more particularly
your just tribute, since this was the third time, that your judgment and medicines rescued me from the grave, permit me to
say, in a manner almost miraculous.

If it be meritorious to have investigated medicines for the cure
of distempers, either overlooked or disregarded by all your predecessors, millions yet unborn will celebrate the man, who wrote
the *Medicinal Dictionary*, and invented the *Fever Powder*.

Let such considerations as these, arm you with constancy against
the impotent attacks of those whose interest interferes with that
of Mankind; and let it not displease you to have those for your
particular enemies, who are foes to the Public in general.

It is no wonder, indeed, that some of the retailers of medicines
should zealously oppose whatever might endanger their Trade,
but 'tis amazing that there should be any Physicians mercenary
and mean enough to pay their court *to*, and ingratiate themselves
with, such persons, by the strongest efforts to prejudice the in-
ventor of the Fever Powder at the expence of honour, dignity, and
conscience. Believe me, however, and let this be a part of your
consolation, that there are very few Physicians in *Britain*, who
were born gentlemen, and whose fortunes place them above such
sordid dependencies, who do not think and speak of you, as I do.

I am, dear Sir,

Your most obliged,

And most humble Servant,

C. SMART.

HYMN
to the SUPREME BEING

I

When *Israel's* ruler on the royal bed
  In anguish and in perturbation lay,
The down reliev'd not his annointed head,
  And rest gave place to horror and dismay.
Fast flow'd the tears, high heav'd each gasping sigh
When God's own prophet thunder'd—MONARCH, THOU MUST DIE.

II

And must I go, th'illustrious mourner cry'd,
  I who have serv'd thee still in faith and truth,
Whose snow-white conscience no foul crime has died
  From youth to manhood, infancy to youth,
Like *David*, who have still rever'd thy word
The sovereign of myself and servant of the Lord!

III

The judge Almighty heard his suppliant's moan,
  Repeal'd his sentence, and his health restor'd;
The beams of mercy on his temples shone,
  Shot from that heaven to which his sighs had soar'd;
The †sun retreated at his maker's nod
And miracles confirm the genuine work of God.

IV

But, O immortals! What had I to plead
  When death stood o'er me with his threat'ning lance,
When reason left me in the time of need,
  And sense was lost in terror or in trance,
My sinking soul was with my blood inflam'd,
And the celestial image sunk, defac'd and maim'd.

* Hezekiah (Isaiah xxxviii).   † Isaiah, chap. xxxviii.

V

I sent back memory, in heedful guise,
  To search the records of preceding years;
Home, like the *raven to the ark, she flies,
  Croaking bad tidings to my trembling ears.
O sun, again that thy retreat was made,
And threw my follies back in to the friendly shade!

VI

But who are they, that bid affliction cease!—
  Redemption and forgiveness, heavenly sounds!
Behold the dove that brings the branch of peace,
  Behold the balm that heals the gaping wounds—
Vengeance divine's by penitence supprest—
She †struggles with the angel, conquers, and is blest.

VII

Yet hold, presumption, nor too fondly climb,
  And thou too hold, O horrible despair!
In man humility's alone sublime,
  Who diffidently hopes he's *Christ's* own care—
O all-sufficient Lamb! in death's dread hour
Thy merits who shall slight, or who can doubt thy power?

VIII

But soul-rejoicing health again returns,
  The blood meanders gentle in each vein,
The lamp of life renew'd with vigour burns,
  And exil'd reason takes her seat again—
Brisk leaps the heart, the mind's at large once more,
To love, to praise, to bless, to wonder and adore.

IX

The virtuous partner of my nuptial bands,
  Appear'd a widow to my frantic sight;

* Gen. viii. 7.   † Gen. xxxii, 24, 25, 26, 27, 28.

My little prattlers lifting up their hands,
 Beckon me back to them, to life, and light;
I come, ye spotless sweets! I come again,
Nor have your tears been shed, nor have ye knelt in vain.

X

All glory to th' ETERNAL, to th' IMMENSE,
 All glory to th' OMNISCIENT and GOOD,
Whose power's uncircumscrib'd, whose love's intense;
 But yet whose justice ne'er could be withstood.
Except thro' him—thro' him, who stands alone,
Of worth, of weight allow'd for all Mankind t'atone!

XI

He rais'd the lame, the lepers he made whole,
 He fix'd the palsied nerves of weak decay,
He drove out Satan from the tortur'd soul,
 And to the blind gave or restor'd the day—
Nay more—far more unequal'd pangs sustain'd,
Till his lost fallen flock his taintless blood regain'd.

XII

My feeble feet refus'd my body's weight,
 Nor wou'd my eyes admit the glorious light,
My nerves convuls'd shook fearful of their fate,
 My mind lay open to the powers of night.
He pitying did a second birth bestow
A birth of joy—not like the first of tears and woe.

XIII

Ye strengthen'd feet, forth to his altar move;
 Quicken, ye new-strung nerves, th' enraptur'd lyre;
Ye heav'n-directed eyes, o'erflow with love;
 Glow, glow, my soul, with pure seraphic fire;
Deeds, thoughts, and words no more his mandates break,
But to his endless glory work, conceive, and speak.

XIV

O! penitence, to virtue near allied,
  Thou can'st new joys e'en to the blest impart;
The list'ning angels lay their harps aside
  To hear the musick of thy contrite heart;
And heav'n itself wears a more radiant face,
When charity presents thee to the throne of grace.

XV

*Chief of metallic forms is regal gold;
  Of elements, the limpid fount that flows;
Give me 'mongst gems the brilliant to behold;
  O'er *Flora's* flock imperial is the rose:
Above all birds the sov'reign eagle soars;
And monarch of the field the lordly lion roars.

XVI

What can with great *Leviathan* compare,
  Who takes his pastime in the mighty main?
What, like the *Sun*, shines thro' the realms of air,
  And gilds and glorifies th' ethereal plain—
Yet what are these to man, who bears the sway;
For all was made for him—to serve and to obey.

XVII

Thus in high heaven charity is great,
  Faith, hope, devotion hold a lower place;
On her the cherubs and the seraphs wait,
  Her, every virtue courts, and every grace;
See! on the right, close by th' Almighty's throne,
In him she shines confest, who came to make her known.

XVIII

Deep-rooted in my heart then let her grow,
  That for the past the future may atone;

* Pind. Olymp. 4.

That I may act what thou hast giv'n to know,
That I may live for THEE and THEE alone,
And justify those sweetest words from heav'n,
"THAT HE SHALL LOVE THEE MOST* TO WHOM THOU'ST
  MOST FORGIVEN."

* Luke vii, 41, 42, 43.

EDITIONS

Hymn to the Supreme Being . . . 1756.   *Poems,* 1791. (Text.)

Selections from
Rejoice in the Lamb

From the "For" Section

vii

For I am not without authority in my jeopardy, which I derive
inevitably from the glory of the name of the Lord.

For I bless God whose name is Jealous—and there is a zeal to
deliver us from everlasting burnings.

For in my existimation is good even amongst the slanderers and
my memory shall arise for a sweet savour unto the Lord.

For I bless the PRINCE of PEACE and pray that all the guns may be
nail'd up, save such are for the rejoicing days.

For I have abstained from the blood of the grape and that even
at the Lord's table.

For I have glorified God in GREEK and LATIN, the consecrated
languages spoken by the Lord on earth.

For I meditate the peace of Europe amongst family bickerings
and domestic jars.

For the HOST is in the WEST—the Lord make us thankful unto
salvation.

For I preach the very GOSPEL of CHRIST without comment & with
this weapon shall I slay envy.

For I bless God in the rising generation, which is on my side.

For I have translated in the charity, which makes things better &
I shall be translated myself at the last.

For he that walked upon the sea, hath prepared the floods with
the Gospel of peace.

For the merciful man is merciful to his beast, and to the trees
that give them shelter.

For he hath turned the shadow of death into the morning, the
Lord is his name.

For I am come home again, but there is nobody to kill the calf
or to pay the musick.

For the hour of my felicity, like the womb of Sarah, shall come
at the latter end.

For I shou'd have avail'd myself of waggery, had not malice been multitudinous.

For there are still serpents that can speak—God bless my head, my heart & my heel.

For I bless God that I am of the same seed with Ehud, Mutius Scaevola, and Colonel Draper.

For the word of God is a sword on my side—no matter what other weapon a stick or a straw.

For I have adventured myself in the name of the Lord, and he hath mark'd me for his own.

For I bless God for the Postmaster general & all conveyancers of letters under his care especially Allen & Shelvock.

For my grounds in New Canaan shall infinitely compensate for the flats & maynes of Staindrop Moor.

For the praise of God can give to a mute fish the notes of a nightingale.

For I have seen the White Raven & Thomas Hall of Willingham & am myself a greater curiosity than both.

For I look up to heaven which is my prospect to escape envy by surmounting it.

For if Pharaoh had known Joseph, he woud have blessed God & me for the illumination of the people.

For I pray God to bless improvements in gardening till London be a city of palm-trees.

For I pray to give his grace to the poor of England, that Charity be not offended & that benevolence may increase.

For in my nature I quested for beauty, but God, God hath sent me to sea for pearls.

For there is a blessing from the STONE of JESUS which is founded upon hell to the precious jewell on the right hand of God.

For the nightly Visitor is at the window of the impenitent, while I sing a psalm of my own composing.

For there is a note added to the scale, which the Lord hath made fuller, stronger & more glorious.

For I offer my goat as he browses the vine, bless the Lord from chambering & drunkeness.

For there is a traveling for the glory of God without going to Italy or France.

For I bless the children of Asher for the evil I did them & the good I might have received at their hands.

For I rejoice like a worm in the rain in him that cherishes and from him that tramples.

For I am ready for the trumpet & alarm to fight to die & to rise again.

For the banish'd of the Lord shall come about again, for so he hath prepared for them.

For sincerity is a jewel which is pure & transparent, eternal & inestimable.

For my hands and my feet are perfect as the sublimity of Naphtali and the felicity of Asher.

For the names and number of animals are as the names and number of the stars.

For I pray the Lord Jesus to translate my MAGNIFICAT into verse and represent it.

For I bless the Lord Jesus from the bottom of Royston Cave to the top of King's Chapel.

For I am a little fellow, which is intitled to the great mess by the benevolence of God my father.

For I this day made over my inheritance to my mother in consideration of her infirmities.

For I this day made over my inheritance to my mother in consideration of her age.

For I this day made over my inheritance to my mother in consideration of her poverty.

For I bless the thirteenth of August, in which I had the grace to obey the voice of Christ in my conscience.

For I bless the thirteenth of August, in which I was willing to run all hazards for the sake of the name of the Lord.

For I bless the thirteenth of August, in which I was willing to be called a fool for the sake of Christ.

For I lent my flocks and my herds and my lands at once unto the Lord.

For nature is more various than observation tho' observers be innumerable.

For Agricola is Γεωργος.

For I pray God to bless POLLY in the blessing of Naomi and assign her to the house of DAVID.

For I am in charity with the French who are my foes and Moabites because of the Moabitish woman.

For my Angel is always ready at a pinch to help me out and to keep me up.

For CHRISTOPHER must slay the Dragon with a PAEON's head.

For they have seperated me and my bosom, whereas the right comes by setting us together.

For Silly fellow! Silly fellow! is against me and belongeth neither to me nor my family.

For he that scorneth the scorner hath condescended to my low estate.

For Abiah is the father of Joab and Joab of all Romans and English Men.

For they pass me by in their tour, and the good Samaritan is not yet come.

For I bless God in the behalf of TRINITY COLLEGE in CAMBRIDGE & the society of PURPLES in LONDON.

For I have a nephew CHRISTOPHER to whom I implore the grace of God.

For I pray God bless the CAM—Mr. HIGGS & Mr. & Mrs. WASHBOURNE as the drops of the dew.

For I pray God bless the king of Sardinia and make him an instrument of his peace.

For I am possessed of a cat, surpassing in beauty, from whom I take occasion to bless Almighty God.

For I pray God for the professors of the University of Cambridge to attend & to amend.

For the Fatherless Children and widows are never deserted of the Lord.

viii

For I pray God be gracious to the house of Stuart and consider their afflictions.

For I pray God be gracious to the seed of Virgil to Mr. GOODMAN SMITH of King's and Joseph STUD.

For I give God the glory that I am a son of ABRAHAM a PRINCE of the house of my fathers.

For my brethren have dealt deceitfully as a brook, and as the stream of brooks that pass away.

For I bless God for my retreat at CANBURY, as it was the place of the nativity of my children.

For I pray God to give them the food which I cannot earn for them any otherwise than by prayer.

For I pray God bless the Chinese which are of ABRAHAM and the Gospel grew with them at the first.

For I bless God in the honey of the sugar-cane and the milk of the cocoa.

For I bless God in the libraries of the learned & for all the book-sellers in the world.

For I bless God in the strength of my loins and for the voice which he hath made sonorous.

For tis no more a merit to provide for oneself, but to quit all for the sake of the Lord.

For there is no invention but the gift of God, and no grace like the grace of gratitude.

For grey hairs are honourable and tell every one of them to the glory of God.

For I bless the Lord Jesus for the memory of GAY, POPE and SWIFT.

For all good words are from GOD and all others are cant.

For I am enobled by my ascent and the Lord hath raised me above my Peers.

For I pray God bless my Lord CLARENDON and his seed for ever.

For there is silver in my mines and I bless God that it is rather there than in my coffers.

For I blessed God in St. James's Park till I routed all the company.

For the officers of the peace are at variance with me and the watchman smites me with his staff.

For I am the seed of the WELCH WOMAN and speak the truth from my heart.

For they lay wagers touching my life.—God be gracious to the winners.

For the piety of Rizpah is imitable in the Lord—wherefore I pray for the dead.

For the Lord is my ROCK and I am the bearer of his CROSS.

For I am like a frog in the brambles, but the Lord hath put his whole armour upon me.

For I was a Viper-catcher in my youth and the Lord delivered me from his venom.

For I rejoice that I attribute to God, what others vainly ascribe to feeble man.

For I am ready to die for his sake—who lay down his life for all mankind.

For the son of JOSHUA shall prevail against the servant of Gideon —Good men have their betters.

For my seed shall worship the Lord JESUS as numerous & musical as the grashoppers of Paradise.

For I pray God to turn the council of Ahitophel into foolishness.

For the learning of the Lord increases daily, as the sun is an improving angel.

For I pray God for a reformation amongst the women and the restoration of the veil.

For beauty is better to look upon than to meddle with and tis good for a man not to know a woman.

For the Lord Jesus made him a nosegay and blessed it & he blessed the inhabitants of flowers.

For a faithful friend is the medicine of life, but a neighbour in the Lord is better than he.

For I stood up betimes in behalf of LIBERTY, PROPERTY and No EXCISE.

For they began with grubbing up my trees & now they have excluded the planter.

For I am the Lord's builder and free & accepted MASON in CHRIST JESUS.

For I bless God in all gums & balsams & every thing that ministers relief to the sick.

For the Sun's at work to make me a garment & the Moon is at work for my wife.

For tall and stately are against me, but humiliation on humiliation is on my side.

For I have a providential acquaintance with men who bear the names of animals.

For I bless God to Mr. Lion Mr. Cock Mr. Cat Mr. Talbot Mr. Hart Mrs. Fysh Mr. Grub, and Miss Lamb.

For they throw my horns in my face and reptiles make themselves wings against me.

For I bless God for the immortal soul of Mr. Pigg of DOWNHAM in NORFOLK.

For I fast this day even the 31st of August N. S. to prepare for the SABBATH of the Lord.

For the bite of an Adder is cured by it's greese & the malice of my enemies by their stupidity.

For I bless God in SHIPBOURNE FAIRLAWN the meadows the brooks and the hills.

For the adversary hath exasperated the very birds against me, but the Lord sustain'd me.

For I bless God for my Newcastle friends the voice of the raven and heart of the oak.

For I bless God for every feather from the wren in the sedge to the CHERUBS & their MATES.

For I pray the Lord JESUS that cured the LUNATICK to be merciful to all my brethren and sisters in these houses.

For they work me with their harping-irons, which is a barbarous instrument, because I am more unguarded than others.

For the blessing of God hath been on my epistles, which I have written for the benefit of others.

For I bless God that the CHURCH of ENGLAND is one of the SEVEN evn the candlestick of the Lord.

For the ENGLISH TONGUE shall be the language of the WEST.

For I pray Almighty CHRIST to bless the MAGDALEN HOUSE & to forward a National purification.

For I have the blessing of God in the three POINTS of manhood, of the pen, of the sword, & of chivalry.

For I am inquisitive in the Lord, and defend the philosophy of the scripture against vain deceit.

For the nets come down from the eyes of the Lord to fish up men to their salvation.

For I have a greater compass both of mirth and melancholy than another.

For I bless the Lord JESUS in the innumerables, and for ever & ever.

For I am redoubted, and redoubtable in the Lord, as is THOMAS BECKET my father.

For I have had the grace to GO BACK, which is my blessing unto prosperity.

For I paid for my seat in St. PAUL's, when I was six years old & took possession against the evil day.

For I am descended from the steward of the island blessed be the name of the Lord Jesus king of England.

For the poor gentleman is the first object of the Lord's charity & he is the most pitied who hath lost the most.

For I am in twelve HARDSHIPS, but he that was born of a virgin shall deliver me out of all.

For I am safe, as to my head, from the female dancer and her admirers.

For I pray for CHICHISTER to give the glory to God, and to keep the adversary at bay.

For I am making to the shore day by day, the Lord Jesus take me.

For I bless the Lord JESUS upon RAMSGATE PIER—the Lord forward the building of harbours.

For I bless the Lord JESUS for his very seed, which is in my body.

For I pray for R and his family, I pray for Mr. Becher, and I bear for the Lord JESUS.

For I pray to God for Nore, for the Trinity house, for all lighthouses, beacons and buoys.

For I bless God that I am not in a dungeon, but am allowed the light of the Sun.

For I pray God for the PYGMIES against their featherd adversaries, as a deed of charity.

For I pray God for all those, who have defiled themselves in matters inconvenient.

For I pray God be gracious to CORNELIUS MATTHEWS name and connection.

ix

For I am under the same accusation with my Saviour—for they said, he is besides himself.

For I pray God for the introduction of new creatures into this island.

For I pray God for the ostriches of Salisbury Plain, the beavers of the Medway & silver fish of Thames.

For Charity is cold in the multitude of possessions, & the rich are covetous of their crumbs.

For I pray to be accepted as a dog without offence, which is best of all.

For I wish to God and desire towards the most High, which is my policy.

OF FLOWERS

Let Esdras bless Christ Jesus with the Rose and his people, which is a nation of living sweetness. (ii, 22)

For there was no rain in Paradise because of the delicate construction of the spiritual herbs and flowers. (xii, 14)

For the doubling of flowers is the improvement of the gardners talent.

For the flowers are great blessings.

For the Lord made a Nosegay in the medow with his disciples & preached upon the lily.

For the angels of God took it out of his hand and carried it to the Height.

For a man cannot have publick spirit, who is void of private benevolence.

For there is no Height in which there are not flowers.

For flowers have great virtues for all the senses.

For the flower glorifies God and the root parries the adversary.

For the flowers have their angels even the words of God's Creation.

For the warp and woof of flowers are worked by perpetual moving spirits.

For flowers are good both for the living and the dead.

For there is a language of flowers.

For there is a sound reasoning upon all flowers.

For elegant phrases are nothing but flowers.

For flowers are peculiarly the poetry of Christ.

For flowers are medicinal.

For flowers are musical in ocular harmony.

For the right names of flowers are yet in heaven. God make gardners better nomenclators.

For the Poorman's nosegay is an introduction to a Prince. (xvi, 40-58)

For Flowers can see, and Pope's Carnations knew him. (xvii, 56)

For the art of Agriculture is improving.

For this is evident in flowers.

For [it] is more especially manifest in double flowers.

For earth will get it up again by the blessing of God on the industry of man. (xxiv, 77-80)

The Lord succeed my pink borders. (xxviii, 22)

THE COFFIN, THE CRADLE, AND THE PURSE

For the coffin and the cradle and the purse are all against a man.

For the coffin is for the dead and death came by disobedience.

For the cradle is for weakness and the child of man was originally strong from ye womb.

For the purse is for money and money is dead matter with the stamp of human vanity.

For the adversary frequently sends these particular images out of the fire to those whom they concern.

For the coffin is for me because I have nothing to do with it.

For the cradle is for me because the old Dragon attacked me in it & [I] overcame in Christ.

For the purse is for me because I have neither money nor human friends. (x, 55-62)

OF THE SUN AND THE MOON

For the Sun's at work to make me a garment & the Moon is at work for my wife. (viii, 41)

For the Wedding Garments of all men are prepared in the Sun against the day of acceptation.

For the Wedding Garments of all women are prepared in the Moon against the day of their purification. (ix, 42-43)

For the Sun is an intelligence and an angel of the human form.

For the Moon is an intelligence and an angel in shape like a woman.

For they are together in the spirit every night like man and wife. (xi, 22-24)

For the phenomenon of the horizontal moon is the truth—she appears bigger in the horizon because she actually is so.

For the moon is magnified in the horizon by Almighty God, and so is the Sun.

For she has done her days-work and the blessing of God upon her, and she communicates with the earth.

For when she rises she has been strengthned by the Sun, who cherishes her by night. (xv, 16, 18-20)

OF THE SPIRITUAL MUSICK

For the spiritual musick is as follows.

For there is the thunder-stop, which is the voice of God direct.

For the rest of the stops are by their rhimes.

For the trumpet rhimes are sound bound, soar more and the like.

For the Shawm rhimes are lawn fawn moon boon and the like.

For the harp rhimes are sing ring, string & the like.

For the cymbal rhimes are bell well toll soul & the like.

For the flute rhimes are tooth youth suit mute & the like.

For the dulcimer rhimes are grace place beat heat & the like.

For the Clarinet rhimes are clean seen and the like.

For the Bassoon rhimes are pass, class and the like. God be gracious to Baumgarden.

For the dulcimer are rather van fan & the like and grace place &c are of the bassoon.

For beat heat, weep peep &c are of the pipe.

For every word has its marrow in the English tongue for order and for delight.

For the dissyllables such as able, table &c are the fiddle rhimes.

For all dissyllables and some trissyllables are fiddle rhimes.

For the relations of words are in pairs first.

For the relations of words are sometimes in oppositions.

For the relations of words are according to their distances from the pair. (xviii, 2-20)

OF THE HARP

For God the father Almighty plays upon the Harp of stupendous magnitude and melody.

For innumerable Angels fly out at every touch and his tune is a work of creation.

For at that time malignity ceases and the devils themselves are at peace.

For that time is perceptible to man by a remarkable stillness and
serenity of soul. (x, 25-28)

For the story of Orpheus is of the truth.

For there was such a person a cunning player on the harp.

For he was a believer in the true God and assisted in the spirit.

For he playd upon the harp in the spirit by breathing upon the
strings.

For this will affect every thing that is sustained by the spirit even
every thing in nature. (xxiii, 51-56)

OF COLOURS

For Newton's notion of colours is αλογος unphilosophical.

For the colours are spiritual.

For WHITE is the first and the best.

For there are many intermediate colours before you come to
SILVER.

For the next colour is a lively GREY.

For the next colour is BLUE.

For the next is GREEN of which there are ten thousand distinct
sorts.

For the next is YELLOW wch is more excellent than red, tho Newton makes red the prime. God be gracious to John Delap.

For RED is the next working round the Orange.

For Red is of sundry sorts till it deepens to BLACK.

For black blooms and it is PURPLE.

For purple works off to BROWN which is of ten thousand acceptable shades.

For the next is PALE. God be gracious to William Whitehead.

For pale works about to White again.

Now that colour is spiritual appears inasmuch as the blessing
of God upon all things descends in colour.

For the blessing of health upon the human face is in colour.

For the blessing of God upon purity is in the Virgin's blushes.

For the blessing of God in colour is on him that keeps his virgin.

For I saw a blush in Staindrop Church which was of God's own
colouring.

For it was the benevolence of a virgin shewn to me before the
whole congregation.

For the blessing of God upon the grass is in shades of Green visible to a nice observer as they light upon the surface of the earth.

For the blessing of God unto perfection in all bloom & fruit is by colouring.

For from hence something in the spirit may be taken off by painters.

For Painting is a species of idolatry, tho' not so gross as statuary.

For it is not good to look with [y]earning upon any dead work.

For by so doing something is lost in the spirit & given from life to death. (xix, 4-29)

OF JEOFFRY, HIS CAT

For I will consider my Cat Jeoffry.

For he is the servant of the Living God, duly and daily serving him.

For at the first glance of the glory of God in the East he worships in his way.

For is this done by wreathing his body seven times round with elegant quickness.

For then he leaps up to catch the musk, wch is the blessing of God upon his prayer.

For he rolls upon prank to work it in.

For having done duty and received blessing he begins to consider himself.

For this he performs in ten degrees.

For first he looks upon his fore-paws to see if they are clean.

For secondly he kicks up behind to clear away there.

For thirdly he works it upon stretch with the fore paws extended.

For fourthly he sharpens his paws by wood.

For fiftly he washes himself.

For sixthly he rolls upon wash.

For Seventhly he fleas himself, that he may not be interrupted upon the beat.

For Eightly he rubs himself against a post.

For Ninthly he looks up for his instructions.

For Tenthly he goes in quest of food.

For having consider'd God and himself he will consider his neighbour.

For if he meets another cat he will kiss her in kindness.

For when he takes his prey he plays with it to give it chance.

For one mouse in seven escapes by his dallying.

For when his day's work is done his business more properly begins.

For [he] keeps the Lord's watch in the night against the adversary.

For he counteracts the powers of darkness by his electrical skin & glaring eyes.

For he counteracts the Devil, who is death, by brisking about the life.

For in his morning orisons he loves the sun and the sun loves him.

For he is of the tribe of Tiger.

For the Cherub Cat is a term of the Angel Tiger.

For he has the subtlety and hissing of a serpent, which in goodness he suppresses.

For he will not do destruction, if he is well-fed, neither will he spit without provocation.

For he purrs in thankfulness, when God tells him he's a good Cat.

For he is an instrument for the children to learn benevolence upon.

For every house is incompleat without him & a blessing is lacking in the spirit.

For the Lord commanded Moses concerning the cats at the departure of the Children of Israel from Egypt.

For every family had one cat at least in the bag.

For the English Cats are the best in Europe.

For he is the cleanest in the use of his fore-paws of any quadrupede.

For the dexterity of his defence is an instance of the love of God to him exceedingly.

For he is the quickest to his mark of any creature.

For he is tenacious of his point.

For he is a mixture of gravity and waggery.

For he knows that God is his Saviour.

For there is nothing sweeter than his peace when at rest.

For there is nothing brisker than his life when in motion.

For he is of the Lord's poor and so indeed is he called by benevolence perpetually—Poor Jeoffry! poor Jeoffry! the rat has bit
thy throat.

For I bless the name of the Lord Jesus that Jeoffry is better.

For the divine spirit comes about his body to sustain it in compleat
cat.

For his tongue is exceeding pure so that it has in purity what it
wants in musick.

For he is docile and can learn certain things.

For he can set up with gravity which is patience upon approbation.

For he can fetch and carry, which is patience in employment.

For he can jump over a stick which is patience upon proof
positive.

For he can spraggle upon waggle at the word of command.

For he can jump from an eminence into his master's bosom.

For he can catch the cork and toss it again.

For he is hated by the hypocrite and miser.

For the former is affraid of detection.

For the latter refuses the charge.

For he camels his back to bear the first notion of business.

For he is good to think on, if a man would express himself neatly.

For he made a great figure in Egypt for his signal services.

For he killed the Icneumon-rat very pernicious by land.

For his ears are so acute that they sting again.

For from this proceeds the passing quickness of his attention.

For by stroaking of him I have found out electricity.

For I perceived God's light about him both wax and fire.

For the Electrical fire is the spiritual substance, which God sends
from heaven to sustain the bodies both of man and beast.

For God has blessed him in the variety of his movements.

For, tho he cannot fly, he is an excellent clamberer.

For his motions upon the face of the earth are more than any
other quadrupede.

For he can tread to all the measures upon the musick.

For he can swim for life.

For he can creep. (xxix, 51-60; xx, 1-64)

APHORISMS

Before honour is humility, and he that looketh low shall learn. (ii, 29)

To conquer malice is nobler, than to slay the lion. (iii, 3)

The minister of vengeance is the harbinger of mercy. (iii, 6)

Liberty begetteth insolence, but necessity is the mother of prayer. (iii, 27)

Lively subtlety is acceptable to the Lord. (iii, 29)

Let Huldah bless with the Silkworm—the ornaments of the Proud are from the bowells of their Betters.
Let Susannah bless with the Butterfly—beauty hath wings, but chastity is the Cherub. (iv, 6 & 7)

It is good for man and beast to mend their pace. (iv, 11)

A silly bird is wise unto his own preservation. (v, 48)

For the Glory of God is always in the East, but cannot be seen for the cloud of the crucifixion. (ix, 17)

For the sin against the HOLY GHOST is INGRATITUDE. (xi, 11)

For stuff'd guts make no musick; strain them strong and you shall have sweet melody. (xi, 12)

For every man beareth death about him ever since the transgression of Adam, but in perfect light there is no shadow. (xi, 14)

For Justice is infinitely beneath Mercy in nature and office.
For the Devil himself may be just in accusation and punishment. (xi, 25-26)

For there is a forlorn hope ev'n for impenitent sinners because the furnace itself must be the crown of Eternity. (xi, 35)

For the souls of the departed are embodied in clouds and purged by the Sun. (xi, 53)

For a Man is to be looked upon in that which he excells as on a prospect. (xi, 59)

For where Accusation takes the place of encouragement a man of Genius is driven to act the vices of a fool. (xii, 3)

For GOD neverthless is an extravagant BEING and generous unto loss.
For there is no profit in the generation of man and the loss of millions is not worth God's tear. (xii, 18-19)

For a good wish is well, but a faithful prayer is an eternal benefit. (xii, 31)

The worse the time the better the eternity. (xiii, 50)

There is a way to the terrestrial Paradise upon the knees. (xiv, 47)

For the ends of the world are the accomplishment of great events, and the consummation of periods. (xv, 10)

For man is born to trouble in the body, as the sparks fly upwards in the spirit.
For man is between the pinchers while his soul is shaping and purifying. (xv, 21-22)

For when the nation is at war, it is better to abstain from the punishment of criminals, especially, every act of human vengeance being a check to the grace of God. (xvi, 24)

For a man cannot have publick spirit, who is void of private benevolence. (xvi, 44. *Repeated* xvii, 52)

For many a genius being lost at the plough is a false thought, the divine providence is a better manager. (xvii, 59)

For I prophecy that there will be more mercy for criminals. (xxiii, 65)

For I prophecy that they will not dare to imprison a brother or sister for debt. (xxiii, 72)

EDITION

Rejoice in the Lamb: a Song out of Bedlam, ed. William Force Stead, London, 1939. (Text.)

On Gratitude
To the Memory of M:r Seaton.

O Muse! O Music! Voice & Lyre,
　　Which are together Psalm of Praise
From heav'n the kneeling bard inspire
　　New thoughts, new grace of utterance raise;
That more acceptable with Thee
　　W:t Thy best service may begin
O Rev'rent bent Ride hallow'd Knee,
　　And blefs'd he bleed of for Adam's sin.
Then did the Spirit of a Man
　　Above all height sublimely tow'r,
And there sweet Gratitude began,
　　To claim Supremacy from Pow'r.
But how shall we Rev: step ascend
　　By what the Host approach the Throne? —
Love thou thy brother & thy friend,
　　Whom thou on earth hast seen & known;
For Gratitude may make the *plea
　　Of Love by sisterhood most dear —
How can we read the first degree,
　　If we neglect a step so near;
So shall we take dear Seaton's part
　　When paths of topmost heav'n are trod,
And pay the talent of our heart,
　　Thrown up in Heav'n and told to God.

He knew the art the World despise
　　Might to his Merit be applied
Who when for man he left the Skies
　　By all was hated, scorn'd, denied.
† " The man that gives me Rank & land
　　" Does honour to my glorious name "
Thus God did David's works applaud,
　　And seald for everlasting fame.

And this for SEATON, shall redound
　　To praise, as long as Camus runs;
Since Gratitude by him was crown'd,
　　Who bless'd his Maker & his Sons.

When Spenser virtuous Sydney prais'd
　　When Prior Dorsett hail'd to heaven;
They more by Gratitude were rais'd
　　Then all the Nine & all the Seven.

Then, O ye emulative tribe
　　Of Granta, strains divine pursue;
The glory to the Lord ascribe,
　　Yet honour Seaton's memory too.

† Psalm C. 29   The

The Throne of Excellence accost
And be the post of Prayr maintain'd,
For ~~Paradise~~ Paradise had neer been lost
Had heavnly Gratitude remain'd

Christopher Smart.

"On Gratitude," from the MS. in the Berg Collection

Musical settings by Dr. Nares, from *A Collection of Melodies for the Psalms of David,
according to the Version of Christopher Smart*

A Translation
of the
Psalms of David

Psalm VII

O Lord, my God, I ground my creed
    In thine almighty pow'r;
Preserve me, and their course impede,
    Who chace me to devour.

Lest like the lion and the bear,
    That came upon my fold,
They set about my soul to tear,
    By no rebuke controul'd.

O Lord, if I have done the crime
    Whereof I stand accus'd;
Or hand or heart at any time
    To mischief have abus'd;

If e'er with them that well deserve
    I treacherously deal;
Yea, rather if I cease to serve
    My causeless foe with zeal;

Then let mine enemies be sped,
    Nor give me to respire;
Yea, let them take my life, and tread
    My trophies in the mire.

Stand up, O Lord, and plume thy crest
    Against my rival's rage:
Arise—thy judgment be the test,
    As we the contest wage;

So shall thy congregation make
    Toward thy hallow'd fane;
And therefore for thy people's sake
    Exert thyself again.

The Lord shall judge the common cause,
    My plea, O Christ, admit;
As I have kept thy holy laws
    Mine innocence acquit.

O let all wickedness and lust,
    In penitence conclude;
But govern thou the good and just,
    With grace and peace renew'd.

For God in righteousness explores
    A man's interior part;
The reins, and all the secret pores
    Of his deceitful heart.

My sole security from force
    In God's assistance lies;
To his defence I have recourse,
    Who saves the good and wise.

God is all-gracious to decide
    For those that weep and pray;
Strong in his patience, which is tried
    By sinners every day.

Yet e'en to those that love the dark,
    His vengeance will be slow;
For pity built the floating ark,
    And goodness bent his bow.

His swords are turn'd to shepherd's crooks,
    The breast-plate and the helm;
His darts and spears to pruning hooks,
    To dress the vine-clad elm.

Behold a virgin has conceiv'd,
   By congress undefil'd,
And lost Jeshurun is retriev'd
   By an almighty child.

Lo! he has dug the grave of death,
   Destruction to destroy;
And open'd by his HOLY BREATH
   The way to endless joy.

And all the labour of his love
   To glory shall redound;
In earth beneath, in heaven above
   His truth shall be renown'd.

To this his righteous word reveal'd,
   I will in thanks reply;
And faithfully for ever yield
   That CHRIST is God most high.

Psalm VIII

O Lord, that rul'st the human heart,
How excellent thy name and art,
   In all the world renown'd!
The glorious pillars of thy reign
No flight can reach, nor heav'ns contain,
   Nor exaltation bound!

The very babes and sucklings cry,
Almighty Father, God most high!
   Whom blasphemy profanes—
Thou hear'st and tak'st them by the hand,
Nor can the silenc'd fiend withstand
   The strength that Christ ordains.

I will my soaring thoughts exalt
To yonder heaven's cerulean vault,

Whose height thy fingers form'd;
The moon attended at thy call,
Made marvelously fair, and all
    The stars around her swarm'd!

Lord what is man, that he should find
A place in his Creator's mind
    Or what his whole increase—
A race of rebels vain and weak,
That he should for a moment break
    Upon his Saviour's peace?

An angel quite thou mad'st him not,
A little lower is his lot,
    On earth thou set'st him down;
There his dominion and degree,
To glorify and worship thee
    For glory and a crown.

Him thou deputed to review
The scenes of nature, and subdue
    Thy creatures to his will;
Whose motley numbers own his sway,
And by his strength compell'd obey,
    Or disciplin'd by skill.

All flocks of sheep and droves of kine,
Which as his olive and his vine,
    To man their goodness yield;
And not a beast that can be nam'd,
But may be taken or be tam'd
    In woodland or in field.

In air, in ocean he controuls,
The feather'd millions, finny shoals,
    From minnows to the whale;
Whate'er beneath the waters creep,
Or glide within the yielding deep,
    Or on the surface sail.

O thou that rul'st the human heart,
Supreme of nature and of art,
  How is thy name renown'd!
How blest thy providential care,
In heav'n above, in earth and air,
  And in the vast profound!

Psalm X

Lord, in this disastrous season,
  Why dost thou at distance keep?
Times of turbulence and treason
  Loudly for thine absence weep.

Worldlings for their own false pleasure
  Cruelly the poor intreat;
Deal them not, O God, the measure
  They in craft to Christians mete.

For the self-applauding vicious
  Speak the bravest and the best
Of the griping avaricious,
  Whom God's bounteous laws detest.

There is infinite alliance
  'Twixt ungodliness and pride;
In their thoughts they bid defiance
  To the God their words deride.

Hard their ways are, disregarding
  In what throngs opposers bleed,
While thy love, thy bolts retarding,
  Gives them courage to proceed.

For they've to themselves suggested,
  Tush! we are not like to fall;
Nor shall ever be molested
  With the common lot of all.

Fraught with double-tongu'd expression
  Are their mouths, and base deceit;
With vain lies and lewd transgression,
  Thought and speech they are replete.

In the thievish corners lurking,
  They th'unmansion'd poor prevent:
Blood-shot eyes with terror working,
  On the private stab intent.

Like a lion fierce and greedy,
  Couchant in his secret den,
They're in wait to grind the needy;
  All is prey within their ken.

And without remorse they grind him
  With their teeth for slaughter set;
Whensoe'er the traitors find him
  Caught within their cover'd net.

Formal, with affected meekness,
  Each a seeming saint behaves;
That the poor, thro' want and weakness,
  May become their captain's slaves.

In their hearts themselves they flatter:
  Tush! the Lord beholds us not,
And the knowledge of the matter
  Christ himself has quite forgot.

Rise, O Lord, the cause examine,
  And thy mighty hand uprear;
In the day of war and famine
  For the poor in pow'r appear.

Why should every impious traitor
  Such a foul presumption dare:
Tush! for God, the great Creator,
  Will not for his creatures care.

Murder, theft, and devastation,
   Thou hast seen their ruins lie,
For thy chosen church and nation
   Are forever in thine eye.

To thy goodness for their trial
   The poor destitute appeal;
For with thee is no denial
   When for aid the friendless kneel.

Take from malice thy protection,
   Throw the light on dark disguise,
Purge away each foul affection
   And the wicked shall be wise.

Christ his crown of palms is wreathen,
   And for ever, ever blooms;
King alike of Jews and heathen,
   He th' eternal reign assumes:

Thou hast heard the poor's petition,
   Thou establishest their heart;
And the cry of their condition
   Has ascended where thou art,

That with thy benign compassion
   Thou thine orphans may'st redress
From the men of worldly fashion
   Who are proud when they oppress.

Psalm XVIII

Thee will I love, O Lord, my tow'r,
My Saviour of almighty pow'r
   Is God, in whom I dare;
By whom my conq'ring bands are led,
My buckler in the hour of dread,
   And refuge from despair.

I will invoke the great Supreme
Whose matchless merits are the theme
          Of everlasting praise;
So when the furious warriors chafe,
I shall command the battle safe
          From terror and amaze.

The sorrows of a death-like gloom,
And all the visions of the tomb
          Came threat'ning as at hand;
And blood in such profusion spilt
By swords extravagant of guilt
          My trembling heart unmann'd.

Hell with her agonizing pains,
And horror of eternal chains,
          My vestibule alarm'd;
And by my active health forsook,
A ghastly consternation shook,
          And all my strength disarm'd.

Thro' trouble when my members fail,
O Lord, I will myself avail
          Of thy most holy name;
To thee prefer my soul's complaint,
And from diseases and restraint
          Thy blest protection claim.

So that within thy sacred shrine
Thou shalt thy gracious ears incline,
          As I thy help beseech;
Thy psalmist to the height shall soar,
And up at Heaven's interior door
          Shall thine attention reach.

Strong dread redoubled to convulse
All nature's frame at every pulse,
          And from their topmost height,

Down to the bottom of their base,
The hills were shaken and gave place,
       Because his wrath was great.

Out in his presence issue wreathes
Of lucid smoak, and as he breathes
       Flames from his mouth transpire;
Which rage so vehement and fierce,
The bowels of the earth they pierce,
       And set her mines on fire.

The empyrean at his frown
Was humbled, and the heav'ns came down
       With all the host incens'd
Of Michael summon'd from his seat,
And gathering underneath his feet,
       The darkness was condens'd.

And on the innumerable flight
Of cherubims, the sons of light,
       He rode in grand career;
And bore on the stupendous force
And speed of winged winds his course,
       O'er vaulted space to steer.

A thick tremendous veil he made,
The glorious majesty to shade,
       Where in the midst he storm'd;
And his pavilion was a cloud
Of deepest water, which to shroud,
       His alter'd face he form'd.

But then the brightness which he beam'd,
As he the copious lustre stream'd,
       The dusky scene controuls;
And as the gloom around was clear'd,
From out the central blaze appear'd
       Hail mixt with burning coals.

God also thunder'd—the most high
Pronounc'd his thunder in the sky,
  The rolling pomp to drive;
And at his omnipresent word,
Above, beneath, around occurr'd
  Hailstones and coals alive.

He from his loaded quiver drew
The forked arrows, and they flew
  To make obstruction void;
He bade the heathen wrath avast,
And with the lightning that he cast,
  Their menaces destroy'd.

The secret water springs the while
Were seen ev'n to the source of Nile,
  And in the world beneath,
The pillars of th' inferior arch
Stood naked at the fires that search,
  And his strong vengeance breathe.

His blessed angel he shall send
To fetch me, and in pow'r defend
  From his terrific scourge;
With which he visits all around,
And from the floods of the profound
  I shall to peace emerge.

He shall in love prevent my fall,
Till my worst enemy of all
  With guilty shame shall blush;
And save me from the gross disgust
Of men with ruffian rage robust,
  Whose furious weight would crush.

In that sad hour of pinching need,
They strove my progress to impede,
  And from my point debarr'd;

But Christ the Lord, to whom I pray,
Upheld my goings in the way,
  At once my guide and guard.

He saw my jeopardy discharg'd,
And freedom's ample walk enlarg'd
  With plenty and content;
He set me in a spacious place,
Because I found peculiar grace,
  When kneeling to repent.

The Lord shall my reward prepare,
Because my dealings have been fair,
  And from all treach'ry free;
According to the spotless hue,
With which these harmless hands I shew,
  My recompence shall be.

For I with courage have abode
By God and truth, and kept the road
  Which goes to endless bliss;
Nor have deserted from his cause,
Like men that have not known his laws,
  The godless and remiss.

Because with application strict
I to thy laws my mind addict,
  Their import to discern;
Nor poorly single out a part,
But keep them all with all my heart
  As of the last concern.

I likewise found myself intire,
And pure from every vain desire,
  Lascivious and unclean;
My former follies I eschew'd,
And all the past of life review'd,
  My thoughts from vice to wean:

Wherefore the Lord, whom thus I please,
And which my righteous dealing sees
        With his paternal eyes,
According as my hands are pure,
Shall to my soul in heav'n secure
        The blest immortal prize.

Where saints and holy angels dwell,
Thou shalt in holiness excell,
        And shalt have perfect peace;
Where perfected beyond the sketch
Of Nature, to their utmost stretch,
        Faith, hope and grace increase.

In living waters thou shalt bathe,
And God with purity shall swathe
        Thy loins as with a girth;
And with the clean and undefil'd,
Thou shall be number'd as a child,
        In this thy second birth.

For thou shalt save the poor oppress'd,
And have his grievances redress'd
        By thine immediate aid;
And pompous pride, that is above
The works of charity and love,
        Thou shalt to want degrade.

Thou shalt indulge a farther length
To David's life, and with new strength
        My blazing lamp shall burn;
Again my vessel shall embark,
And God shall dissipate the dark,
        And urge the day's return.

Thro' thee I shall maintain my post,
Nor of the fury of an host,
        Or numbers, make account;

And, as thy present help supports,
Shall leap o'er battlements and forts,
    And every bar surmount.

God's way is just, his word the same,
And proof against the sev'nfold flame,
    When challeng'd to the test;
He is the Saviour and the shield
Of all that in his truth reveal'd
    Their firm affiance rest.

For what is the Supreme, or who
But God Almighty, and all-true
    On his eternal throne;
What is this pow'r and strength of ours,
And what is strength, or what are pow'rs
    But God's, and God alone?

It is the Lord that girds my sword,
Whose grace and might their help afford,
    Calm thought with wrath to mix;
Against each giant foe of Gath,
'Tis he alone directs my path,
    His champion's fame to fix.

His mandates to my feet[1] impart
The swiftness of the nimble hart,
    To run with them that fly;
He takes me up from off the ground,
On which with active speed I bound,
    And sets me up on high.

The Lord has with my forces fought,
And these my hardy members taught
    The battle to sustain;
My hands are practical and apt,
And with their vigour I have snapt
    A bow of steel in twain.

[1] Text has "seat."

Thou'st plac'd salvation's glorious helm
Upon thy servant, and his realm
  E'en to remotest Dan;
I rise augmented from thy rod,
And thy kind chastisement, O God,
  Shall magnify the man.

Thou shalt enlarge me round about,
And whersoe'er I take my rout,
  My pilgrimage equip;
By thee directed I shall move,
And thou shalt keep as in a groove,
  My footsteps lest they slip.

With God and Israel's cause at stake,
I shall their armies overtake,
  Which our perdition seek;
Nor will my rapid courses slack,
Nor bring Jehudah's standard back,
  Till I have made them meek.

I will attack them sword in hand,
Nor shall they my sure stroke withstand,
  While God my arm uplifts;
One shall his thirst of glory glut
With hundreds vanquish'd—ten shall put
  Ten thousand to their shifts.

Thy pow'r shall gird and brace my loins,
Whene'er the fierce encounter joins,
  Thine angel shall aggrieve
The foe that Israel's coast alarms,
Till I by my victorious arms
  Immortal fame atchieve.

Thou'st made mine enemies retreat,
Nor could they, previous of defeat,
  My fair battalia front;

And I shall quell their boistrous boasts,
Invested by the Lord of Hosts,
  With brav'ry scorners want.

Their clamours shall ascend the skies,
But none shall stay to hear their cries
  Of angels or of men;
To God they shall address their suit,
Yet they shall have but little fruit
  To their devotions then.

They came in number, like the dust,
Their weapons in our heart to thrust,
  Like dust they shall recede;
Or crumbled clay before the wind,
Nor shall an atom stay behind,
  To signify their deed.

Thou shalt preserve thy servant's life
From faction and domestick strife,
  However rais'd or spread;
And fresh from every clime and shore,
The heathen shall thy name adore,
  With David at their head.

My swelling sails shall be unfurl'd,
And to reform a distant world,
  Thou shall my fleets convoy;
And nations from thy word remote,
I to thine honour will devote,
  And in thy ways employ.

Soon as my precepts they imbibe,
They shall to their good truth subscribe,
  And their rude manners change;
Yea perjured hypocrites shall throng
To God and Jesus, whom they wrong
  As they themselves estrange.

The stranger shall be taken in,
Redeem'd from slavery and sin,
    Their Saviour to invoke—
Their nature shall no more despond
Of mercy, but embrace the bond
    Of peace and Christ his yoke.

The God of all perfection lives,
And reigns o'er all things, and he gives
    The laurel to my lance;
And I will bless him and applaud
His pow'rful succour, and his laud
    And magnitude advance.

E'en he whose holy angels wage
Their warfare with me, and engage
    Against the strength of stealth,
Of hate and falshood, and confirms
My people in submissive terms
    By plenty, peace and wealth.

He shall my soul's salvation set
O'er those that cruel men abet,
    Still pouring fresh and fresh;
And for my safety shall provide
From every loud blasphemer's pride,
    And from an arm of flesh.

I therefore will my Saviour thank,
And from a faithful heart and frank
    The song of praise produce;
And to the Gentiles will I sing
Of him who guides the warrior's sling,
    Or fills the peaceful cruse.

Great things and prosperous hast thou done
In love to David—and his Son
    Shall ride the royal mule;

King David thy free choice appoints,
And from his loins thy seer anoints
 A man thy tribes to rule.

Psalm XXIX

Ye men of birth and high renown,
Who, zealous for the heav'nly crown,
 Have gallant deeds atchiev'd,
The Lord with thankfulness adore,
The strength, the praise to him restore,
 From whom ye both receiv'd.

Give to the Lord's most holy name
The honour which his merits claim,
 In meekness as ye kneel;
With reverence pay your daily vow;
In seemliness and order bow
 With lively faith and zeal.

The word of infinite command,
August, adorable and grand,
 The water-flood controuls;
And in terrific glory breaks
Upon the billows, and he speaks
 The thunder as it rolls.

The voice of God and pow'r are one,
The mandate which he gives is done
 In all the dread profound;
Vast operative strength and skill,
The proclamation of his will
 Is of majestic sound!

The voice of God in anger drives
The tempest to the mark, and rives
 The cedar-trees in twain,

Yea Lebanon, with all his growth,
Was rifted when the Lord was wroth
    And strawn along the plain.

The lofty mountains huge and steep
At voice of his commandment leap
    Like calves upon the sod,
And Libanus and Sirion too
Bound like young unicorns to do
    Obeisance to their God.

The voice of God divides the flakes
Of torrent fire, his mandate shakes
    The wilderness with fear;
Yea Kadesh with his voice he shocks,
And caverns, mountains, woods and rocks
    With dreadful trembling hear.

The voice of God upon the lawn
Descends and causes hinds to fawn,
    The thicket disarrays;
With terror strikes the human race
Who that tremendous time embrace
    For publick pray'r and praise.

The Lord in highest heav'n ascends,
The while his stedfast course he bends
    All ocean's depth to ford;
From eastern to the western beam,
The Lord is evermore supream,
    Is evermore ador'd.

The Lord shall make his people strong,
With corn and wine our lives prolong
    And cloath us with his fleece;
He shall the bonds of sin unloose,
And on our consciences diffuse
    The blessing of his peace.

Psalm XXXIV

Unceasing thanks, as thus I kneel,
  I will to God return;
And still with eager lips reveal
Th' internal gratitude I feel,
  And zeal to praise with which I burn.

With confidence in Jesus placed,
  My soul herself shall plume;
The poor and by the world disgrac'd,
And those that have themselves abas'd,
  Shall hear, and joyfulness assume.

O take the blessed theme of praise
  Our spirits to expand;
And let us our conceptions raise,
God's glorious name together blaze,
  And faithful worship hand in hand.

The Lord my Saviour I besought,
  And he was quickly found,
And in his arms of mercy caught
My spirit, and to safety brought
  From every terror, every wound.

Illumination beams on all
  That to the Lord aspire;
And, when they to the godhead call,
Nought can abash them, or appal
  In such a duty and desire.

Lo! the poor suff'rers importune
  Their Saviour to attend,
And mercy gives them audience soon,
With speed accomplishes their boon,
  And to their troubles puts an end.

The Lord his ever-blessed dove
    Keeps hov'ring with her wings
For all that cherish fearful love,
And buoy their spirits up above
    The peril of all earthly things.

O hear the summons—"Come and see"
    And God's free grace receive;
Exalted to the first degree,
And of eternal worth is he,
    Who stands determin'd to believe.

O to the Lord your God adhere,
    Ye saints, in trembling dread;
For they which his decrees revere,
And nourish reverence by fear
    Are in all exigencies sped.

The lions in the forest roar,
    And hunger as they quest;
But heroes in the Lord, that soar
To heav'n, and there his face explore,
    Shall have no want of what is best.

Come little children and imbibe
    The nurture of my speech;
And I will list you of my tribe,
God's fear within your heart inscribe,
    And early your Redeemer preach.

What man is he that would prolong
    His pilgrimage on earth,
And live in lusty health and strong,
To see each day the theme of song
    And full of melody and mirth?

O'er all thy craving members reign
    Lest they thy soul defile;

Thy tongue with diligence restrain,
And thine unguarded lips contain
    From idle words and active guile.

All evil thoughts and speech avoid,
    And in the Christian race
Be with perpetual good employ'd,
Seek peace, nor ever be decoy'd
    With ought that leads you from the chace.

The Lord his omnipresent eyes
    From highest heaven's ascent,
The good and righteous supervise,
He hears their pray'rs as they arise
    Towards his throne with ears intent.

God cannot countenance the deeds
    Of them that act amiss,
But from their commerce he recedes,
Until their Saviour's merit pleads
    To reinstate their souls in bliss.

Whene'er the righteous make complaint,
    From heav'n attention stoops;
God has respect unto his saint
The more when he thro' grief is faint,
    And wholly saves him ere he droops.

Christ is the neighbour of the meek,
    Whose nature is renew'd,
And those that by contrition seek,
And with their tears his love bespeak,
    He will within his fold include.

The crosses of the Lord's elect
    Are grievous here below;
But God gives all his pray'rs effect,
And shall his ministers direct
    To snatch him out of all his woe.

He keeps his bones and all intire
From fracture and mischance,
So that his foes, when set on fire
Of hell, they cruelly conspire,
Can only pierce him with a lance.

But mischief from the pit pursues
The wicked as they tread;
And who the grace of God refuse,
Their way from every virtue lose,
To death and desolation led.

The Lord his meritorious cross
Shall ransom all our souls,
And purify our filthy dross,
And they shall not be at a loss,
Whose faith he in his book enrolls.

Psalm XXXVI

My heart within me is advis'd,
And but too sure conviction finds,
How little God is fear'd or priz'd
By men of worldly minds.

For they're self-flatterers to the last,
And supple servants of the times,
Till that, which sets them most aghast,
Detection blaze their crimes.

Their words are foolish and unfair
And full of falsehood and deceit;
Each act of wisdom they forbear,
With all that's good and meet.

They mischief on their couches plan,
The broader way of ruin chuse,

Nor that, whose touch defiles a man,
 Do they at all refuse.

Thy mercy to thy people's faults
 Thou hast in highest heav'n avow'd;
Thy faithfulness itself exalts
 Beyond the topmost cloud.

Thy truth's like mountains strong and steep,
 Which stand with rock-work for their ground,
And all thy judgments dreadful deep
 Are like the vast profound!

Thou, Lord, shalt save both man and beast;
 O how transcendent is thy grace:
Beneath thy wings from first to least
 All flesh themselves shall place.

They from thy stores replenish'd still
 Shall in thy spacious dome be fed;
And of thy pleasures take their fill
 As from the fountain-head.

For in the holiest height with Thee
 In heav'n is life's perennial well,
Light in thy light we there shall see,
 And thence irradiate dwell.

O! with thy charity regal'd
 Let them that know Thee still remain,
And let thy mercy be intail'd
 Upon the good in grain.

O save me from the spurning heel
 Of those, that with proud aspect frown,
Nor let his blow the ruffian deal
 To cast thy servant down.

There are they founder'd in the flood
　　Such as were wicked for reward,
For there's no hope, save in the blood
　　Of Jesus Christ our Lord.

Psalm XLVII

O join your hands with loud applause,
Ye people, and the common cause
　　　　Of Christian zeal attend:
In voice and spirit sing and shout,
By hearty melody devout
　　　　And hymns to God ascend.

For a tremendous God is ours,
Most high, most holy, and the pow'rs,
　　　　The majesty, the might,
And all things glorious, all things great
In empire are subordinate,
　　　　And bow to him of right.

The people from his grace remov'd
Shall in our converse be improv'd,
　　　　And to his altars speed;
The Gentiles thus shall he subdue,
And all the runagates renew
　　　　In Abraham's chosen seed.

For his lov'd tribes he shall select
A better country, and direct
　　　　Our travel to his throne;
And Jacob's glory, Jacob's care,
Which is in gratitude and pray'r,
　　　　Shall reckon to his own.

Christ is gone up, the king of kings,
And joyful acclamation rings,
　　　　As thankless earth he spurns;

The marshall'd cherubs stand in rows,
From inmost heav'n the trumpet blows
    While God from death returns.

In Christ your God the song commence,
Which said "arise let us go hence,"
    By flights of lively praise;
To Christ your king in grateful strain
Raise pealing anthems, and again
    The pealing anthems raise.

By God supream all earth is sway'd,
By him administer'd and made,
    Let us perform our part,
Sing vying for th' immortal prize
In high-wrought verse and heedfull wise,
    Like masters of your art.

The heathen also he controuls,
In whose obnubilated souls
    His image is effac'd;
God sits upon his throne to bless,
His throne by purest holiness
    And boundless mercy plac'd.

Each rebel Jew the church rejoins,
And every prince from Abraham's loins
    Again his fruit shall yield;
For God, whose exaltation soars
O'er heav'n, and whom all earth adores,
    Shall be himself our shield.

Psalm LIV

O God, the name to which I pray,
    Of boundless love and pow'r,
O pass, if possible, away
    This bitter cup and hour.

Yet if these drops must thus be spilt,
 Thou, Father, knowest best;
And be it rather as thou wilt,
 Than to my soul's request.

Lo! strangers to thy truth arise,
 Nor put their trust in thee;
And Herod, leagu'd with Pilate, vies
 To nail me to the tree.

But God shall raise from stripes and scorn
 The Lamb betray'd and kill'd;
And on the third triumphant morn
 This temple shall rebuild.

Then thou shalt greater grace supply
 To have the worst redeem'd;
And truth shall make them free to die
 For him they once blasphem'd.

A victim patient and resign'd
 I for the cross prepare,
And bless thy name, because I find
 Such consolation there.

For he has caus'd me to respire,
 And all my vows have thriv'n;
Mine eye has seen my heart's desire
 In every foe forgiv'n.

Psalm LXVIII

Arouse—and let thy foes disperse,
Thou master of the universe,
 Arouse thee from on high;
Take up the trumpet and alarm,
And at the terror of thine arm
 Let those that hate thee fly.

Like as afflicting smoke's dispell'd,
Let them be driv'n away and quell'd,
  As wax before the fire,
Let fraud at thine effulgence fail,
And let the multitudes in mail
  Before my God retire.

But let the men of righteous seed,
Accepted in their father's deed,
  Rejoice before the shrine;
Yea, let them shout till heav'n resounds,
There is no need of end or bounds
  To joyfulness divine.

Give praise—with songs your praises blend,
And as your thoughts to heav'n ascend,
  And leave the world beneath,
Extol his universal name,
Who rides on the celestial flame,
  In IAH, which all things breathe.

The father of the friendless child,
To keep the damsel undefil'd,
  And judge the widow's cause,
Is God upon his righteous throne,
Whence he the hands to rapine prone
  O'ersees and overawes.

Thy Lord domestick peace creates,
And those his Mercy congregates,
  Who solitary dwell;
The slave delivers from his chain,
But rebels in dry wastes remain,
  And where no waters well.

When thou Jehovah led the way,
Before thy people in array,
  From Egypt's barb'rous coast;

Thro' boundless wilds exposed and parch'd,
In pillar'd majesty thou march'd
    The captain of the host.

The earth in ecstasy gave place,
With vast vibrations on her base
    The present God she found;
Ev'n Israel's God—the heav'ns dissolv'd,
And Sinai's mount in clouds involv'd,
    Felt all his rocks rebound.

O God, thou bad'st the heav'ns dispense
The bread of thy benevolence,
    Down with the daily dew;
And fixt the people of thy pow'r,
Amidst their doubtings by a show'r
    Miraculous and new.

Therein thy congregation dwelt,
E'en midst the manna, which thou dealt
    So plentiful and pure;
Thy goodness to confirm the weak,
Thy charity to bless and break
    The largess for the poor.

God, in stupendous glory deck'd,
His gracious covenant direct,
    Came down from heav'n to teach;
Great was the trembling and the fear
Of crouds, that rush'd that word to hear,
    They were enjoin'd to preach.

Each talking tyrant at the head
Of thousands and ten thousands fled,
    They fled with all their might;
And all Judea's blooming pride,
The spouse, the damsel and the bride,
    Dispos'd the spoil at night.

Though ye the bitter bondage wept,
And midst Rhamnesian tripods slept,
    Hereafter is your own;
Ye shall as turtle-doves unfold
The silver plumage wing'd with gold,
    And make melodious moan.

When kings were scatter'd for our sake,
And God alarm'd his host to take
    His vengeance on the foe;
On Israel's countenance benign
He made his radiant grace to shine
    As bright as Salmon's snow.

Jehovah's hill's a noble heap,
And ev'n as Bashan's spiry steep,
    From which the cedars nod;
And Zion's mount herself sublimes,
And swells her goodly crest and climbs
    To meet descending God.

Ye haughty hills that leap so high,
What is th' exertion that ye try?
    This is God's hallow'd mount,
On whose blest top the glories play,
And where the Lord desires to stay
    While we his praise recount.

The chariots of the Lord are made
Of angels in a cavalcade
    Ev'n twenty thousand strong,
Those thousands of the first degree,
O'er Sinai—in the midst is HE,
    And bears the pomp along.

God is gone up from whence he rose;
With gifts accepted for his foes,
    His loaded altars smoke;

Captivity, from chains repriev'd,
Is made his captive, and receiv'd
　　To thy most blessed yoke.

God is our help from every ill,
And gives to every want its fill,
　　For us and all our race;
By him we're every hour review'd,
To him the daily pray'r's renew'd
　　For daily bread and grace.

God, that great God whom we profess,
Is all-benevolent to bless,
　　Omnipotent to save;
In God alone is our escape,
From death and all the gulphs that gape,
　　From terror and the grave.

God shall not send his blessing down
To rest upon the hoary crown
　　Of those which grace resist;
But shall afflict the heads of all,
That after his repeated call
　　To penitence, persist.

From Bashan, which they pass'd of yore,
Said God, I will my tribes restore,
　　And bring them back again;
Where Abr'ham worshipp'd and was bless'd,
Of Canaan they shall be possess'd,
　　Emerging from the main.

That thy baptized foot may tread,
Where proud blasphemers laid their head,
　　By judgments unreclaim'd;
And that thy shepherd's dogs may chace
Thy flocks into their pleasant place,
　　Who made the earth asham'd.

They've seen (their errors to disprove)
My God in blest procession move,
    The pomp of God my king;
Accordant to the train below,
The dances rise, the streamers flow,
    And holy flow'rs they fling.

The goodly shew the singers lead,
The minstrels next in place proceed,
    With musick sweet and loud;
The damsels, that with wild delight
The brisk-resounding timbrels smite,
    Are in the mid-most crowd.

O thou Jeshurun, yield thy thanks,
All ages, sexes, tribes and ranks,
    In congregated bands;
To God united thanks restore,
Brought from the heart its inmost core,
    And with protesting hands.

There Benjamin in triumph goes,
Least, but in love the Lord, of those
    That dwell in tents and bow'rs;
And Judah next to the most high,
With Zebulon and Naphtali
    Their princedoms and their powr's.

God to the sires of all the tribes
Some great peculiar gift ascribes,
    To each his talents told;
The loan with such long-suff'ring lent,
Do thou establish and augment
    Ten thousand thousand fold.

From this thy temple which we lay,
To thee the homage they shall pay,
    To thee the praise impute;

Kings shall their annual gifts renew,
And give Melchisedec his due,
    The glory and the fruit.

Rebuke the spearmen with thy word,
Those calves and bulls of Bashan's herd,
    Which from our ways abhor;
Let them pay toll, and hue the wood,
Which are at enmity with good,
    And love the voice of war.

The nobles from the sons of Ham,
Shall bring the bullock and the ram,
    Idolatrous no more;
The Morians soon shall offer alms,
And bow their heads, and spread their palms,
    God's mercy to implore.

Ye blessed angels of the Lord,
Of nations and of kings the ward,
    That further thanks and pray'r,
To Jesus Christ your praise resound,
Collected from the regions round
    Your tutelary care.

In other days before the sev'n,
Upon that ante-mundane heav'n,
    In glorious pomp he rode—
He sends a voice, which voice is might,
In inconceivable delight
    Th' acknowledg'd word of God.

Ye heroes foremost in the field
That couch the spear, or bear the shield,
    Bless God that ye prevail;
His splendour is on Israel's brow,
He stands all-pow'rful on the prow
    Midst all the clouds that sail.

O God, all miracle thou art,
Ev'n thou the God of Israel's heart
　　Within thy holy shrine,
Thou shalt with strength and pow'r protect,
Thy people in the Lord elect,
　　Praise, endless praise be thine.

Psalm LXXIV

Lord Jesus, why dost thou retard
　　The grace thou lov'st to send,
And all thy pastoral regard
　　In kindling wrath suspend?

O think upon thy chosen seed,
　　Reproach'd and disesteem'd,
Which, as thy holy word decreed,
　　Thy precious blood redeem'd.

O think upon Jehudah's race,
　　The tribe so much thine own,
And on fair Zion's special place,
　　Where thou hast fixt thy throne.

Prepare thy blessed feet, and come
　　With peace angelic shod,
And purge away the dross and scum,
　　That stain the house of God.

Thy foes display their flags and boast
　　That they thy battles fight,
And schismatics maintain their post
　　Amongst the sons of light.

The servile hand that hew'd the wood
　　From out the stately trees,
Was, in his place, ordain'd to good,
　　And shap'd his work to please.

But now these artizans untune
    The musick that they made,
The carvers break each fair festoon,
    And counteract their trade.

Nay more, they've carried force and fire
    Against each shrine around;
And levell'd, in their godless ire,
    Thy temple with the ground.

Yea, in their wishes they combine
    That not a church should stand,
And thus incendiaries mine
    The faith of all the land.

No signs the wonted grace attest—
    The services unsung;
And few to prophesy the best,
    And learn each sacred tongue.

O God, how long shall traitors sting,
    And hiss with spite and guile,
And with th' establish'd church and king
    Their Saviour Christ revile?

Why dost thou our defence withdraw
    At this so great alarm,
Nor keepest Antichrist in awe
    By thine almighty arm?

For Christ, my king from long ago,
    Is with me to this hour;
All hope above, and help below,
    Are solely from his pow'r.

That pow'r astonish'd floods avow'd,
    Dividing heap from heap;
Thou smote the dragons as they plough'd
    The waters of the deep.

The huge Leviathan was stunn'd
　　At that stupendous roar
Of billows, breaking to refund
　　The fishes on the shore.

The living springs and streams profuse
　　Thy people to supply,
Thy mandate could from rocks educe,
　　And made the river dry.

The day is subject to thy rule,
　　The night to thy decree,
The blessed sunshine and the cool
　　Are made and chang'd by thee.

Thou by thy wisdom hast ordain'd
　　The borders of the world,
And summer's genial heat maintain'd,
　　And wintry winds unfurl'd.

Consider, Lord, how men blaspheme
　　The honour of thy name,
And fools, in their ambitious dream,
　　Have lost the sense of shame.

Let not thy turtle-dove be sold,
　　To crowds and ruffian rage,
Nor from the prostrate poor withhold
　　Thy love for such an age!

Thy gracious covenant review,
　　For in this earth beneath
The worldlings dark designs pursue,
　　And fell revenge they breathe.

Let not the simple man depart
　　Abash'd at fruitless pray'r;
But give the poor a joyful heart
　　Thy glory to declare.

Arise, O God, thy cause support,
   Thine own eternal cause,
Reclaim the folly that in sport
   Contemns thy name and laws.

O let thy words of comfort drown
   The voice of rank excess,
And bring their gross presumption down
   To worship and to bless.

Psalm CIV

Bless thou the Lord, my soul—how great,
O Lord, what a stupendous weight
   Of honours crown thy name;
Thou'rt cloath'd with majesty and might,
And glories how exceeding bright
   Come clust'ring on thy fame!

With light, which thou hast purer made,
As with a robe thou art array'd,
   Whose pow'r the world upholds;
And hang'st the skies in beauteous blue,
Wav'd like a curtain to the view,
   Down heav'n's high dome in folds.

His chamber-beams in floods he shrouds,
His chariots are the rolling clouds
   Upon th'etherial arch;
And on the rapid winds their wings
Majestical, the king of kings
   Walks in his awful march.

The guardian spirits know their post,
His heralds are th' angelic host
   Obedient to his will;
The delegated lightnings fly,
And flames are sent on embassy
   His mandates to fulfill.

Fair and full-finished at her birth,
Firm at the first he fixt the earth,
    And wrought her bases fast;
Her deep foundations has he girt,
That as the lively springs exert,
    Her state of rest might last.

Upon the surface deep and wide
Thou pouredst out the flowing tide,
    Like some loose garment spread;
The rising waters stood around,
And swoln above the level ground,
    O'ertop the mountain's head.

But at the thunder of thy word
Their inundations were deterr'd,
    And thy rebuke obey'd;
And to the centre from the top,
Th' unfathom'd ocean to a drop
    Was pacify'd and laid.

Then up into the hills they go,
And down upon the vales below
    Again their way they find;
Till at such places they abide,
And in those due directions glide
    Thy wisdom has assign'd.

Thou over-rul'st the liquid mass,
And in the bounds they may not pass
    Thou shalt their floods restrain;
The way that is prescrib'd they learn
For ever, nor shall they return
    To cover earth again.

The living springs at his command
Are sent a succour to the land,
    For rivers the resource;

Which as by stooping woods they curve
'Mongst intermingl'd hills preserve
    Their interrupted course.

All beasts that haunt the distant groves,
Frequent the lucid stream in droves,
    As need and nature rule,
And asses of the wild assuage
Their thirst, and the meridian age
    Of sultry sun-beams cool.

Near them thro' blossoms bursting ripe
The birds upon the perches pipe,
    As boughs the herbage shield;
And while each other they salute,
The trees from every quiv'ring shoot,
    Melodious musick yield.

He from his chambers dew distills,
And waters with his rain the hills
    Where'er their summits soar;
The vales, with sweet luxuriance clad,
Make all the face of nature glad
    With never-failing store.

He laid the verdant turf to graze,
That earth the due supplies might raise
    Of annual food and wealth;
And fragrant herbs and flow'rs profuse
The seasons on the field produce
    For pleasure and for health.

He planted on the rock the vine,
To glad the heart of man with wine,
    And crown the thankful bowl;
And to exhilarate the face,
He gave the cruse, and broke in grace
    His bread sustains the soul.

The trees with precious balsam sweat,
Which Grace in seemly rows has set
  By her almighty pow'r;
And Lebanon, which God perfumes,
His crest with stately cedar plumes,
  Whose tufted tops embow'r.

The feather'd families of air
Contrive their cunning fabricks there,
  What time the sexes mix;
The storks for elevation seek
To loftier firs with bolder beak
  Their pensile house to fix.

The kid that brouses on the thyme,
Looks from the precipice sublime,
  And every peril braves;
The skulking conies dwell secure,
And for defence their young immure
  In quarries and in caves.

He taught the silver moon her way,
Her monthly and nocturnal sway,
  Where'er she wanes or grows;
The glorious globe that gilds the skies
Is conscious of his early rise,
  And his descent he knows.

The lines of light and shade to mark
Is thine, thou bidst the night be dark,
  Beneath whose solemn gloom
The forest-beasts forsake their den,
And all that shun the walks of men,
  Their wonted haunts resume.

The lions rouse to fill the scene,
With eyes of baleful lightning keen
  Upon the desart rude;

And as in surly-sounding tone
They make the hollow caverns groan,
    From God require their food.

But at the glancing of the dawn,
Ere yet the sun-beams o'er the lawn
    The burnish'd orb unveil;
Alarm'd they flee their nightly round,
And in their place with peace profound
    Their weary'd limbs regale.

While man, frail nature to sustain,
Awakes to labour and to pain,
    Till from the wish'd-for west
Th' approaches of the dusky eve
Give to his toil a short reprieve,
    And send him home to rest.

How manifold thy works are made,
O Lord—by thankful man survey'd,
    What an exhaustless theme!
In wisdom didst thou all dispense,
How with thy vast munificence
    Heav'n, earth, air, all things teem!

So does the sea, whose shelvy rocks
And depths with numberless he stocks
    From life's eternal fount;
Some in the nether crannies skulk,
And some of huge enormous bulk
    The swelling floods surmount.

There go the ships from shore to store,
Of distant climes the diff'rent shore
    To take and to discharge;
There that Leviathan resorts,
Which at thy blessed bidding sports
    At leisure and at large.

All these upon thy love depend,
And on thy providence attend
    Their daily wants to urge;
And as the stated hour revolves,
The bread is broke, the dew dissolves
    Upon the rising surge.

They gather that which is diffus'd,
Nor ought is wasted or abus'd,
    So has thy wisdom will'd;
Thy bounteous hand prepares a feast,
And all from greatest to the least
    Thou fillest, and they're fill'd.

Thou hid'st thy face—however brief
Thy absence, it is instant grief
    Of infinite degree;
'Tis thine to give, and to withdraw
Their breath, and by a stablish'd law
    They are, or cease to be.

But by succession they survive,
And sense and pow'r to move derive,
    As from thy spirit sent;
Anew their moulded dust is warm'd—
Ev'n earth herself by thee reform'd,
    Shall other scenes present.

The glorious majesty and love
Of God shall have no bounds, above
    All mortal change and chance;
The Lord shall heav'n's whole choir employ
In anthems of exceeding joy
    To see his works advance.

Abash'd at his tremendous look,
The earth with strong commotions shook,
    Which all her awe bespoke;

He touch'd the hills, their summits nod,
And at the weighty hand of God
　　　They totter, and they smoke.

That goodness which these years prolongs,
Shall give new spirit to my songs
　　　As measure to my span;
While I my life and limbs possess,
The bounteous author will I bless
　　　With all the might of man.

As in the spirit I repeat
His praise, my musings shall be sweet,
　　　To just refinement wrought;
Yea, while I yet suppress my voice,
To thee, O Lord, will I rejoice
　　　In melody of thought.

The men, by carnal sins entic'd,
Must fall before the rod of Christ,
　　　Confounded and amaz'd;—
Praise thou the Lord, my soul apart—
Praise ye, who hear with voice and heart—
　　　The Lord our God be prais'd.

Psalm CXXXIV

Attend to the musick divine
　　　Ye people of God with the priest,
At once your Hosanna combine
　　　As meekly ye bow to the east.

Ye servants that look to the lights
　　　Which blaze in the house of the Lord,
And keep up the watch of the nights
　　　To bless each apartment and ward.

The holy of holies review,
　　　And lift up your hands with your voice,

And there sing your anthems anew,
    In praise to Jehova rejoice.

The Lord that made heav'n and earth,
    Which rules o'er the night and the day,
His blessing bestow on your mirth,
    And hear you whenever ye pray.

Psalm CXXXVII

Pensive we sat the silent hours
Where by the Babylonian tow'rs
    At large the waters stray,
Till mem'ry brought thee to our eyes,
O Zion, then the tears and sighs
    Burst out and made their way.

No matter for our harps—our care
Was not on mirth and musick there,
    All solace we declin'd;
We sate and suffer'd them in view
To hang as bended, or as blew
    The willows or the wind.

When they, that led our captive train,
Bade us our heavy hearts refrain
    From grief to joys extreme;
Thus they commanded their request,
"Sing us a song, and sing your best,
    And Zion be the theme!"

What, in a land by God abhorr'd,
Shall we profane unto the Lord
    The consecrated songs;
And Israel's harp and hands employ,
To strike up symphonies of joy
    'Mongst foreigners and wrongs?

Jerusalem! O blest in woe,
If I forget thee, or forego
    When heav'n and nature call,

May this right hand, and God's own heart
Forget his spirit, and her art
     To touch the strings at all!

May my tongue to my palate cleave
If I forget thee when I grieve;
     If to all realms on earth
I not Jerusalem prefer,
Jerusalem! and harp on her
     When most my might in mirth!

O Lord, when it shall be fulfill'd
That thou Jerusalem rebuild,
     Remember unto good,
How "down with it," th' insulting band
Cry'd, "down with it, and mar the land
     Where all that splendour stood."

Renown'd the man! that shall reward
And serve thee as thou'st serv'd the Lord,
     Thou shalt thy turn deplore;
There's desolation too for thee,
Thou daughter of calamity,
     And Babylon no more!

But he is greatest and the best,
Who spares his enemies profest,
     And Christian mildness owns;
Who gives his captives back their lives,
Their helpless infants, weeping wives,
     And for his sin atones.

Psalm CXLVII

Hosanna—musick is divine,
When in the praise the psalmists join,
     And each good heart is warm;

Yea, joy is sweetest so renew'd,
And all the rites of gratitude
     Are rapture to perform.

The Lord fair Salem shall replace,
And set upon his ancient base
     Hananiel's goodly tow'r;
Make captives free, the barren big,
And under his own vine and fig
     All Jacob re-embow'r.

He shall the broken heart repair,
And for all sickness and despair
     A cure in Christ provide;
And heal the wounded and the bruis'd,
His oil into their sores infus'd,
     And soothing balm applied.

Tho' their bright swarms the sand surpass,
Of every magnitude and class
     He knows th' etherial flames;
The numb'rer of their host is He,
And to his summons "here we be,"
     They answer by their names.

For God is magnitude immense,
His prowess is omnipotence
     That knows no date or end;
His wisdom infinitely great,
And all duration, depth and height,
     His mysteries transcend.

The Lord with approbation sees
The meek, and from his faithful knees
     He lifts him up on high;
But spurns the sinner and unjust,
And leaves low luxury and lust
     To worms that never die.

Sing praises all degrees and ranks,
As in the pray'r of general thanks
    The holy church commune;
As to the touch the harp revives,
Sing praises with your lips and lives
    To Christ the word and tune.

He the blue heav'n in beauty shrouds,
And ballances the plumy clouds
    Which for the rain he wrings;
He causes the mild dew to drop,
And grass upon the mountain top
    In tufted verdure springs.

For every thing that moves and lives,
Foot, fin, or feather, meat he gives,
    He deals the beasts their food
Both in the wilderness and stall,
And hears the raven's urgent call,
    And stills her clam'rous brood.

And yet his maker has no need
Of the train'd ox, or prancing steed,
    Tho' thunder cloath his chest;
And man that manages the rein,
Is but a creature brief and vain
    With such proportion blest.

But God is pleas'd with duteous fear,
Men with clean hands and conscience clear,
    Which at thy mercy-gate
With ceaseless application knock,
And patient on him as their rock
    For sure redemption wait.

O Sion, praise the Lord, and thou,
Fair Salem, to his praises bow
    Thine olives and thy palms;

Are there afflicted? let them pray,
But mirth shall dedicate her day
    To hymns and festive psalms.

For by his might the Lord supports
Thy mounds, and fortifies thy forts,
    Thy brazen bars he nails;
Thy sportive children fill the streets,
Thy foe without the wall retreats,
    Nor want within prevails.

He sheathes the sword and blunts the spears,
And thy redoubtable frontiers
    Barbarian inroads scorn;
That thou may'st in thy peace possess
The blessings of a social mess,
    And flour of choicest corn.

He sends his word upon the earth
To call conception into birth,
    And kind with kind to match;
And to sustain all human race,
The blessed angels of his grace
    Make infinite dispatch.

His snow upon the ground he teems,
Like bleaching wool beside the streams,
    To warm the tender blade;
Like ashes from the furnace cast,
His frost comes with the northern blast
    To pinch and to pervade.

Like vitreous fragments o'er the field,
In ice the waters are congeal'd,
    Their liquid swiftness lost;
The breath steams on the sharpen'd air,
And who so hardy as to bear
    The quickness of his frost!

He sends the word of his command
To melt and loosen all the land,
 And let the floods at large;
He blows, and with the genial breeze,
The fount and river by degrees
 Their usual tale discharge.

His word to Jacob he disclos'd,
When he upon the stones repos'd
 And worship'd in a trance;
And laws to Israel enjoin'd
When o'er the nations of mankind
 He bade his tribes advance.

Such wond'rous love has not been shown,
But to the patriarch's seed alone
 His duty to requite;
And judgments on the rest impend,
Till Jesus make them comprehend
 His ways, his truth and light.

Psalm CXLVIII

Hosanna to the king
 On his eternal throne,
Let heaven's high convex ring
 With pray'r and praise alone!
Praise him which treads th' etherial vault,
And with the theme your strains exalt.

Praise him, cherubic flights,
 And ye seraphic fires,
Angelical delights
 With voices, lutes and lyres;
And vie who shall extol him most,
Ye blest innumerable host!

Praise him, thou source of heat,
　　Great ruler of the day,
And thou serenely sweet,
　　O moon, his praise display;
Praise him ye glorious lights that are,
The planet and the sparkling star.

Praise him ye heav'ns above
　　The highest heav'n sublime,
Where tun'd to truth and love
　　The spheres symphonious chime;
Praise him where holy spirits lave,
Ye waters of eternal wave.

Let them to praise his name
　　With choral musick flow;
For from his word they came,
　　He spake and it was so;
His are the glorious, great and fair,
For he commanded, and they were.

For he hath made them fast
　　For ever and again;
For ever they shall last,
　　And in their spheres remain;
In all their movements seek or shun,
The law that he commands is done.

Praise ye the Lord of earth,
　　All ye that dwell therein,
And leap with active mirth,
　　Ye fish of ev'ry fin;
Praise ye, that hide where ocean sleeps,
Ye dragons of unfathom'd deeps.

Ye meteors, fire and hail,
　　With ev'ry cloud that snows,

As o'er the land they sail,
　　And various wind that blows
The rapid terror of the storm,
At once his mandate to perform.

Ye mountains of the air,
　　And hills of less degree,
And you ye groves that bear
　　On ev'ry goodly tree
The summer fruits, and vernal bloom,
And lofty cedars of perfume.

Ye beasts that haunt the wild,
　　From servile bondage loose,
Ye cattle tame and mild
　　For man's domestic use,
Ye reptiles of the ground adore,
Ye birds sing praises, as ye soar.

Praise him, each scepter'd seer
　　Advanc'd to hold the helm,
And to his praise appear,
　　Ye people of the realm;
Ye princes by the world renown'd,
And judges, that the law expound.

Ye youths the maids engage
　　In melody divine,
Let infancy with age
　　To praise the Lord combine,
Whose name, whose merits have no end,
But measure and immense transcend.

He shall exalt the crest
　　Of his peculiar fold,
And all the wise and blest
　　This festival shall hold;

Ev'n Jacob's sons and Judah's bands,
Whose faith, whose firm allegiance stands.

OR THIS:

HALLELUJAH! kneel and sing
Praises to the heav'nly king;
To the God supremely great,
Hallelujah in the height!

Praise him, archangelic band,
Ye that in his presence stand;
Praise him, ye that watch and pray,
Michael's myriads in array.

Praise him, sun, at each extreme
Orient streak, and western beam,
Moon and stars of mystic dance,
Silv'ring in the blue expanse.

Praise him, O ye heights, that soar
Heav'n and heav'n for evermore;
And ye streams of living rill,
Higher yet, and purer still.

Let them praise his glorious name,
From whose fruitful word they came,
And they first began to be
As he gave the great decree.

Their constituent parts he founds
For duration without bounds,
And their covenant has seal'd,
Which shall never be repeal'd.

Praise the Lord on earth's domains,
And the mutes that sea contains,
Ye that on the surface leap,
And ye dragons of the deep.

Batt'ring hail, and fires that glow,
Steaming vapours, plumy snow,
Wind and storm his wrath incurr'd,
Wing'd and pointed at his word.

Mountains of enormous scale,
Ev'ry hill, and ev'ry vale,
Fruit-trees of a thousand dyes,
Cedars that perfume the skies.

Beasts that haunt the woodland maze,
Nibbling flocks, and droves that graze;
Reptiles of amphibious breed,
Feather'd millions form'd for speed;

Kings, with Jesus for their guide,
Peopl'd regions far and wide,
Heroes of their country's cause,
Princes, judges of the laws;

Age and childhood, youth and maid,
To his name your praise be paid;
For his word is worth alone,
Far above his crown and throne.

He shall dignify the crest
Of his people rais'd and blest,
While we serve with praise and pray'rs
All, in Christ, his saints and heirs.

EDITIONS

A Translation of the Psalms of David, 1765. (Text.)
Blunden, *A Song to David*, etc., 1924, had fragments
from Ps. civ, and cxlvii.

Hymns
& Spiritual Songs
for the Fasts and Festivals
of the
Church of England

Hymn I

NEW YEAR

Word of endless adoration,
　　Christ, I to thy call appear;
On my knees in meek prostration
　　To begin a better year.

Spirits in eternal waiting,
　　*Special ministers of pray'r,
Which our welcome antedating,
　　Shall the benediction bear.

Which, the type of vows completed,
　　Shall the wreathed garland send,
While new blessings are intreated,
　　And communicants attend.

Emblem of the hopes beginning,
　　Who the budding rods shall bind,
Way from guiltless nature's winning,
　　In good-will to human kind.

Ye that dwell with cherub-turtles
　　Mated in that upmost light,
Or parade† amongst the myrtles,
　　On your steeds of speckl'd white.

　* Tobit xxii, 15. [Apparently a misprint; the
reference should be Tobit xii, 15.]
　† Zec. i. 8.

Ye that sally from the portal
 Of yon everlasting bow'rs,
Sounding symphonies immortal,
 Years, and months, and days, and hours.

But nor myrtles, nor the breathing
 Of the never-dying grove,
Nor the chaplets sweetly wreathing,
 And by hands angelic wove;

Not the musick or the mazes
 Of those spirits aptly tim'd,
Can avail like pray'r and praises
 By the Lamb himself sublim'd.

Take ye therefore what ye give him,
 Of his fulness grace for grace,
Strive to think him, speak him, live him,
 Till you find him face to face.

Sing like David, or like Hannah,
 As the spirit first began,
To the God of heights hosanna!
 Peace and charity to man.

Christ his blessing universal
 On th'arch-patriarch's seed bestow,
Which attend to my rehearsal
 Of melodious pray'r below.

Hymn II
CIRCUMCISION

When Abraham was bless'd,
And on his face profess'd
 The Saviour Christ hereafter born,
"Thou pilgrim and estrang'd,

Thy name," said God, "is chang'd,
Thy lot secur'd from want and scorn.

O Abraham, my friend,
My covenant attend,
  Which Shilo's self shall not repeal,
Chastise from carnal sin
Thy house and all thy kin,
  Thy faith by circumcision seal."

The promis'd Shilo came,
And then receiv'd the name
  Of Jesus, Saviour of the soul;
As he the law fulfill'd
Which checks the fleshly-will'd,
  And o'er the passion gives controul.

O clean and undefil'd!
Thou shalt not be beguil'd
  By youthful heat and female art,
To thee the strains belong
Of that mysterious song
  Where none but virgins bear a part.

Come every purer thought,
By which the mind is wrought
  From man's corruption, nature's dust;
Away each vain desire,
And all the fiends that fire
  The soul to base and filthy lust.

Ye swans that sail and lave
In Jordan's hallow'd wave,
  Ah sweet! ah pensive! ah serene!
Thou rose of maiden flush,
Like Joseph's guiltless blush,
  And herb of ever-grateful green;

Ye lilies of perfume,
That triumph o'er the loom,
   And gaudy greatness far outshine;
And thou the famous tree,
Whose name is chastity,
   And all the brilliants of the mine;

Ye doves of silver down
That plume the seraph's crown,
   All, all the praise of Jesus sing,
The joy of heav'n and earth,
And Christ's eternal worth,
   The pearl of God the Father's ring.

Let elegance, the flow'r
Of words, in tune and pow'r,
   Find some device of cleanest choice
About that gem to place—
"This is my HEIR of GRACE,
   In whose perfections I rejoice."

Hymn III

EPIPHANY

GRACE, thou source of each perfection,
   Favour from the height thy ray;
Thou the star of all direction,
   Child of endless truth and day.

Thou that bidst my cares be calmer,
   Lectur'd what to seek and shun,
Come, and guide a western palmer
   To the Virgin and her Son.

Lo! I travel in the spirit,
   On my knees my course I steer
To the house of might and merit
   With humility and fear.

Poor at least as John or Peter
    I my vows alone prefer;
But the strains of love are sweeter
    Than the frankincense and myrrh.

Neither purse nor scrip I carry,
    But the books of life and pray'r;
Nor a staff my foe to parry,
    'Tis the cross of Christ I bear.

From a heart serene and pleasant
    'Midst unnumber'd ills I feel,
I will meekly bring my present,
    And with sacred verses kneel.

Muse, through Christ the Word, inventive
    Of the praise so greatly due;
Heav'nly gratitude retentive
    Of the bounties ever new;

Fill my heart with genuine treasures,
    Pour them out before his feet,
High conceptions, mystic measures,
    Springing strong and flowing sweet.

Come, ye creatures of thanksgiving,
    Which are harmoniz'd to bless,
Birds that warble for your living,
    Beasts with ways of love express.

Thou the shepherd's faithful fellow,
    As he lies by Cedron's stream,
Where soft airs and waters mellow
    Take their Saviour for their theme.

Thou too gaily grave domestic,
    With whose young fond childhood plays,
Held too mean for verse majestic,
    First with me thy Maker praise.

Brousing kids, and lambkins grazing,
    Colts and younglings of the drove,
Come with all your modes of praising,
    Bounding through the leafless grove.

Ye that skill the flow'rs to fancy,
    And in just assemblage sort,
Pluck the primrose, pluck the pansy,
    And your prattling troop exhort.

"Little men, in Jesus mighty,
    And ye maids that go alone,
Bodies chaste, and spirits flighty,
    Ere the world and guilt are known.

"Breath so sweet, and cheeks so rosy—
    Put your little hands to pray,
Take ye ev'ry one a posy,
    And away to Christ, away."

Youth, benevolence, and beauty,
    In your Saviour's praise agree,
Which this day receives our duty,
    Sitting on the virgin's knee.

That from this day's institution
    Ev'ry penitent in deed,
At his hour of retribution,
    As a child, through him may speed.

Hymn VI

THE PRESENTATION OF CHRIST
IN THE TEMPLE

Preserver of the church, thy spouse,
    From sacrilege and wrong,
To whom the myriads pay their vows,

Give ear, and in my heart arouse
  The spirit of a nobler song.

When Hiero built, from David's plan,
  The house of godlike style,
And Solomon, the prosp'rous man,
Whose reign with wealth and fame began,
  O'erlaid with gold the glorious pile;

Great was the concourse of mankind
  The structure to review;
Such bulk with sweet proportion join'd
The labours of a vaster mind,
  In all directions grand and true.

And yet it was not true and grand
  The Godhead to contain;
By whom immensity is spann'd,
Which has eternal in his hand
  The globe of his supreme domain.

Tho' there the congregation knelt
  The daily debt to pay,
Tho' there superior glories dwelt,
Tho' there the host their blessings dealt,
  The highest GRACE was far away.

At length another fane arose,
  The fabrick of the poor;
And built by hardship midst her foes,
One hand for work and one for blows,
  Made this stupendous blessing sure:

That God should in the world appear
  Incarnate—as a child—
That he should be presented here,
At once our utmost doubts to clear,
  And make our hearts with wonder wild.

Present ye therefore, on your knees,
  Hearts, hands resign'd and clean;
Ye poor and mean of all degrees,
If he will condescend and please
  To take at least what orphans glean—

I speak for all—for them that fly,
  And for the race that swim;
For all that dwell in moist and dry,
Beasts, reptiles, flow'rs and gems to vie
  When gratitude begins her hymn.

Praise him ye doves, and ye that pipe
  Ere buds begin to stir;
Ev'n every finch of every stripe,
And thou of filial love the type,
  O stork! that sit'st upon the fir.

Praise him thou sea, to whom he gave
  The shoal of active mutes;
(Fit tenants of thy roaring wave)
Who comes to still the fiends, that rave
  In oracles and school disputes.

By Jesus number'd all and priz'd,
  Praise him in dale and hill;
Ye beasts for use and peace devis'd,
And thou which patient and despis'd,
  Yet shalt a prophecy fulfill.

Praise him ye family that weave
  The crimson to be spread
There, where communicants receive,
And ye, that form'd the eye to grieve,
  Hid in green bush or wat'ry bed.

Praise him ye flow'rs that serve the swarm
  With honey for their cells;

Ere yet the vernal day is warm,
To call out millions to perform
   Their gambols on your cups and bells.

Praise him ye gems of lively spark,
   And thou the pearl of price;
In that great depth or caverns dark,
   Nor yet are wrested from the mark,
     To serve the turns of pride and vice.

Praise him ye cherubs of his breast,
   The mercies of his love,
Ere yet from guile and hate profest,
The phenix makes his fragrant nest
   In his own paradise above.

Hymn VIII

ST. MATTHIAS

Hark! the cock proclaims the morning,
   Match the rhime, and strike the strings;
Heav'nly muse, embrace the warning,
   Raise thy voice, and stretch thy wings.

Lo! the poor, alive and likely
   Midst desertion and distress,
Teach the folk that deal obliquely,
   They had better bear and bless.

If we celebrate Matthias,
   Let us do it heart and soul;
Nor let worldly reasons bias
   Our conceptions from their goal.

As the fancy cools and rambles,
   Keep her constant, keep her chaste;
Ward from wine, and from the shambles,
   Sight and appetite, and taste.

Tho' thy craving bowels murmur
    And against thy pray'r rebell,
Yet be firmer still, and firmer
    In the work begun so well.

Sick and weakly, pris'ners, strangers,
    Cold in nakedness we lie;
Train'd in hunger, thirst and dangers,
    As in exercise to die.

All avail not to dispirit
    Toil, determin'd to succeed;
And we trust in Christ his merit,
    As we have his woes to plead.

Yea, our lot is fallen fairer
    Than the sons of wealth and pride;
While our Saviour is a sharer
    In all hardships that betide.

Hard and precious are together,
    Stripes and wounds are endless gain;
If with him the storm we weather
    With him also we shall reign.

We shall take the traitors' places
    And their forfeit office hold,
And to Christ shall show our faces,
    Not betray'd by us or sold.

Lord, our spirits disencumber,
    From the world our hearts dismiss;
Let us reckon to the number
    Of thy saints in fruitful bliss.

Let the few of Christ be hearty
    In the cause they bleed to win,
And religion make her party
    Good against the pow'r of sin.

Let us pray—by self-denial
    Every sense to Christ resign,
Till we from the fiery trial
    Pure as purity refine.

Hymn IX

THE ANNUNCIATION OF THE
BLESSED VIRGIN

O Purity, thou test
Of love amongst the blest,
How excellent thou art,
The Lord Jehovah's heart,
    Whose sweet attributes embrace,
    Every virtue, praise and grace.

Thou fair and good dispos'd,
'Midst glories undisclos'd,
Inspire the notes to play
Upon the virgin's day;
    High above all females nam'd,
    And by Gabriel's voice proclaim'd.

Glad herald, ever sent
Upon some blest event,
But never sped to men
On such a charge till then—
    When his Saviour's feet he kiss'd,
    To promulge his birth dismiss'd.

Hail mystery! thou source
Of nature's plainest course,
How much this work transcends
Thine usual means and ends—
    Wherefore call'd, we shall not spare
    Louder praise, and oft'ner prayer.

But if the work be new,
So shou'd the song be too,
By every thought that's born
In freshness of the morn;
    Every flight of active wings,
    Every shift upon the strings.

To praise the mighty hand
By which the world was mann'd,
Which dealt to great and small
Their talents clear of all;
    Kind to kind by likeness linkt,
    Various all, and all distinct.

Praise him seraphic tone
Of instruments unknown,
High strains on golden wire,
Work'd by etherial fire;
    Blowing on unceasing chords,
    "King of kings, and lord of lords."

Praise Hannah, of the three,
That sang in Mary's key;
With her that made her psalm
Beneath the bow'ring palm;
    With the dame—Bethulia's boast,
    Honour'd o'er th' Assyrian host.

Praise him faith, hope, and love
That tend Jehovah's dove;
By men from lust repriev'd
As females best conceiv'd;
    To remount the man and muse
    Far above all earthly views.

Hymn X

THE CRUCIFIXION OF OUR
BLESSED LORD

The world is but a sorry scene,
Untrue, unhallow'd, and unclean,
    And hardly worth a man;
The fiend upon the land prevails,
And o'er the floods in triumph sails
    Do goodness all she can.

How many works for such a day?
How glorious? that ye scourge and slay
    Ye blind, by blinder led;
All hearts at once devising bad,
Hands, mouths against their Maker mad,
    With Satan at the head—

Are these the race of saints profest,
That for authorities contest,
    And question and debate?
Yet in so foul a deed rebell,
Beyond example, ev'n from hell,
    To match its barb'rous hate.

Behold the man! the tyrant said,
As in the robes of scoff array'd
    And crown'd with thorns he stood;
And feigning will to let him go
He chose Barabbas, open foe
    Of human kind and good.

And was it He, whose voice divine,
Could change the water into wine,
    And first his pow'r averr'd;
Which fed in Galilea's groves
The fainting thousands with the loaves
    And fishes of his word!

And was it He, whose mandate freed
The palsied suppliant, and in deed
    The sabbath-day rever'd;
Which bade the thankful dumb proclaim
The Lord omnipotent by name,
    Till loosen'd deafness heard!

And was it He, whose hand was such,
As lighten'd blindness at a touch,
    And made the lepers whole;
Could to the dropsy health afford,
And to the lunatic restor'd
    Serenity of soul!

The daughter that so long a term
By Satan's bonds had been infirm,
    Was rescued and receiv'd;
Yea, with the foes of faith and hope
His matchless charity cou'd cope,
    When Malchus was reliev'd.

The woman in his garment's hem
Conceiv'd a prevalence to stem
    The sources of her pain;
He calls—the dead from death arise,
And as their legions he defies
    The dev'ls descend again.

His irresistable command
Convey'd the vessel to the land,
    As instant as his thought;
He caus'd the tempest to forget
Its rage, and into Peter's net
    The wond'rous capture brought.

The roarings of the billows cease
To hear the gospel of his peace
    Upon the still profound—

He walk'd the waves—and at his will,
The fish to pay th' exactor's bill
　　To Judah's coast was bound.

The wither'd hand he saw and cur'd,
And health from gen'ral ail secur'd
　　Where'er disease was rife;
And was omniscient to tell
The woman at the patriarch's well
　　The story of her life.

But never since the world was known,
One so stupendous as his own,
　　And rich of vast event;
From love ador'd, as soon as seen,
Had not his hated message been
　　To bid the world repent.

Ah, still desirous of a king,
To give voluptuous vice its swing
　　With passions like a brute;
By Jesus Christ came truth and grace,
But none indulgence, pension, place,
　　The slaves of SELF to suit.

The Lord on Gabbatha they doom,
Before the delegate of Rome,
　　Deserted and exposed—
They might have thought on Israel's God,
Which on the sapphire pavement trod,
　　To sev'nty seers disclos'd.

They might have thought upon the loss
Of Eden, and the dreadful cross
　　That happen'd by a tree;
Ere yet with cursed throats they shout
To bring the dire event about,
　　Tho' prophesy'd to be.

O God, the bonds of sin enlarge,
Lay not this horror to our charge,
 But as we fast and weep,
Pour out the streams of love profuse,
Let all the pow'rs of mercy loose,
 While wrath and vengeance sleep.

Hymn XI

EASTER DAY

Awake—arise—lift up thy voice,
 Which as a trumpet swell,
Rejoice in Christ—again rejoice,
 And on his praises dwell.

The muse at length, no more perplext
 In search of human wit,
Shall kneel her down, and take her text
 From lore of sacred writ.

My lot in holy ground was cast,
 And for the prize I threw;
And in the path by thousands past
 The Lord shall make me new.

O let the people, with the priest,
 Adorn themselves to pray,
And with their faces to the east
 Their adoration pay.

Let us not doubt, as doubted some,
 When first the Lord appear'd;
But full of faith and rev'rence come
 What time his voice is heard.

And ev'n as John, who ran so well,
 Confess upon our knees

The prince that locks up death and hell,
    And has himself the *keys.

'Tis He that puts all hearts in tune
    With strings that never jar,
And they that rise to praise him soon,
    Shall win the †Morning Star.

The morning star, and pearl of price,
    And ‡stone of lucid white,
Are all provocatives from vice,
    To heav'n and true delight.

O Gladness! that suspend'st belief
    For fear that rapture dreams;
Thou also hast the tears of grief,
    And failst in wild extreams.

Tho' Peter make a clam'rous din,
    Will he thy doubts destroy?
Will little Rhoda let him in,
    Incredulous with joy?

And thus thro' gladness and surprize
    The saints their Saviour treat;
Nor will they trust their ears and eyes
    But by his hands and feet.

These hands of lib'ral love indeed
    In infinite degree,
Those feet still frank to move and bleed
    For millions and for me.

A watch, to slavish duty train'd,
    Was set by spiteful care,
Lest what the sepulchre contain'd
    Should find alliance there.

* Rev. i. 18.   † Rev. ii. 28.
‡ Rev. ii. 17.

Herodians came to seal the stone
  With Pilate's gracious leave,
Lest dead and friendless, and alone,
  Should all their skill deceive.

O dead arise! O friendless stand
  By seraphim ador'd—
O solitude! again command
  Thy host from heav'n restor'd.

Watchmen sleep on, and take your rest,
  And wake when conscience stings;
For Christ shall make the grave his nest
  Till God return his wings.

He died—but death itself improv'd
  To triumph o'er the foe,
And preach'd, as God's great spirit mov'd,
  To sinners chain'd below.

The souls that perish'd in the flood
  He bid again to bliss;
And caus'd his rod with hope to bud
  From out the dread abyss.

The seventh day above the week
  Still would he keep and bless;
The pain'd to sooth, the lost to seek,
  And grievance to redress.

Yet never such a day before
  Of holy work was spent,
While hardship infinite he bore
  That malice might relent.

And whether from success exempt
  The story is not told;
But sure most glorious was th' attempt,
  Whose fame in heav'n's enroll'd.

And each man in his spirit knows
     That mercy has no bound;
And from that upmost zenith flows
     The lowest depth to sound.

And therefore David calls for praise
     From all the gulphs that yawn,
Our thoughts by greater strokes to raise
     Than e'er before were drawn.

Beyond the height that science kens,
     Where genius is at home;
And poets take their golden pens
     To fill th' immortal tome.

Ye that for psalmody contend,
     Exert your trilling throats;
And male and female voices blend
     With joy's divinest notes.

By fancy rais'd to Zion's top
     Your swelling organ join;
And praise the Lord on every stop
     Till all your faces shine.

With sweetest breath your trumpets fill'd,
     Shall forward strength and grace;
Then all your warbling measures build
     Upon the grounding bass.

The boxen pipe, for deepness form'd,
     Involve in strains of love,
And flutes, with inspiration warm'd,
     Shall imitate the dove.

Amongst the rest arouse the harp,
     And with a master's nail;
And from the quick vibrations carp
     The graces of the scale.

The flow'rs from every bed collect,
    And on the altar lift;
And let each silver vase be deckt
    With nature's graceful gift.

And from the steeple's summit stream
    The flag of golden gloss,
Exposing to the glancing beam
    The glorious English cross;

And let the lads of gladness born
    The ringers be renew'd;
And as they usher'd in the morn,
    Let them the day conclude.

Hymn XII

ST. MARK

Pull up the bell-flow'rs of the spring,
And let the budding greenwood ring
    With many a chearful song;
All blessing on the human race,
From CHRIST, evangelist of grace,
    To whom these strains belong.

To whom belong the tribe that vie
In what is musick to the eye,
    Whose voice is "stoop to pray"—
While many colour'd tints attire
His fav'rites, like the golden wire,
    The beams on wind flow'rs play.

To whom belong the dress and airs
Of nature in her warbling pairs,
    And in her bloomy pride;
By whom the man of pray'r computes
His year, and estimates the fruits
    Of every time and tide.

To whom the sacred penman cries,
And as he heav'nwards lifts his eyes,
 With meekness kneels him down;
Then what inspiring truth indites,
His strengthen'd memory recites,
 The tale of God's renown.

O holy Mark! ordain'd in youth
To be historian of the truth
 From heav'ns first fountain brought;
And Christ his hand was on thy head,
To bless thee that thou shouldst be read,
 And in his churches taught.

And tho', as Peter's scribe and son,
Thou mightst a charity have done
 To cover his disgrace;
Yet strictly charg'd thou wouldst not spare
At large the treason to declare,
 And in its order place.

Thus in the church, to cleanse our sin,
By fair confession we begin,
 And in thanksgiving end;
And they that have the Lord deny'd,
Must not come there the crime to hide,
 But promise to amend.

Then let us not this day refuse,
With joy to give the Christian dues
 To Lazars at the door;
"O for the name and love of Christ
Spare one poor dole from all your grist,
 One mite from all your store!"

And those that in by-places lurk,
Invite with overpay to work,
 Thy garner'd hay to fill;

And worship on the new mown sod,
And active to the Lord thy God,
    Keep lust and conscience still.

Hymn XIII

ST. PHILIP AND ST. JAMES

Now the winds are all composure,
    But the breath upon the bloom,
Blowing sweet o'er each inclosure,
    Grateful off'rings of perfume.

Tansy, calaminth and daisies,
    On the river's margin thrive;
And accompany the mazes
    Of the stream that leaps alive.

Muse, accordant to the season,
    Give the numbers life and air;
When the sounds and objects reason
    In behalf of praise and pray'r.

All the scenes of nature quicken,
    By the genial spirit fann'd;
And the painted beauties thicken
    Colour'd by the master's hand.

Earth her vigour repossessing
    As the blasts are held in ward;
Blessing heap'd and press'd on blessing,
    Yield the measure of the Lord.

Beeches, without order seemly,
    Shade the flow'rs of annual birth,
And the lily smiles supremely
    Mention'd by the Lord on earth.

Couslips seize upon the fallow,
    And the cardamine in white,
Where the corn-flow'rs join the mallow,
    Joy and health, and thrift unite.

Study sits beneath her arbour,
    By the bason's glossy side;
While the boat from out its harbour
    Exercise and pleasure guide.

Pray'r and praise be mine employment,
    Without grudging or regret,
Lasting life, and long enjoyment,
    Are not here, and are not yet.

Hark! aloud, the black-bird whistles,
    With surrounding fragrance blest,
And the goldfinch in the thistles
    Makes provision for her nest.

Ev'n the hornet hives his honey,
    Bluecap builds his stately dome,
And the rocks supply the coney
    With a fortress and an home.

But the servants of their Saviour,
    Which with gospel-peace are shod,
Have no bed but what the paviour
    Makes them in the porch of God.

O thou house that hold'st the charter
    Of salvation from on high,
Fraught with prophet, saint, and martyr,
    Born to weep, to starve and die!

Great to-day thy song and rapture
    In the choir of Christ and WREN
When two prizes were the capture
    Of the hand that fish'd for men.

To the man of quick compliance
    Jesus call'd, and Philip came;
And began to make alliance
    For his master's cause and name.

James, of title most illustrious,
    Brother of the Lord, allow'd;
In the vineyard how industrious,
    Nor by years nor hardship bow'd!

Each accepted in his trial,
    One the CHEERFUL one the JUST;
Both of love and self-denial,
    Both of everlasting trust.

Living they dispens'd salvation,
    Heav'n-endow'd with grace and pow'r;
And they dy'd in imitation
    Of their Saviour's final hour.

Who, for cruel traitors pleading,
    Triumph'd in his parting breath;
O'er all miracles preceding
    His inestimable death.

Hymn XIV

THE ASCENSION OF OUR LORD JESUS CHRIST

"And other wond'rous works were done
    No mem'ry can recall;
Which were they number'd every one,
Not all the space beneath the sun
    Cou'd hold the fair detail of all."

The text is full, and strong to do
    The glorious subject right;
But on the working mind's review

The letter's like the spirit true,
    And clear and evident as light.

For not a particle of space
    Where'er his glory beam'd,
With all the modes of site and place,
But were the better for his grace,
    And up to higher lot redeem'd.

For all the motley tribe that pair,
    And to their cover skim,
Became his more immediate care,
The raven urgent in his pray'r,
    And those that make the woodland hymn.

For every creature left at will
    The howling WASTE to roam,
Which live upon the blood they spill,
From his own hands receive their fill,
    What time the desart was his home.

They knew him well, and could not err,
    To him they all appeal'd;
The beast of sleek or shaggy fur,
And found their natures to recur
    To what they were in Eden's field.

For all that dwell in depth or wave,
    And ocean—every drop—
Confess'd his mighty pow'r to save,
When to the floods his peace he gave,
    And bade careering whirlwinds stop.

And all things meaner, from the worm
    (Probationer to fly)
To him that creeps his little term,
And countless rising from the sperm
    Shed by sea-reptiles, where they ply.

These all were bless'd beneath his feet,
  Approaching them so near;
Vast flocks that have no mouths to bleat,
With yet a spirit to intreat,
  And in their rank divinely dear.

For on some special good intent,
  Advancement or relief,
Or some great evil to prevent,
Or some perfection to augment,
  He held his life of tears and grief.

'Twas his the pow'rs of hell to curb,
  And men possess'd to free;
And all the blasting fiends disturb
From seed of bread, from flow'r and herb,
  From fragrant shrub and stately tree.

The song can never be pursu'd
  When Infinite's the theme—
For all to crown, and to conclude,
He bore and bless'd ingratitude,
  And insult in its worst extreme.

And having then such deeds atchiev'd
  As never man before,
From scorn and cruelty repriev'd,
In highest heav'n he was receiv'd,
  To reign with God for evermore.

Hymn XVI

TRINITY SUNDAY

If Jesus be reveal'd,
There is no truth conceal'd
For honour or for awe,
That tends to drive or draw

To the hope of heav'nly bliss,
From the dread of hell's abyss.

If oracles be mute,
And every dull dispute
Of ostentatious gloom
In Athens or in Rome;
We should, sure, amend our ways
By submission, pray'r and praise.

O Three! of blest account
To which all sums amount,
For if the church has two
The work of pray'r to do,
God himself, th' Almighty word,
Will be there to make the third.

One Lord, one faith, one font,
Are all good christians want
To make the fiend retreat,
And build the saint compleat;
Where the Godhead self-allied,
Faith, hope, charity reside.

Man, soul and angel join
To strike up strains divine;
O blessed and ador'd,
Thine aid from heav'n afford;
Holy, Holy, Holy Three,
Which in One, as One agree.

For angel, man and soul
Make up upon the whole,
One individual here,
And in the highest sphere;
Where with God he shall repose,
From whose image first he rose.

Ye books, that load the shelves,
To lead us from ourselves,
Where things, in doubt involv'd,
Are rather made than solv'd;
  Render to the dust and worm
  All ye question or affirm.

Ye poets, seers and priests,
Whose lore the spirit feasts,
And keep the banquet on,
From Moses ev'n to John;
  On your truth I will regale,
  "Which is great and must prevail."

The Trinity is plain,
So David's psalms maintain,
—Who made not God his boast
But by the HOLY GHOST;
  Thence prophetick to record
  All the suff'rings of the Lord.

Yet all the Scriptures run
That God is great and one,
Or else there is no cause
Of nature or her laws;
  To controul and comprehend
  All beginning, course and end.

Hymn XVIII

ST. BARNABAS

Daring as the noon-tide ray
On the summer's longest day,
  Is the truth of Christ supreme;
Proving at its sacred touch,
Whether Ophir's gold be such,
  Or a shift to seem.

Joses, who can doubt thee now,
Who will not thy faith allow,
   With thy lands, for Christ, at sale?
By foul lucre undefil'd,
In the spirit Jesus' child,
   Son of comfort, hail!

For a substance to endure
Hast thou listed with the poor,
   Triumph o'er thyself atchiev'd—
Thee thy Saviour God inrolls
In the calendar of souls,
   Sainted and receiv'd.

Heroes of the Christian cause,
Candidates for God's applause,
   —Leaving all for Christ his sake;
Scorning temporal reward,
Ready to confess the Lord
   At the cross or stake.

Shew your everlasting store
To one great believer more,
   And your ghostly gifts impart—
Grutching treasures for the moth,
To the Lord he pledg'd his troth,
   And ally'd his heart.

Hence instructed, let us learn
Heav'n and heav'nly things to earn,
   And with want by pray'r to cope;
To the Lord your wealth resign;
Distribution is divine;
   Misers have no hope.

Hymn XIX

THE NATIVITY OF ST. JOHN THE BAPTIST

Great and bounteous BENEFACTOR,
　　We thy gen'rous aid adjure,
Shield us from the foul exactor,
　　And his sons, that grind the poor.

Lo the swelling fruits of summer,
　　With inviting colours dy'd,
Hang, for ev'ry casual comer,
　　O'er the fence projecting wide.

See the corn for plenty waving,
　　Where the lark secur'd her eggs—
In the spirit then be saving,
　　Give the poor that sings and begs.

Gentle nature seems to love us
　　In each fair and finish'd scene,
All is beauteous blue above us,
　　All beneath is cheerful green.

Now when warmer rays enlighten
　　And adorn the lengthen'd time,
When the views around us brighten,
　　Days a rip'ning from their prime,

She that was as barren reckon'd,
　　Had her course completely run,
And her dumb-struck husband beckon'd
　　For a pen to write a son.

JOHN, the child of Zacharias,
　　Just returning to his earth,
Prophet of the Lord Messias,
　　And fore-runner of his birth.

He too martyr'd, shall precede him,
   Ere he speed to heav'n again,
Ere the traitors shall implead him,
   And the priest his God arraign.

John beheld the great and holy,
   Hail'd the love of God supreme;
O how gracious, meek, and lowly,
   When baptiz'd in Jordan's stream!

If from honour so stupendous
   He the grace of pow'r deriv'd,
And to tyrants was tremendous,
   That at fraud and filth conniv'd;

If he led a life of rigour,
   And th' abstemious vow obey'd;
If he preach'd with manly vigour,
   Practis'd sinners to dissuade;

If his voice by fair confession
   Christ's supremacy avow'd;
If he check'd with due suppression
   Self-incitements to be proud;

Vice conspiring to afflict him
   To the death that ends the great,
Offer'd him a worthy victim
   For acceptance in the height.

Hymn XXII

ST. BARTHOLOMEW

"Behold an Israelite indeed,
   In whom there is no guile,"—
Whom neither wordly ways mislead,
   Nor treach'rous thoughts defile.

SINCERITY, belov'd of Christ,
    For him herself has kept,
And neither purchas'd, nor intic't,
    With him has smil'd and wept.

Her Jesus in his arms infolds,
    And to his church ascribes—
She wears the precious ring that holds
    Each jewel of the tribes.

Gold is not very gold, nor myrrh
    True myrrh, nor rubies glow,
If first not try'd and prov'd by her
    That they indeed are so.

She is a fountain from the truth,
    And floods embracing all;
Hypocrisy shall gnash its tooth
    Whene'er it hears her call.

Who then amongst mankind can thrive
    That has such ghostly worth?
The saint must needs be flay'd alive,
    Possessing her on earth.

Come then, or sword, or fire, or ax,
    Devour me branch and stem,
I will not fail to pay the tax
    Of life for such a gem.

Hymn XXIV

ST. MICHAEL AND ALL ANGELS

Angelic natures, great in arms
    Against the dragon and his pow'rs,
Whom Michael's excellence alarms
    From highest heav'n's imperial tow'rs;

Ye that in Christ his church attend
    What time the services are sung,
And your propitious spirits blend
    With our united heart and tongue.

O come, celestial watch and ward,
    As in the closet I adore,
My fellow-servants of the Lord,
    To whom these measures I restore.

If Satan's malice was withstood
    Where Moses cold and breathless lay,
Give Michael, patient, meek, and good,
    Through Christ, the glory of the day.

If Tobit's charitable soul,
    A type of Jesus Christ to come,
Was blessed from the poor man's dole
    Ev'n to the social sparrow's crumb;

If to the living and the dead
    His hand was rich in deeds of love,
First Raphael from his Master fled
    By mandate in the heights above.

If Zacharias was inform'd
    That God his pious pray'rs should crown,
The barren womb to ripeness warm'd,
    'Twas Gabriel brought the tidings down.

Hail mighty princes in the height,
    Which o'er stupendous works preside
Of vast authority and weight—
    But there are other pow'rs beside.

These, one for every man, are sent
    God in the spirit to reveal,
To forward ev'ry good event,
    And each internal grief to heal.

Hymn XXXII

THE NATIVITY OF OUR LORD AND SAVIOUR
JESUS CHRIST

Where is this stupendous stranger?
    Swains of Solyma, advise;
Lead me to my Master's manger,
    Shew me where my Saviour lies.

O Most Mighty! O Most Holy!
    Far beyond the seraph's thought,
Art thou then so mean and lowly
    As unheeded prophets taught?

O the magnitude of meekness!
    Worth from worth immortal sprung;
O the strength of infant weakness,
    If eternal is so young!

If so young and thus eternal,
    Michael tune the shepherd's reed,
Where the scenes are ever vernal,
    And the loves be love indeed!

See the God blasphem'd and doubted
    In the schools of Greece and Rome;
See the pow'rs of darkness routed,
    Taken at their utmost gloom.

Nature's decorations glisten
    Far above their usual trim;
Birds on box and laurels listen,
    As so near the cherubs hymn.

Boreas now no longer winters
    On the desolated coast;
Oaks no more are riv'n in splinters
    By the whirlwind and his host.

Spinks and ouzles sing sublimely,
"We too have a Saviour born";
Whiter blossoms burst untimely
On the blest Mosaic thorn.

God all-bounteous, all-creative,
Whom no ills from good dissuade,
Is incarnate, and a native
Of the very world he made.

EDITIONS

A Translation of the Psalms of David, 1765. (Text.)

Blunden, *A Song to David*, etc., 1924, has Hymns xxii and xxxii complete, and portions of Hymns ii, vi, xi, xii.

A Song to David

DAVID the Son of *Jesse* said, and the *Man*
who was *raised up on High*, the *Anointed
of the* GOD of *Jacob*, and the *sweet Psalmist of Israel* said, The SPIRIT OF THE LORD
spake by *Me*, and HIS WORD was in my
Tongue.—2 *Sam.* xxiii. 1, 2.

Contents

Invocation, ver. 1, 2, 3.—The excellence and lustre of David's
character in twelve points of view, ver. 4; proved from the history of his life, to ver. 17.—He consecrates his genius for consolation and edification.—The subjects he made choice of—the Supreme Being—angels; men of renown; the works of nature in
all directions, either particularly or collectively considered, to ver.
27—He obtains power over infernal spirits, and the malignity
of his enemies; wins the heart of Michael, to ver. 30.—Shews that
the pillars of knowledge are the monuments of God's works in
the first week, to ver. 38.—An exercise upon the decalogue, from
ver. 40 to 49.—The transcendent virtue of praise and adoration,
ver. 50 and 51.—An exercise upon the seasons, and the right use
of them, from ver. 52 to 64.—An exercise upon the senses, and
how to subdue them, from ver. 65 to 71.—An amplification in
five degrees, which is wrought up to this conclusion, That the
best poet which ever lived was thought worthy of the highest
honour which possibly can be conceived, as *the Saviour of the
world was ascribed to his house, and called his son in the body.*

A SONG TO DAVID

I

O THOU, that sit'st upon a throne,
With harp of high majestic tone,
    To praise the King of kings;
And voice of heav'n-ascending swell,
Which, while its deeper notes excell,
    Clear, as a clarion, rings:

II

To bless each valley, grove and coast,
And charm the cherubs to the post
    Of gratitude in throngs;
To keep the days on Zion's mount,
And send the year to his account,
    With dances and with songs:

III

O Servant of God's holiest charge,
The minister of praise at large,
    Which thou may'st now receive;
From thy blest mansion hail and hear,
From topmost eminence appear
    To this the wreath I weave.

IV

Great, valiant, pious, good, and clean,
Sublime, contemplative, serene,
    Strong, constant, pleasant, wise!
Bright effluence of exceeding grace;
Best man!—the swiftness and the race,
    The peril, and the prize!

V

Great—from the lustre of his crown,
From Samuel's horn and God's renown,
    Which is the people's voice;
For all the host from rear to van,
Applauded and embrac'd the man—
    The man of God's own choice.

VI

Valiant—the word, and up he rose—
The fight—he triumph'd o'er the foes,
    Whom God's just laws abhor;

And arm'd in gallant faith he took
Against the boaster, from the brook,
    The weapons of the war.

VII

Pious—magnificent and grand;
'Twas he the famous temple plann'd:
    (The seraph in his soul)
Foremost to give the Lord his dues,
Foremost to bless the welcome news,
    And foremost to condole.

VIII

Good—from Jehudah's genuine vein,
From God's best nature good in grain,
    His aspect and his heart;
To pity, to forgive, to save,
Witness En-gedi's conscious cave,
    And Shimei's blunted dart.

IX

Clean—if perpetual prayer be pure,
And love, which could itself innure
    To fasting and to fear—
Clean in his gestures, hands, and feet,
To smite the lyre, the dance compleat,
    To play the sword and spear.

X

Sublime—invention ever young,
Of vast conception, tow'ring tongue
    To God th'eternal theme;
Notes from yon exaltations caught,
Unrival'd royalty of thought,
    O'er meaner strains supreme.

XI

Contemplative—on God to fix
His musings, and above the six
    The sabbath-day he blest;
'Twas then his thoughts self-conquest prun'd,
And heavenly melancholy tun'd,
    To bless and bear the rest.

XII

Serene—to sow the seeds of peace,
Rememb'ring, when he watch'd the fleece,
    How sweetly Kidron purl'd—
To further knowledge, silence vice,
And plant perpetual paradise
    When God had calm'd the world.

XIII

Strong—in the Lord, who could defy
Satan, and all his powers that lie
    In sempiternal night;
And hell, and horror, and despair
Were as the lion and the bear
    To his undaunted might.

XIV

Constant—in love to God THE TRUTH,
Age, manhood, infancy, and youth—
    To Jonathan his friend
Constant, beyond the verge of death;
And Ziba, and Mephibosheth,
    His endless fame attend.

XV

Pleasant—and various as the year;
Man, soul, and angel, without peer,
    Priest, champion, sage and boy;

In armour, or in ephod clad,
His pomp, his piety was glad;
   Majestic was his joy.

XVI

Wise—in recovery from his fall,
Whence rose his eminence o'er all,
   Of all the most revil'd;
The light of Israel in his ways,
Wise are his precepts, prayer and praise,
   And counsel to his child.

XVII

His muse, bright angel of his verse,
Gives balm for all the thorns that pierce,
   For all the pangs that rage;
Blest light, still gaining on the gloom,
The more than Michal of his bloom,
   Th' Abishag of his age.

XVIII

He sung of God—the mighty source
Of all things—the stupendous force
   On which all strength depends;
From whose right arm, beneath whose eyes,
All period, pow'r, and enterprize
   Commences, reigns, and ends.

XIX

Angels—their ministry and meed,
Which to and fro with blessings speed,
   Or with their citterns wait;
Where Michael with his millions bows,
Where dwells the seraph and his spouse,
   The cherub and her mate.

XX

O DAVID, scholar of the Lord!
Of God and Love—the Saint elect
    For infinite applause—
To rule the land, and briny broad,
To be laborious in his laud,
    And heroes in his cause.

XXI

The world—the clustring spheres he made,
The glorious light, the soothing shade,
    Dale, champaign, grove, and hill;
The multitudinous abyss,
Where secrecy remains in bliss,
    And wisdom hides her skill.

XXII

Trees, plants, and flow'rs—of virtuous root;
Gem yielding blossom, yielding fruit,
    Choice gums and precious balm;
Bless ye the nosgay in the vale,
And with the sweetners of the gale
    Enrich the thankful psalm.

XXIII

Of fowl—e'en ev'ry beak and wing
Which chear the winter, hail the spring,
    That live in peace or prey;
They that make music, or that mock,
The quail, the brave domestic cock,
    The raven, swan, and jay.

XXIV

Of fishes—ev'ry size and shape,
Which nature frames of light escape,
    Devouring man to shun:

The shells are in the wealthy deep,
The shoals upon the surface leap,
   And love the glancing sun.

XXV

Of beasts—the beaver plods his task;
While the sleek tygers roll and bask,
   Nor yet the shades arouse;
Her cave the mining coney scoops;
Where o'er the mead the mountain stoops,
   The kids exult and brouse.

XXVI

Of gems—their virtue and their price,
Which hid in earth from man's device,
   Their darts of lustre sheathe;
The jasper of the master's stamp,
The topaz blazing like a lamp
   Among the mines beneath.

XXVII

Blest was the tenderness he felt
When to his graceful harp he knelt,
   And did for audience call;
When satan with his hand he quell'd,
And in serene suspense he held
   The frantic throes of Saul.

XXVIII

His furious foes no more malign'd
As he such melody divin'd,
   And sense and soul detain'd;
Now striking strong, now soothing soft,
He sent the godly sounds aloft,
   Or in delight refrain'd.

XXIX

When up to heav'n his thoughts he pil'd,
From fervent lips fair Michal smil'd,
    As blush to blush she stood;
And chose herself the queen, and gave
Her utmost from her heart, "so brave,
    And plays his hymns so good."

XXX

The pillars of the Lord are sev'n,
Which stand from earth to topmost heav'n;
    His wisdom drew the plan;
His WORD accomplish'd the design,
From brightest gem to deepest mine,
    From CHRIST enthron'd to man.

XXXI

Alpha, the cause of causes, first
In station, fountain, whence the burst
    Of light, and blaze of day;
Whence bold attempt, and brave advance,
Have motion, life, and ordinance,
    And heav'n itself its stay.

XXXII

Gamma supports the glorious arch
On which angelic legions march,
    And is with sapphires pav'd;
Thence the fleet clouds are sent adrift,
And thence the painted folds, that lift
    The crimson veil, are wav'd.

XXXIII

Eta with living sculpture breathes,
With verdant carvings, flow'ry wreathes
    Of never-wasting bloom;

In strong relief his goodly base
All instruments of labour grace,
    The trowel, spade, and loom.

XXXIV

Next Theta stands to the Supreme—
Who form'd, in number, sign, and scheme,
    Th' illustrious lights that are;
And one address'd his saffron robe,
And one, clad in a silver globe,
    Held rule with ev'ry star.

XXXV

Iota's tun'd to choral hymns
Of those that fly, while he that swims
    In thankful safety lurks;
And foot, and chapitre, and niche,
The various histories enrich
    Of God's recorded works.

XXXVI

Sigma presents the social droves,
With him that solitary roves,
    And man of all the chief;
Fair on whose face, and stately frame,
Did God impress his hallow'd name,
    For ocular belief.

XXXVII

OMEGA! GREATEST and the BEST,
Stands sacred to the day of rest,
    For gratitude and thought;
Which bless'd the world upon his pole,
And gave the universe his goal,
    And clos'd th' infernal draught.

XXXVIII

O David, scholar of the Lord!
Such is thy science, whence reward,
    And infinite degree;
O strength, O sweetness, lasting ripe!
God's harp thy symbol, and thy type
    The lion and the bee!

XXXIX

There is but One who ne'er rebell'd,
But One by passion unimpell'd,
    By pleasures unintic't;
He from himself his semblance sent,
Grand object of his own content,
    And saw the God in Christ.

XL

Tell them I am, Jehova said
To Moses; while earth heard in dread,
    And smitten to the heart,
At once above, beneath, around,
All nature, without voice or sound,
    Replied, O Lord, Thou art.

XLI

Thou art—to give and to confirm,
For each his talent and his term;
    All flesh thy bounties share:
Thou shalt not call thy brother fool;
The porches of the Christian school
    Are meekness, peace, and pray'r.

XLII

Open, and naked of offence,
Man's made of mercy, soul, and sense;
    God arm'd the snail and wilk;

Be good to him that pulls thy plough;
Due food and care, due rest, allow
    For her that yields thee milk.

XLIII

Rise up before the hoary head,
And God's benign commandment dread,
    Which says thou shalt not die:
"Not as I will, but as thou wilt,"
Pray'd He whose conscience knew no guilt;
    With whose bless'd pattern vie.

XLIV

Use all thy passions!—love is thine,
And joy, and jealousy divine;
    Thine hope's eternal fort,
And care thy leisure to disturb,
With fear concupiscence to curb,
    And rapture to transport.

XLV

Act simply, as occasion asks;
Put mellow wine in season'd casks;
    Till not with ass and bull:
Remember thy baptismal bond;
Keep from commixtures foul and fond,
    Nor work thy flax with wool.

XLVI

Distribute: pay the Lord his tithe,
And make the widow's heart-strings blithe;
    Resort with those that weep:
As you from all and each expect,
For all and each thy love direct,
    And render as you reap.

XLVII

The slander and its bearer spurn,
And propagating praise sojourn
    To make thy welcome last;
Turn from old Adam to the New;
By hope futurity pursue;
    Look upwards to the past.

XLVIII

Controul thine eye, salute success,
Honour the wiser, happier bless,
    And for thy neighbour feel;
Grutch not of mammon and his leaven,
Work emulation up to heaven
    By knowledge and by zeal.

XLIX

O David, highest in the list
Of worthies, on God's ways insist,
    *The genuine word repeat.
Vain are the documents of men,
And vain the flourish of the pen
    That keeps the fool's conceit.

L

Praise above all—for praise prevails;
Heap up the measure, load the scales,
    And good to goodness add:
The gen'rous soul her Saviour aids,
But peevish obloquy degrades;
    The Lord is great and glad.

LI

For ADORATION all the ranks
Of angels yield eternal thanks,
    And DAVID in the midst;

* Ps. cxix.

With God's good poor, which, last and least
In man's esteem, thou to thy feast,
   O blessed bride-groom, bidst.

LII

For ADORATION seasons change,
And order, truth, and beauty range,
   Adjust, attract, and fill:
The grass the polyanthus cheques;
And polish'd porphyry reflects,
   By the descending rill.

LIII

Rich almonds colour to the prime
For ADORATION; tendrils climb,
   And fruit-trees pledge their gems;
And *Ivis with her gorgeous vest
Builds for her eggs her cunning nest,
   And bell-flowers bow their stems.

LIV

With vinous syrup cedars spout;
From rocks pure honey gushing out,
   For ADORATION springs:
All scenes of painting croud the map
Of nature; to the mermaid's pap
   The scaled infant clings.

LV

The spotted ounce and playsome cubs
Run rustling 'mongst the flow'ring shrubs,
   And lizards feed the moss;
For ADORATION †beasts embark,
While waves upholding halcyon's ark
   No longer roar and toss.

* Humming-bird.
† There is a large quadruped that preys upon fish, and provides himself with a
piece of timber for that purpose, with which he is very handy.

LVI

While Israel sits beneath his fig,
With coral root and amber sprig
   The wean'd advent'rer sports;
Where to the palm the jasmin cleaves,
For ADORATION 'mong the leaves
   The gale his peace reports.

LVII

Increasing days their reign exalt,
Nor in the pink and mottled vault
   Th' opposing spirits tilt;
And, by the coasting reader spy'd,
The silverlings and crusions glide
   For ADORATION gilt.

LVIII

For ADORATION rip'ning canes
And cocoa's purest milk detains
   The western pilgrim's staff;
Where rain in clasping boughs inclos'd,
And vines with oranges dispos'd,
   Embow'r the social laugh.

LIX

Now labour his reward receives,
For ADORATION counts his sheaves
   To peace, her bounteous prince;
The nectarine his strong tint imbibes,
And apples of ten thousand tribes,
   And quick peculiar quince.

LX

The wealthy crops of whit'ning rice,
'Mongst thyine woods and groves of spice,
   For ADORATION grow;

And, marshall'd in the fenced land,
The peaches and pomegranates stand,
   Where wild carnations blow.

LXI

The laurels with the winter strive;
The crocus burnishes alive
   Upon the snow-clad earth:
For ADORATION myrtles stay
To keep the garden from dismay,
   And bless the sight from dearth.

LXII

The pheasant shows his pompous neck;
And ermine, jealous of a speck
   With fear eludes offence:
The sable, with his glossy pride,
For ADORATION is descried,
   Where frosts the wave condense.

LXIII

The chearful holly, pensive yew,
And holy thorn, their trim renew;
   The squirrel hoards his nuts:
All creatures batten o'er their stores,
And careful nature all her doors
   For ADORATION shuts.

LXIV

For ADORATION, DAVID's psalms
Lift up the heart to deeds of alms;
   And he, who kneels and chants,
Prevails his passions to controul,
Finds meat and med'cine to the soul,
   Which for translation pants.

LXV

For ADORATION, beyond match,
The scholar bulfinch aims to catch
    The soft flute's iv'ry touch;
And, careless on the hazle spray,
The daring redbreast keeps at bay
    The damsel's greedy clutch.

LXVI

For ADORATION, in the skies,
The Lord's philosopher espies
    The Dog, the Ram, and Rose;
The planets ring, Orion's sword;
Nor is his greatness less ador'd
    In the vile worm that glows.

LXVII

For ADORATION* on the strings
The western breezes work their wings,
    The captive ear to sooth.—
Hark! 'tis a voice—how still, and small—
That makes the cataracts to fall,
    Or bids the sea be smooth.

LXVIII

For ADORATION, incense comes
From bezoar, and Arabian gums;
    And from the civet's furr.
But as for pray'r, or ere it faints,
Far better is the breath of saints
    Than galbanum and myrrh.

LXIX

For ADORATION from the down
Of dam'sins to th' anana's crown,
    God sends to tempt the taste;

* Æolian harp.

And while the luscious zest invites
The sense, that in the scene delights,
    Commands desire be chaste.

LXX

For ADORATION, all the paths
Of grace are open, all the baths
    Of purity refresh;
And all the rays of glory beam
To deck the man of God's esteem,
    Who triumphs o'er the flesh.

LXXI

For ADORATION, in the dome
Of Christ the sparrows find an home,
    And on his olives perch:
The swallow also dwells with thee,
O man of God's humility,
    Within his Saviour's CHURCH.

LXXII

Sweet is the dew that falls betimes,
And drops upon the leafy limes;
    Sweet Hermon's fragrant air:
Sweet is the lily's silver bell,
And sweet the wakeful tapers smell
    That watch for early pray'r.

LXXIII

Sweet the young nurse with love intense,
Which smiles o'er sleeping innocence;
    Sweet when the lost arrive:
Sweet the musician's ardour beats,
While his vague mind's in quest of sweets,
    The choicest flow'rs to hive.

LXXIV

Sweeter in all the Strains of love,
The language of thy turtle dove,
    Pair'd to thy swelling chord;
Sweeter with ev'ry grace endu'd,
The glory of thy gratitude,
    Respir'd unto the Lord.

LXXV

Strong is the horse upon his speed;
Strong in pursuit the rapid glede,
    Which makes at once his game:
Strong the tall ostrich on the ground;
Strong through the turbulent profound
    Shoots *xiphias to his aim.

LXXVI

Strong is the lion—like a coal
His eye-ball—like a bastion's mole
    His chest against the foes:
Strong the gier-eagle on his sail,
Strong against tide, th' enormous whale
    Emerges, as he goes.

LXXVII

But stronger still, in earth and air,
And in the sea, the man of pray'r;
    And far beneath the tide;
And in the seat to faith assign'd,
Where ask is have, where seek is find,
    Where knock is open wide.

LXXVIII

Beauteous the fleet before the gale;
Beauteous the multitudes in mail,
    Rank'd arms and crested heads:

* The sword-fish.

Beauteous the garden's umbrage mild,
Walk, water, meditated wild,
　　And all the bloomy beds.

LXXIX

Beauteous the moon full on the lawn;
And beauteous, when the veil's withdrawn,
　　The virgin to her spouse:
Beauteous the temple deck'd and fill'd,
When to the heav'n of heav'ns they build
　　Their heart-directed vows.

LXXX

Beauteous, yea beauteous more than these,
The shepherd king upon his knees,
　　For his momentous trust;
With wish of infinite conceit,
For man, beast, mute, the small and great,
　　And prostrate dust to dust.

LXXXI

Precious the bounteous widow's mite;
And precious, for extreme delight,
　　*The largess from the churl:
Precious the ruby's blushing blaze,
And †alba's blest imperial rays,
　　And pure cerulean pearl.

LXXXII

Precious the penitential tear;
And precious is the sigh sincere,
　　Acceptable to God:
And precious are the winning flow'rs,
In gladsome Israel's feast of bow'rs,
　　Bound on the hallow'd sod.

* Sam. xxv. 18.　　　　　† Rev. xi. 17.

LXXXIII

More precious that diviner part
Of David, ev'n the Lord's own heart,
   Great, beautiful, and new:
In all things where it was intent,
In all extreams, in each event,
   Proof—answ'ring true to true.

LXXXIV

Glorious the sun in mid career;
Glorious th' assembled fires appear;
   Glorious the comet's train:
Glorious the trumpet and alarm;
Glorious th' almighty stretch'd-out arm;
   Glorious th' enraptur'd main:

LXXXV

Glorious the northern lights astream;
Glorious the song, when God's the theme;
   Glorious the thunder's roar:
Glorious hosanna from the den;
Glorious the catholic amen;
   Glorious the martyr's gore:

LXXXVI

Glorious—more glorious is the crown
Of Him, that brought salvation down
   By meekness, call'd thy Son;
Thou at stupendous truth believ'd,
And now the matchless deed's atchiev'd,
   DETERMIN'D, DAR'D, and DONE.

EDITIONS

A Song to David, London, 1763.
New Translation of the Psalms, London, 1765. (Text.)
A Song to David, ed. Harvey, London, 1819.
Gilfillan's *Less Known British Poets*, London, 1860, vol. III.
A Song to David, ed. F.H.D. and H.C.M., London, 1895.

A Song to David, ed. J. R. Tutin, London, 1898.

A Song to David (No. 5 of vol. vi, *The Bibelot*, Portland, Maine), ed. C. F. Richardson, May, 1900.

A Song to David, ed. R. A. Streatfield, London, 1901.

A Song to David, ed. J. R. Tutin, Cottingham near Hull, 1904.

A Song to David, ed. J. R. Tutin, Cottingham near Hull, 1904 (Orinda Booklets, no. 4).

A Song to David (De la Mare booklets), London, 1906.

A Song to David, ed. Blunden, London, 1924.

A Song to David, ed. Percival Serle, Melbourne, 1924.

A Song to David, facsimile of the first edition, Cambridge, 1927.

A Song to David (Augustan Books of Poetry, Benn), London, 1931.

Oxford Book of Eighteenth Century Verse.

A Song to David, ed. Anthony Hillyer, Los Angeles, 1934.

Minor Poems,
1761-1768

The 100th Psalm, for a Scotch Tune

Rejoice in God, ye blithesome lands,
With all your voices all your hands,
 Bent knees and faces prone;
With mickle gladness and content
Your goodly songs and selves present
 Before his awful throne.

Nought in ourselves but life and limb,
We are the workmanship of him,
 He is our God be sure;
Our shepherd too, as well ye ken,
He feeds us congregated men,
 Like sheep upon the moor.

O gang your way and gang with glee,
Into his courts with melody,
 And do his goodness right.
His gates are not too straight nor strong
To keep out sicke a lively song,
 And sicke a menceful sight.

For gracious is the Lord our rest,
Sith by his merits we are blest,
 And rescued from our crimes,
And us his just degrees he learns,
For sires to teach their bonny barnes,
 Through all succeeding times.

EDITION

Christian's Magazine, ii, 349, Supplement from January to June, 1761. (Text.)

An Epistle to John Sherratt, Esq.

Haec mihi semper erunt imis infixa medullis,
Perpetuusque ANIMI debitor HUJUS ero.
        Ovid de Trist. Eleg. iv.

Of all the off'rings thanks can find,
None equally delights the mind;
Or charms so much, or holds so long
As gratitude expres'd in song.
We reckon all the BOOK of GRACE
By verses, as the source we trace,
And in the spirit all is great
By number, melody and weight.
By nature's light each heathen sage,
Has thus adorn'd th' immortal page;
Demosthenes and Plato's prose,
From skill in mystic measure flows;
And ROLT's sublime, historic stile,
Is better that the Muses smile.
Take then from hartiness profest,
What in the bard's conceit is best;
The golden sheaf desertion gleans
For want of better helps and means.

Well nigh sev'n years had fill'd their tale,
From Winter's urn to Autumn's scale,
And found no friend to grief and *Smart*,
Like Thee and Her, thy sweeter part;
Assisted by a friendly* pair
That chose the side of CHRIST and PRAY'R,
To build the great foundation laid,
By one †sublime, transcendent maid.
'Tis well to signalize a deed,
And have no precedent to plead;
'Tis blessing as by God we're told,

* Mr. and Mrs. Rolt.
† Miss A.F.S.———. Of Queen's-square.

To come and visit friends in hold;
Which skill is greater in degree,
If goodness set the pris'ner free.
'Tis you that have in my behalf,
Produc'd the robe and kill'd the calf;
Have hail'd the *restoration day*,
And bid the loudest music play.
If therefore there is yet a note
Upon the lyre, that I devote,
To gratitude's divinest strains,
One gift of love for thee remains;
One gift above the common cast,
Of making fair memorials last.

Not He whose highly finish'd piece,
Outshone the chissel'd forms of Greece;
Who found with all his art and fame,
‡A partner in the house I claim;
Not he that pencils CHARLOTTE's eyes
And boldly bids for ROMNEY's prize;
Not both the seats, where arts commune
Can blazon like a word in tune;
But this our young scholasticks con,
As warrant from th' *Appulian* Swan.
Then let us frame our steps to climb,
Beyond the sphere of chance and time,
And raise our thoughts on HOLY WRIT,
O'er mortal works and human wit.
The lively acts of CHRISTIAN LOVE,
Are treasur'd in the rolls above;
Where Archangelic concerts ring,
And God's accepted poets sing.
So Virtue's plan to parry praise,
Cannot obtain in after days,
Atchievements in the Christian cause,
Ascend to sure and vast applause;
Where Glory fixes to endure

‡ Mr. Roubilliac's first wife was a Smart, descended from
the same Ancestors as Mr. Christopher Smart.

All precious, permanent and pure.
Of such a class in such a sphere,
Shall thy distinguish'd deed appear;
Whose spirit open and avow'd
Array'd itself against the croud,
With chearfulness so much thine own;
And all thy motive God alone;
To run thy keel across the boom,
And save my vessel from her doom,
And cut her from the pirate's port,
Beneath the cannon of the fort,
With colours fresh, and sails unfurl'd,
Was nobly dar'd to beat the world;
And stands for ever on record,
IF TRUTH AND LIFE BE GOD AND LORD.

E D I T I O N

Poems, 1763. (Text.)

On Gratitude

TO THE MEMORY OF MR. SEATON

O Muse! O Music![1] Voice & Lyre,
   Which are together Psalm of Praise
From heav'n the kneeling bard inspire
   New thoughts, new grace of utt'rance raise,
That more acceptable with Thee
   We thy best service may begin
O thou that bent thine hallow'd knee,
   And[2] bless'd to bleed for Adam's sin.
Then did the Spirit of a Man
   Above all height sublimely towr,
And then[3] sweet Gratitude began
   To claim Supremacy from Pow'r.
But how shall we those[4] steps ascend
   By which the Host approach the Throne?
Love thou thy brother & thy friend,
   Whom thou on earth has seen & known.

For Gratitude may make the *plea
    Of Love by Sisterhood most dear—
How can we reach the first degree
    If we neglect a step so near?
So shall we take dear *Seaton's* part
    When paths of topmost heav'n are trod,
And pay the talent of our heart
    Thrown up ten thousand fold to God.
He knew the art the World dispise
    Might to his Merit be applied
Who when for man he left the skies
    By all was hated, scorn'd, denied.
†"The man that gives me thanks & laud
    Does honour to my glorious name"
Thus God did David's works applaud
    And⁵ seal'd for everlasting fame.
And this for SEATON shall redound
    To praise, as long as *Camus* runs;
Sure Gratitude by him was crown'd,
    Who bless'd her Maker & her Sons.
When *Spencer* virtuous *Sydney* prais'd
    When *Prior Dorsett* hail'd to heav'n;
They more by Gratitude were rais'd
    Than all the *Nine* & all the *Sev'n*.
Then, O ye emulative tribe⁶
    Of Granta, strains divine persue;
The glory to the Lord ascribe,
    Yet honour Seaton's memory too.
The Throne of Excellence accost
    And be the post of Pray'r maintain'd;
For Paradise had ne'er been lost
    Had heav'nly Gratitude remain'd.

* I John, iv. 20.   † Psalm i. 23.

EDITION

Text: holograph in Henry W. and Albert A. Berg Collection in New York
  Public Library, reproduced (p. 122) by permission.
Variants from John Drinkwater, *A Book for Bookmen*, New York, 1927 (the
  only previous printing):
1 "O Muse! O Muse!"   4 "these"
2 "Had"   5 "Had"
3 "Had the"   6 "bribe"

An Invitation to Dr. Nares

Smart sends his compliments & pray'rs
Health and long life to Dr. Nares—
But the chief business of the card
Is 'come to dinner with the bard,'
Who makes a mod'rate share of wit
Put on the pot & turn the spit.
'Tis said the Indians teach their sons
The use of bows instead of guns,
And, e'er the striplings dare to dine,
They shoot their victuals off a pine.
The Publick is as kind to me
As to his child a Cherokee;
And if I chance to hit my aim,
I chuse to feast upon the game;
For panegyric or abuse
Shall make the quill procure the goose;
With apple-sauce & Durham mustard
And codling pye o'erlaid with custard.
Pray please to signify with this
My love to Madam, Bob, and Miss
Likewise to Nurse & little Poll
Whose praise so justly you extoll.

P.S.   I have (don't think it a chimaera)
      Some good sound port & right Madeira.

EDITION

Notes and Queries, 3rd Series, x, 506. (Text.)
(MS in Library of Pembroke College).

Song

Where shall Caelia fly for shelter,
    In what secret grove or cave?
Sighs and sonnets sent to melt her
    From the young, the gay, the brave.

Tho' with prudish airs she starch her,
     Still she longs, and still she burns;
Cupid shoots like Hayman's archer
     Wheresoe'er the damsel turns.

Virtue, wit, good sense, and beauty,
     If discretion guide us not,
Sometimes are the ruffian's booty,
     Sometimes are the booby's lot:
Now they're purchased by the trader,
     Now commanded by the peer;
Now some subtle mean invader
     Wins the heart, or gains the ear.

O discretion, thou'rt a jewel,
     Or our grand-mammas mistake;
Stinting flame and baiting fuel,
     Always careful and awake!
Wou'd you keep your pearls from tramplers,
     Weigh the licence, weigh the banns.
Mark my song upon your samplers,
     Wear it on your knots and fans.

E D I T I O N S

Ode to . . . Northumberland, 1764.
Blunden, *A Song to David,* etc., 1924. (Text.)

On a Bed of Guernsey Lilies

Ye beauties! O how great the sum
     Of sweetness that ye bring,
On what a charity ye come
     To bless the latter spring!
How kind the visit that ye pay,
Like strangers on a rainy day,
     When heartiness despair'd of guests:
No neighbour's praise your pride alarms,
No rival flow'r surveys your charms,
     Or heightens, or contests!

Lo, thro' her works gay nature grieves
　How brief she is and frail,
As ever o'er the falling leaves
　Autumnal winds prevail.
Yet still the philosophic mind
Consolatory food can find,
　And hope her anchorage maintain:
We never are deserted quite;
'Tis by succession of delight
　That love supports his reign.

E D I T I O N S

Ode to . . . Northumberland, etc., 1764.
General Advertiser, 20 Dec., 1764.
Blunden: *A Song to David*, etc., 1924. (Text.)
Oxford Book of Eighteenth Century Verse.

The Sweets of Evening

The sweets of Evening charm the mind,
　Sick of the sultry day;
The body then no more confin'd,
But exercise with freedom join'd,
　When Phoebus sheathes his ray.

The softer scenes of nature soothe
　The organs of our sight;
The Zephyrs fan the meadows smooth,
And on the brook we build the booth
　In pastoral delight.

While all-serene the summer moon
　Sends glances thro' the trees,
And Philomel begins her tune,
Asterie too shall help her soon
　With voice of skilful ease.

A nosegay, every thing that grows,
　And music, every sound

To lull the sun to his repose;
The skies are colour'd like the rose
    With lively streaks around.

Of all the changes rung by Time
    None half so sweet appear,
As those when thoughts themselves sublime,
And with superior natures chime
    In fancy's highest sphere.

EDITIONS

Northumberland, 1764.
Poems, 1791.
Plumptre's *A Collection of English Songs*, iii, 70 (1824).
Blunden, *A Song to David*, etc., 1924. (Text.)
    Stanza 2 is omitted by Hunter. Plumptre also omits this stanza and introduces
the following variants: line 5: "the sun" for "Phoebus"; line 11: "noon" for
"moon"; line 13: "The nightingale" for "And Philomel"; line 14: "The plaintive
quail" for "Asterie too."

Lyrics from *Hannah*

Is not Genious heav'nly Fire,
    Thoughts so great and Words so free,
Heighten'd on the living Lyre
    Giv'n from God and Giv'n to Thee?
Are not these the way to Fame
    Tow'ring from th' immortal Page,
Is not *Hannah* then a Name
    Glorious to the latest Age?
                            Act 1, p. 7

There is no Part of Heav'n so high,[1]
    But is accessible with ease,
If faithful Diligence apply
    Upon her never-wearied Knees.
By Pray'r the Miracle is done,
By Pray'r th' eternal Prize is won.

---

[1] This poem is printed in Plumptre's *A Collection of English Songs*
(1824), ii, 375, entitled "Prayer."

But if with Lips and Heart in tune
  The Lute's soft Symphonies unite,
Sweet Hymnist, thou must have thy Boon
  Or Heav'n itself shall lose its Light.
By Pray'r the Miracle is done,
By Pray'r th' eternal Prize is won.
              Act i, p. 8

Every Bird that pipes a Note,
Every Shrub that bears a bloom,
  Thine Unkindnesses upbraid;
Grateful is the Linnet's Throat,
Grateful is the Bay's Perfume,
  And to God their Tribute's paid.

But the Monster of our Scorn,
He whom Men and Angels hate,
  And ev'n Heathen Schools despise;
(Better had he ne'er been born)
Is that odious base Ingrate,
  Who his God and Truth denies.
              Act ii, p. 12

Female tempers ebb and flow,
  With the Bounty of their Lovers;
Spirits never are so low,
  But a Gift their State recovers.

Sparing Hands and niggard Hearts,
  Are the Source of true Dejection;
He that all his Wealth imparts,
  Yields Endearment in Perfection.
              Act ii, p. 14

Sweeter sleeps the Village Hind[1]
Than the Rulers of Mankind,

[1] This is printed in Plumptre's *A Collection of English Songs* (1824), ii, 321, under the title "The Village Hind" with "Almighty Wing" for "Almighty's Wing" in line 11.

But the Son of rough Repose
Neither Taste nor Learning knows.

Clear of Envy or Excess
Some a level State possess,
Tho' from Ignorance disjoin'd
Not by Knowledge much refin'd.

All in due Proportion blest
Have their Fare and take their Rest,
Underneath th' Almighty's Wing,
From the Beggar to the King.

                    Act III, p. 15

EDITION

Hannah. An Oratorio, London, 1764. (Text.)

Lyrics from *Abimelech*

Ah, memory, my cruel foe,
How much you daily work for woe!
    The past upon the present hour,
How I was miss'd, you bring to view,
And all my former scenes renew.
    My ev'ning walks, my fav'rite bow'r;

The friendships I was wont to share,
The flow'rs I nursed with so much care;
    My garden, grotto, and my bees,
And, all these little griefs above,
My mother's and my sisters' love,
    And father's blessing on my knees.

Yet, taunter of the past delight,
That urgest grief in such despight,
    Some soothing pow'rs to thee belong:
Do not those soothing pow'rs refuse,
But, as the mother of the Muse,
    Shape all my sorrows into song.

                    Part I, p. 5-6

There is no rose to minds in grief;
    There is no lilly for despair;
Tears and distraction are relief,
    And yews and willows we must wear.

All nature's blandishments are vain
    From flow'ry turf, or azure sky,
And grottoes, where the groans of pain
    In sadly sounding echoes die.
                  Part II, p. 11

Tho' yon tall almond blooms no more,
'Tis not because its sweets are o'er
    On each aspiring shoot—
Attend to what the starlings sing,
Another year, another spring,
The buds to gayer pride shall bring.
    It now prepares for fruit.
                  Part II, p. 12

EDITION

Abimelech, An Oratorio, London, 1768. (Text.)

A Translation of the Works of Horace

Book I, Ode IV

TO SEXTIUS, A PERSON OF CONSULAR DIGNITY

A grateful change! Favonius, and the spring
    To the sharp winter's keener blasts succeed;
Along the beach, with ropes, the ships they bring,
    And launch again, their wat'ry way to speed.

No more the plowmen in their cots delight,
    Nor cattle are contented in the stall;
No more the fields with hoary frosts are white,
    But Cytherean Venus leads the ball.

She, while the moon attends upon the scene,
    The Nymphs and decent Graces in the set,
Shakes with alternate feet the shaven green,
    While Vulcan's Cyclops at the anvil sweat.

Now we with myrtle shou'd adorn our brows,
    Or any flow'r that decks the loosen'd sod;
In shady groves to Faunus pay our vows,
    Whether a lamb or kid delight the God.

Pale death alike knocks at the poor man's door,
    O happy Sextius, and the royal dome;
The whole of life forbids our hope to soar,
    Death and the shades anon shall press thee home.

And when into the shallow grave you run,
    You cannot win the monarchy of wine,
Nor doat on Lycidas, as on a son,
    Whom for their spouse all little maids design.

Book I, Ode V

TO PYRRHA

Say what slim youth, with moist perfumes
    Bedaub'd, now courts thy fond embrace,
There, where the frequent rose-tree blooms,
    And makes the grot so sweet a place?
Pyrrha, for whom with such an air
Do you bind back your golden hair?

So seeming in your cleanly vest,
    Whose plainness is the pink of taste—
Alas! how oft shall he protest
    Against his confidence misplac't,
And love's inconstant pow'rs deplore,
And wondrous winds, which, as they roar,

Throw black upon the alter'd scene—
    Who now so well himself deceives,
And thee all sunshine, all serene
    For want of better skill believes,
And for his pleasure has presag'd
Thee ever dear and disengag'd.

Wretched are all within thy snares,
    The inexperienc'd and the young!
For me the temple witness bears
    Where I my dropping weeds have hung,
And left my votive chart behind
To him that rules both wave and wind.

Book I, Ode XXIII

TO CHLOE

Me, Chloe, like a fawn you fly,
That seeks in trackless mountains high
    Her tim'rous dam again;

Alarm'd at every thing she hears,
The woods, the winds excite her fears,
        Tho' all those fears are vain.

For if a tree the breeze receives,
That plays upon the quiv'ring leaves
        When spring begins to start;
Or if green lizards, where they hide,
Turn but the budding bush aside,
        She trembles knees and heart.

But I continue my pursuit,
Not like the fierce Getulian brute,
        Or tyger, to assail,
And thee of[1] life and limbs bereave—
Think now at last 'tis time to leave
        Thy mother for a male.

[1] Text has "of thee."

Book I, Ode XXXVIII

TO HIS SERVANT

Persian pomps, boy, ever I renounce them:
Scoff o' the plaited coronet's refulgence;
Seek not in fruitless vigilance the rose-tree's
        Tardier offspring.

Mere honest myrtle that alone is order'd,
Me the mere myrtle decorates, as also
Thee the prompt waiter to a jolly toper
        Hous'd in an arbour.

Book II, Ode IV

TO XANTHIUS PHOCEUS

O Phoceus, think it no disgrace
To love your maid, since Thetis' heir,

Tho' proud, of old was in your case,
    Briseis was so fair.
The slave Tecmessa at her feet
Saw her lord Ajax; Atreus' son
Lov'd his fair captive in the heat
    Of conquest, that he won,
When, beat by that Thessalian boy,
The Phrygian host was disarray'd,
And Hector's death the fall of Troy
    An easy purchase made.
Who knows what wealth thou hast to claim,
Rich parents may thy Phyllis grace,
Surely the Gods have been to blame
    To one of royal race.
You cannot think her meanly born,
Nor worthless cou'd her mother be,
Whose heart has such ingenuous scorn
    For wealth, and love for thee.
Her face, her limbs so form'd t'engage,
I praise with a safe conscience still—
Shun to suspect a man, whose age
    Is going down the hill.

Book II, Ode VIII

TO JULIA BARINE

If any punishment or curse
Had made thee thy false oath bewail;
Hadst thou but been one tooth the worse,
    Or lost a single nail;
I shou'd have kept my faith—but thou
Shin'st out more tempting and more fair,
And art, by breaking of thy vow,
    Our youth's peculiar care.
'Tis profit, therefore, to deceive
Thy mother's ashes in a breath,
Stars, moon, and silent heav'n to grieve,
    And Gods, exempt from death.

Yes, Venus laughs, and nymphs, well known
For mock-simplicity, deride,
And love still whetting on a stone
        His darts in crimson dy'd.
But add to this new dupes abound,
New slaves, nor will the old relent,
Tho' sworn to quit her impious pound,
        Where their fond hearts are pent.
At thee the jealous mothers pine,
At thee old churls, and maids new wed,
Lest by that winning air of thine
        Their spouses be misled.

Book II, Ode XVIII

Gold or iv'ry's not intended
        For this little house of mine,
Nor Hymettian arches, bended
        On rich Afric pillars, shine.

For a court I've no ambition,
        As not Attalus his heir,
Nor make damsels of condition
        Spin me purple for my wear.

But for truth and wit respected,
        I possess a copious vein,
So that rich men have affected
        To be number'd of my train.

With my Sabine field contented,
        Fortune shall be dunn'd no more;
Nor my gen'rous friend tormented
        To augment my little store.

One day by the next's abolish'd,
        Moons increase but to decay;

You place marbles to be polish'd
  Ev'n upon your dying day.

Death unheeding, though infirmer,
  On the sea your buildings rise,
While the Baian billows murmur,
  That the land will not suffice.

What tho' more and more incroaching,
  On new boundaries you press,
And in avarice approaching,
  Your poor neighbours dispossess;

The griev'd hind his gods displaces
  In his bosom to convey,
And with dirty ruddy faces
  Boys and wife are driven away.

Yet no palace grand and spacious
  Does more sure its lord receive,
Than the seat of death rapacious,
  Whence the rich have no reprieve.

Earth alike to all is equal,
  Whither would your views extend?
Kings and peasants in the sequel
  To the destin'd grave descend.

There, tho' brib'd, the guard infernal
  Would not shrewd Prometheus free;
There are held in chains eternal
  Tantalus, and such as he.

There the poor have consolation
  For their hard laborious lot;
Death attends each rank and station,
  Whether he is call'd or not.

Book III, Ode XXV

TO BACCHUS

Bacchus, with thy spirit fraught,
Whither, whither am I caught?
To what groves and dens am driv'n,
Quick with thought, all fresh from heav'n?
In what grot shall I be found,
While I endless praise resound,
Caesar to the milky way
And Jove's synod to convey?
Great and new, as yet unsung
By another's lyre or tongue,
Will I speak—and so behave,
As thy sleepless dames, that rave
With enthusiastic face,
Seeing Hebrus, seeing Thrace,
And, where feet barbarian go,
Rhodope so white with snow.
How I love to lose my way,
And the vastness to survey
Of the rocks and desarts rude,
With astonishment review'd!
O of nymphs, that haunt the stream,
And thy priestesses supreme!
Who, when strengthen'd at thy call,
Can up-tear the ash-trees tall,
Nothing little, nothing low,
Nothing mortal will I show.
'Tis adventure—but 'tis sweet
Still to follow at thy feet,
Wheresoe'er you fix your shrine,
Crown'd with foliage of the vine.

Book IV, Ode VII

TO L. MANLIUS TORQUATUS

The melted snow the verdure now restores,
　　And leaves adorn the trees;
The season shifts—subsiding to their shores
　　The rivers flow with ease.
The Grace, with nymphs and with her sisters twain,
　　Tho' naked dares the dance—
That here's no permanence the years explain,
　　And days, as they advance.
The air grows mild with zephyrs, as the spring
　　To summer cedes the sway,
Which flies when autumn hastes his fruits to bring,
　　Then winter comes in play.
The moons their heav'nly damages supply—
　　Not so the mortal star—
Where good Eneas, Tullus, Ancus lie,
　　Ashes and dust we are.
Who knows if heav'n will give to-morrow's boon
　　To this our daily pray'r?
The goods you take to keep your soul in tune,
　　Shall scape your greedy heir.
When you shall die, tho' Minos must acquit
　　A part so nobly play'd;
Race, eloquence, and goodness, from the pit
　　Cannot restore your shade.
For nor Diana's heav'nly pow'r or love,
　　Hippolytus revives;
Nor Theseus can Perithous remove
　　From his Lethean gives.

Epode III

TO MAECENAS

Has any young profligate been so perverse,
　　To slay his old grandsire in wrath;

Why let him eat garlick (not hemlock is worse)
   What stomachs have clowns to their broth?

O what is this poison that's burning within?
   Has venom of vipers infus'd
Deceiv'd me! or, as the reward of my sin,
   Canidia the viands abus'd!

Medea, beyond all the Argonaut wights,
   When she captain Jason bespoke;
She made him take this as an unction of nights,
   Before the wild bulls cou'd be broke.

With this she prepar'd certain presents she made,
   A desp'rate revenge in her view;
And having Creusa to take them betray'd,
   Away on her dragon she flew.

Sure ne'er on the thirsty Apulia before,
   Arose such a muggy offence;
Nor did the gift-shirt that poor Hercules wore,
   Stick closer or burn more intense.

If ever such stuff you again shou'd affect,
   With a trick and a jest in your head;
May your wife, hand to mouth, your fond kisses reject,
   Or lie on the post of the bed.

Book I, Epistle IV

TO ALBIUS TIBULLUS

Tibullus, whom I love and praise,
Mild judge of my prosaic lays,
Can I account for your odd turn,
Who in Pedanian groves sojourn:
Are you now writing to out-please
The works of Cassius, or at ease,

And silence, range the healthy wood,
Studious of all things wise and good?
Thou'rt not a form without a heart,
For heav'n was gracious to impart
A goodly person, fine estate,
Made for fruition, fortunate.
What more for her most fav'rite boy,
Cou'd a nurse image, to enjoy,
Than to be wise, and ably taught,
To speak aloud his noble thought,
To whom grace, fame, and body sound,
Might to pre-eminence abound,
With table of ingenious fare,
And purse with money still to spare?
—'Twixt hope and care, 'twixt fear and strife,
Think every day the last of life.
Beyond your wish some happy day,
Shall come your grief to over-pay.
Me sleek and fat, as fat can be,
I hope you'll shortly come to see:
When you've a mind to laugh indeed
At pigs of the Lucretian breed.

Book I, Epistle XX

TO HIS BOOK

You seem to cast, my vent'rous book,
Towards the town a wishful look,
That thee the chapmen may demand,
Where Janus, and Vertumnus stand;
When polish'd by the binder's art.—
Both keys and seals, with all your heart,
You hate, and every thing refuse
Which all your modest volumes chuse.
You grudge that you are shewn to few,
Desirous of the public view,
On other principles compil'd—
Away then, since you are so wild—

When once set off there's no return—
Soon shall you say with much concern—
Ah! wretch, what wou'd I, when your pride
Is by some reader mortified,
And in some narrow nook you stick,
When curiosity is sick,
But if the augur do not dream,
In wrath for this your desp'rate scheme;
At Rome you'll be a welcome guest,
As long as you are new at least.
But when all dirty you become,
In witness of the vulgar thumb,
Or groveling book-worms you must feed,
Or for us Utica shall speed;
Or bundled up in pack-thread chain,
Be sent a transport into Spain.
The good adviser, all the while,
To whom you gave no heed, will smile:
As he who from the mountain threw
The sulky ass, that wou'd not do
His bus'ness—"then go down the hill—
"Who'd save an ass against his will."
This destiny too must remain—
Thee faultring dotage shall detain
About the city-skirts to teach
The boys their rudiments of speech.
And when the fervency of day
Brings you more hearers, you must say,
That poor and meanly born at best,
I spread my wings beyond my nest,
And what you from my birth subtract,
You for my virtues must exact;
That peace or war, I still was great,
With the first pillars of the state,
Short-siz'd, and prematurely gray,
Form'd for th' intensity of day,
With passion ev'n to phrenzy seiz'd,
But very easily appeas'd.
If any person by the bye

Shou'd ask how old I am, reply,
That when the fasces were assign'd,
To Lepidus and Lollius join'd,
I was full out, and fairly told,
Four times eleven Decembers old.

EDITION

A Translation of the Works of Horace, London, 1767. (Text.) ("To Pyrrha"
and "To Bacchus" were reprinted by Blunden, *A Song to David*, etc., 1924.)

Hymns

for the Amusement of Children

Hymn iii. Charity

O Queen of virtues, whose sweet pow'r
Does o'er the first perfections tow'r,
Sustaining in the arms of love
All want below, all weal above.

With thee, O let my thoughts conceive,
For all the very best believe;
Predict, pronounce for all the best,
And be by bearing all things blest.

To suffer long, and still be kind
In holy temperance of mind,
Rejoice that truth is on my side,
As free from envy as from pride.

Both tongues and prophecies shall cease,
And painful knowledge cede to peace;
And time and death o'er all prevail,
But Charity shall never fail.

Then guide, O Christ, this little hand,
To deal thy bounties round the land;
To clothe and feed the hungry poor,
And to the stranger ope my door.

My cup of water, Christ, is free
For all that love and thirst for thee;
With wisdom many a soul to win,
And loose the irksome bonds of sin.

Make me, O Christ, tho' yet a child,
To virtue zealous, errors mild,
Profess the feelings of a man,
And be the Lord's Samaritan.

Hymn vi. Mercy

O Sweet—attentive to the pray'r,
Ye forward hope and slave despair;
Tho' Christ his blood divinely spill'd,
Tremendous ruin to rebuild.

Tho' high above the great and just,
Yet thou descendest to the dust;
Both to the sovereign and the slave,
Nor quitt'st the monument and grave.

O let me like the righteous die,
And so I shall if thou art by!
The phial in thy hand uprears
My Saviour's blood, my Saviour's tears.

Come, Cherub, come, possess my soul,
All wrath and bitterness controul;
If thou thy charming pow'rs bestow,
I'll show thee to my veriest foe.

Hymn xi. Beauty

FOR A DAMSEL

CHRIST, keep me from the self-survey
    Of beauties all thine own;
If there is beauty, let me pray,
    And praise the Lord alone.

Pray—that I may the fiend withstand,
    Where'er his serpents be;

Praise—that the Lord's almighty hand
    Is manifest in me.

It is not so—my features are
    Much meaner than the rest;
A glow-worm cannot be a star,
    And I am plain at best.

Then come, my love, thy grace impart,
    Great Saviour of mankind;
O come, and purify my heart,
    And beautify my mind.

Then will I thy carnations nurse,
    And cherish every rose;
And empty to the poor my purse,
    'Till grace to glory grows.

Hymn xiii. Elegance

'Tis in the spirit that attire,
    Th' investiture of saints in heav'n,
Those robes of intellectual fire,
    Which to the great elect are giv'n.

"Bring out to my returning son
    The robes for elegance the best";
Thus in the height it shall be done,
    And thus the penitent be blest.

'Tis in the body that sweet mien
    Ingenuous Christians all possess,
Grace, easy motions, smiles serene,
    Clean hands and seemliness of dress.

Whoever has thy charming pow'rs
    Is amiable as Kidron's* swan,
Like holy Esdras feeds on flow'rs,
    And lives on honey like St. John.

* David.

Hymn xvi. Learning

Come, come with emulative strife,
To learn the way, the truth, and life,
   Which Jesus is in one;
In all sound doctrines he proceeds,
From Alpha to Omega leads,
   E'en Spirit, Sire, and Son.

Sure of th' exceeding great reward,
Midst all your learning learn the Lord—
   This was thy doctrine Paul;
And this thy lecture should persuade,
Tho' thou hadst more of human aid,
   Than thy blest brethren all.

Humanity's a charming thing,
And every science of the ring,
   Good is the classic lore;
For these are helps along the road,
That leads to Zion's blest abode,
   And heav'nly muse's store.

But greater still in each respect,
He that communicates direct
   The tutor of the soul;
Who without pain, degrees or parts,
While he illuminates our hearts,
   Can teach at once the whole.

Hymn xxi. Generosity

That vast communicative mind,
That form'd the world and human kind
   And saw that all was right;
Or was thyself, or came from thee,
Stupendous generosity,
   Above all lustre bright.

"Not* for themselves the bees prepare
Their honey, and the fleecy care
   Not for themselves are shorn:
Not for themselves the warblers build,
Not for themselves the lands are till'd,
   By them that tread the corn."

The Lord shed on the Holy Rood,
His infinitely gen'rous blood,
   Not for himself, but all;
Yea e'en for them that pierc'd his side,
In patient agony he dy'd,
   To remedy the fall.

O highly rais'd above the ranks
Of angels—he could e'en give thanks
   Self-rais'd, and self-renew'd—
Then who can praise, and love and fear
Enough?—since he himself, 'tis clear,
   Is also gratitude.

* Virgil.

Hymn xxii. Gratitude

I upon the first creation
   Clap'd my wings with loud applause,
Cherub of the highest station,
   Praising, blessing, without pause.

I in Eden's bloomy bowers
   Was the heav'nly gard'ner's pride,
Sweet of sweets, and flow'r of flow'rs,
   With the scented tinctures dy'd.

Hear, ye little children, hear me,
   I am God's delightful voice;
They who sweetly still revere me,
   Still shall make the wisest choice.

Hear me not like Adam trembling,
    When I walk'd in Eden's grove;
And the host of heaven assembling
    From the spot the traitor drove.

Hear me rather as the lover
    Of mankind, restor'd and free;
By the word ye shall recover
    More than that ye lost by me.

I'm the Phoenix of the Singers
    That in upper Eden dwell:
Hearing me Euphrates lingers,
    As my wond'rous tale I tell.

'Tis the story of the graces,
    Mercies without end or sum;
And the sketches and the traces
    Of ten thousand more to come.

List, my children, list within you,
    Dread not ye the tempter's rod;
Christ our gratitude shall win you,
    Wean'd from earth, and led to God.

Hymn xxiv. Melancholy

O pluck me quick the raven's quill,
    And I will set me down,
My destin'd purpose to fulfill,
But with this interrupted skill,
    Of thought and grief profound.

How to begin, and how depart
    From this sad fav'rite theme,
The man of sorrow in my heart,
I at my own ideas start,
    As dread as Daniel's dream.

As soon as born the infant cries,
 For well his spirit knows,
A little while and then he dies,
A little while and down he lies
 To take a stern repose.

But man's own death is not th' event
 For which most tears are due;
Wife, children, to the grave are sent,
Or friends, to make the heart repent
 That it such blessings knew.

O thou, which on the mountain's brow
 By night didst pray alone;
In the cold night didst pay thy vow,
And in humiliation bow
 To thrones and pow'rs thine own:

Tell us, for thou the best can tell,
 What Melancholy means?
A guise in them that wear it well,
That goes to music to dispel
 Dark thoughts and gloomier scenes.

Say, didst thou solitude desire,
 Or wert thou driven away
By rank desertion to retire,
Without or bed, or food, or fire,
 For all thy foes to pray.

Yet thou didst preach of future bliss,
 Peace permanent above,
Of truth and mercy's holy kiss.
Those joys, which none that love thee miss,
 O give us grace to love.

Hymn xxv. Mirth

If you are merry, sing away,
 And touch the organs sweet;

This is the Lord's triumphant day,
Ye children, in the gall'ries gay,
　　Shout from each goodly seat.

It shall be May to-morrow's morn,
　　A-field then let us run,
And deck us in the blooming thorn,
Soon as the cock begins to warn,
　　And long before the sun.

I give the praise to Christ alone,
　　My pinks already show;
And my streak'd roses fully blown
The sweetness of the Lord make known,
　　And to his glory grow.

Ye little prattlers, that repair
　　For cowslips in the mead,
Of those exulting colts beware,
But blythe security is there
　　Where skipping lambkins feed.

With white and crimson laughs the sky,
　　With birds the hedge-rows ring;
To give the praise to God most High,
And all the sulky fiends defy,
　　Is a most joyful thing.

Hymn xxvii. Good-Nature to Animals

The man of mercy (says the Seer)
　　Shows mercy to his beast;
Learn not of churls to be severe,
　　But house and feed at least.

Shall I melodious pris'ners take
　　From out the linnet's nest,
And not keep busy care awake
　　To cherish ev'ry guest?

What, shall I whip in cruel wrath
    The steed that bears me safe;
Or 'gainst the dog, who plights his troth,
    For faithful service chafe?

In the deep waters throw thy bread,
    Which thou shalt find again,
With God's good interest on thy head,
    And pleasure for thy pain.

Let thine industrious silk-worms reap
    Their wages to the full,
Nor let neglected Dormice sleep
    To death within thy wool.

Know when the frosty weather comes,
    'Tis charity to deal
To Wren and Redbreast all thy crumbs,
    The remnant of thy meal.

Tho' these some spirits think but light,
    And deem indifferent things;
Yet they are serious in the sight
    Of CHRIST, the King of Kings.

Hymn xxix. Long-Suffering of God

One hundred feet from off the ground
    That noble Aloe blows;
But mark ye by what skill profound
    His charming grandeur rose.

One hundred years of patient care
    The gard'ners did bestow;
Toil and hereditary pray'r
    Made all this glorious show.

Thus man goes on from year to year
And bears no fruit at all,
But gracious God, still unsevere,
Bids show'rs of blessings fall.

The beams of mercy, dews of grace,
Our Saviour still supplies;
And then, the soul regains her place,
And sweetens all the skies.

Hymn xxxiii. For SATURDAY

Now's the time for mirth and play,
Saturday's an holiday!
Praise to heav'n unceasing yield,
I've found a lark's nest in the field.

A lark's nest? Then your play-mate begs
You'd spare herself and speckled eggs;
Soon she shall ascend and sing
Your praises to the Eternal King.

Hymn xxxiv. For SUNDAY

Arise—arise—the Lord arose
On this triumphant day:
Your souls to piety dispose,
Arise to bless and pray.

Ev'n rustics do adorn them now,
Themselves in roses dress;
And to the clergyman they bow,
When he begins to bless.

Their best apparel now arrays
The little girls and boys;

And better than the preacher, prays
For heaven's eternal joys.

EDITIONS

[*Hymns for the Amusement of Children*, London, 1770.] No copies recorded.
[A second edition.] No copies recorded.
Hymns for the Amusement of Children. By Christopher Smart, M. A. Third
Edition. London . . . MDCCLXXV. (Apparently unique copy in the Bod-
leian Library.)
Hymns for the Amusement of Children, Philadelphia, 1791. (Apparently unique
copy in American Antiquarian Society Library.) (Text.)

Notes on the Poems

MINOR POEMS, 1735-1756

UNDER this general title, I have collected a small group of short pieces which seem to represent fairly the journalistic verse Smart produced in great quantity during the years before his breakdown. They recall his three love affairs, his residence at Cambridge, his scribbling for the magazines, and certain of his early friendships in London. The prologue to *A Trip to Cambridge* is almost the only surviving fragment from any of his entertainments designed for the theater, if we except the oratorios of his later period and a few prologues and epilogues for other people's plays.

Only the fables call for any extended comment. During the years from 1750 to 1755, Smart produced some twenty pieces in this form, all in the same manner and of more or less equal merit. Seven of them appeared in the *Midwife*; five were printed in the *Gentleman's Magazine* during 1754-1755; the rest were not printed until later, five of them not seeing publication until Hunter collected them in 1791.

It is perhaps not too much to suggest that Newbery may have been chiefly responsible for Smart's attempts as a fabulist; certainly so astute a publisher must have recognized that verse of this sort was readily salable. At any rate, when Smart fell ill one of the first projects that occurred to Newbery as a means of raising some money for Mrs. Smart and the children was to advertise a collection of "tales and fables." Why he abandoned this scheme we have no way of knowing, but we may suppose that he decided the available material would make too thin a volume.

After his recovery, Smart never took up the writing of fables very seriously again. He did do two—"Reason and Imagination" and "Munificence and Modesty," both published in 1763—but in ideas and in treatment they are much nearer to the other poetry of his later period than to the early fables. In 1765 he published a *Poetical Translation of the Fables of Phaedrus* (whom he had imitated in at least one of his early pieces[1]) but he never set his hand again to the composition of original fables, having found something better to do with his talents.

Smart's fables were fairly popular, if we may judge by the fre-

---

[1] "The Pig" in the *Phaedrus* is a reworking of the version Smart had published in *The Midwife* in 1752.

quency with which individual ones were reprinted in various magazines and anthologies of the period. "Care and Generosity," for instance, was printed at least seven times in the eighteenth century, "The Teapot and the Scrubbing-Brush" six times, and "The Bag-Wig and Tobacco Pipe" and "Reason and Imagination" five times each. The modern reader would hardly care to see them so often, but if we could recapture the eighteenth-century taste for moralized tales and fables we should value them more highly. When they were first collected in the 1791 edition, the *Monthly Review* announced: "We are inclined to believe that, after Gay, Smart is the most agreeable metrical fabulist in our language; his versification is less polished, and his apologues in general are perhaps less correct, than those of Gay and Moore; but in originality, in wit, and in humour, the preference seems due to Smart." Whether today we really like these pieces or not, they offer another proof of Smart's versatility, and his rather surprising ability to tackle a hack job under pressure and turn out a creditable performance.

"The Force of Innocence" is apparently the earliest in print of a group of some half dozen poems addressed to Miss Anna Maria Carnan, whom the poet later married. He made his declaration of love in "The Lass with the Golden Locks," which Arne, at some time or other, set to music. In 1752 or 1753 the lady was greeted on her birthday with the "Ode on the 26th of January" and again in 1754 with "On My Wife's Birthday." In 1754 the "Ode to a Virginia Nightingale" mentioned Mrs. Smart's nursing her husband through an illness, and in July of the same year was printed the amusing "Invitation to Mrs. Tyler" to attend a party on the anniversary of their wedding. The last poem in which Mrs. Smart is mentioned is the "Hymn to the Supreme Being," but all that is said of her there is that Smart, in his illness, failed to recognize her or their children. There is, indeed, in none of the poems to Mrs. Smart the same note of ardent affection that one finds in all the Harriet Pratt poems. With the exception of the first two, they are all little pieces written on such occasions as birthdays and anniversaries, and none of them displays any emotion or lyrical fervor comparable with that which Smart demonstrates in his religious poetry, for example.

These poems add their negative evidence to the theory that Smart's marriage, whatever else it may have represented in his life, did not result from any grand passion. In *Rejoice in the Lamb*, Smart speaks of his absent wife with a detached kindness (his usual phrase is "God be gracious to my wife"); only in the early poems did he refer to her as "Nancy." After his release from confinement she is never

mentioned in his work at all. This is not unnatural, for no man so
situated could forget that in the midst of his afflictions his wife had
taken their children and left him completely. An outsider may feel
that she was justified, and certainly the evidence of contemporaries
indicates that Mrs. Smart was a highly respectable, and even estimable
woman. It is obvious that in her marriage with Smart she was sorely
tried. Nevertheless, it is also perfectly evident that there was never
any profound love between them.

The child whose death called forth "To the Memory of Master
N———" was John Newbery, the son of the printer and the former
Mrs. Carnan; in other words, the half-brother of Mrs. Smart. The
pieces to Mrs. Tyler and to Mr. Powell display Smart's light and
bantering manner (which never deserted him, incidentally; see the
"Invitation to Dr. Nares," p. 236). Their graceful wit, set off by
amusing "burla" rhymes, entitle them to a place among those poems
of his which we can re-read with pleasure.

The Seaton Poems

When Thomas Seaton, vicar of Ravenstone, Bucks., died in 1741,
he left a will which contained the following provision: "I give my
Kislingbury estate to the University of Cambridge for ever; the rents
of which shall be disposed of yearly by the Vice-Chancellor for the
time being, as he the Vice-Chancellor, the Master of Clare-Hall, and
the Greek Professor for the time being, or any two of them, shall
agree. Which three persons aforesaid shall give out a subject, which
subject shall, for the first year, be one or other of the Perfections or
Attributes of the Supreme Being, and so the succeeding years, till
the subject be exhausted; and afterwards the subject shall be either
Death, Judgment, Heaven, Hell, Purity of Heart, &c. or whatsoever
else may be judged by the Vice-Chancellor, Master of Clare-Hall,
Greek Professor, to be most conducive to the honour of the Supreme
Being and recommendation of Virtue. And they shall yearly dispose
of the rent of the above estate to that Master of Arts, whose Poem
on the subject given shall be best approved by them. Which Poem I
ordain to be always in English, and to be printed; the expence of
which shall be deducted out of the product of the estate, and the
residue given as a reward for the Composer of the Poem, or Ode,
or Copy of Verses."

The executors, not satisfied to let the estate pass into the hands of
the university, brought suit to alter the clause. The case dragged on,
and it was not until 1750 that the university was able to make the

first award. The first subject was "The Eternity of the Supreme Being," and the first winner was Christopher Smart. His name stands
at the head of a list of poets whose productions continue, by the grace
of Thomas Seaton, to the present day.

"Eternity" set a fairly high standard for prize pieces, and for six
years Smart was the chief beneficiary of the Seaton awards. (He did
not compete in 1754.) His five Seaton poems were very highly regarded by his contemporaries. Almost every biographical notice or
anecdotal reference to him during the eighteenth century mentions
them as his crowning achievement. They came to be regarded as the
best of all the poems that were written for the Seaton prizes during
the succeeding years, and later prize-winners imitated and even
plagiarized them. Another significant bit of testimony to the continued reputation of Smart's poems is offered by *Providence: an
Oratorio*, a composition of one Mr. Fisher, published in London in
1777. According to the title page of this production, "the recitatives
are selected from the Cambridge Prize Poems of the late ingenious
Mr. Christopher Smart; except where the necessity of a proper connection obliged the compiler occasionally to add a few lines." When
Hunter's edition was published in 1791, the reviewers again selected
the Seaton poems as the best of Smart's works.

They have not fared so well at the hands of later critics. Oliver
Elton[1] considers them "seldom readable," and Edmund Blunden has
observed that "their main recommendation is that they show Smart
already praising the omnipotent by way of admiring precious stones,
the deeps of the sea, tropical fruits, and all the ranks and orders of
creation."[2] No one else, so far as I know, has in recent years bothered
to comment upon them at all.

However, the five prize-winning poems are of peculiar interest to
the student of Smart's poetry, for they present a unified group of
religious meditations composed during the period of busy journalistic
activity in London. Aside from the "Hymn to the Supreme Being"
and a few short pieces, they are the only religious verse that can safely
be attributed to him before he found his real medium in the period
of his confinement.

At first glance, the Seaton poems seem to have little in common
with the bulk of Smart's religious poetry. Since they are written in
what the eighteenth century called "Miltonic verse," they naturally
have none of the highly lyrical quality that distinguishes all his other
poetry on religious themes. But a closer examination reveals many

[1] *A Survey of English Literature, 1750-1780*, New York, 1928, ii, 83.
[2] *A Song to David*, etc., p. 16.

elements which enable us to see that they really fit into an unbroken continuity of development.

Structurally, the poems are very simple. The ideas are arranged in easy progressions and are developed in logical paragraphs. Within the paragraph, one method of development is found that is characteristic of much of his other poetry. This is the habit of listing "the catalogue of lovely things in earth, and sea, and sky." In describing the end of the world in *Eternity* (61-98) he names over all the seemingly permanent objects of creation which are to perish in that catastrophe, and not content here he repeats his catalogue in a condensed form at the beginning of his next paragraph (99-106). Almost the entire poem on *Immensity* is made up of similar catalogues. This listing of example after example to illustrate his main theme is characteristic of the other Seaton poems as well. Here, as so often in the later poems, he uses a sequence which includes the main groups of birds, fish, trees or flowers, precious stones, animals, and man. Some of his grandest effects he achieved later by combining this catalogue with the repeated word or phrase, as in the "adoration" section of *A Song to David*, and in the "Praise Him" stanzas of "Hymn VI, The Presentation of Christ in the Temple" in *Hymns and Spiritual Songs*. The idea came to him, no doubt, from many poems in the Psalter and in the Book of Common Prayer.

Another point of contact with Smart's other poetry is seen in the prominence given to the theme of gratitude to God for the gift of life, since this is the very keystone in the arch of all his later work. Gratitude is a Virtue, personified in the form of a cherub (*Omniscience*, 6-9) and her home on earth is in the Church (*Goodness*, 71-80). The expression of gratitude is not confined to man, for Smart had already formed the conception that all life is a grand paean of praise to the Creator. He had realized that every object of the material world contributes to this chorus, and had decided that this participation, at least on the part of members of the animal kingdom, was conscious and voluntary. One of the most charming things about Smart's interpretation of nature is his willingness to acknowledge that even those instruments in the universal orchestra which offend his own ears produce a discord which, in Pope's phrase, is really "harmony not understood." In *Goodness*, he remarks of the "invoking ravens":

> And tho' their throats coarse ruttling hurt the ear
> They mean it all for music, thanks and praise
> They mean, and leave ingratitude to man. (Lines 56-59)

Years later he wrote into his "magnificat":

> Let Ehud rejoice with Onocrotalus, whose braying is for the
> glory of God, because he makes the best musick in his power.
> (*Rejoice in the Lamb*, v. 19)

The choice of "Miltonic" verse for these poems doubtless increased
their impressiveness to men of the middle eighteenth century, but
today it seems regrettable. The ideas of the poems are pleasant and
interesting, if not profound, but for the modern reader the pieces are
rather dull. The blight of Miltonism had already ruined Thomson,
as well as a host of lesser lights, and it is not surprising that most
of the grace and power of Smart is crushed under the same deadening
tradition. Fortunately, after 1756 Smart never returned to this style
of writing. If he had continued to use it, his lyric genius would never
have flowered.

Within the pompous distortions of "Miltonic" rhetoric, however,
there is a wealth of experiment in the details of verse technique. One
who has the patience will find in the Seaton poems ample evidence
of Smart's painstaking care in the study of versification. Such devices as repetitions, parallel constructions, contrasts and paradoxes,
are used in abundance. That Smart was carefully training his ear
is evidenced by the most elaborate experiments with every kind of
alliteration and with the more subtle harmonic qualities of vowel
sounds. It is his absolute mastery of these technical devices that accounts for the sheer beauty of much of his greatest work, and the
Seaton poems as a group offer one of the best places to study the
methods by which the young poet taught himself his craft.

Hymn to the Supreme Being

This poem is one of the most personal, and certainly the most
pathetic, of all Smart's works. As he says in his dedication, he had
suffered at least three attacks of "fevers" since his arrival in London.
They had apparently been quite severe, but after each Smart had
rallied his forces and taken up his life again with the sure conviction
that he was well. His gratitude for the second recovery had been
expressed to his wife; now after the third attack he is quick to offer
his thanks to his physician. It is difficult to resist the attraction of
such a character.

Dr. James, to whom the poem is dedicated, made quite a reputation with his fever powders. They were sold through Newbery's
establishment, and the publisher took every opportunity to "puff"

them. He even wrote into "Goody Two Shoes," for the enlightenment of the young, the information that Goody's grandmother died because she was in a part of the world where the famous powders were unobtainable. He must have published with great delight a poem that was such an excellent piece of advertising.

The reviewers did not take kindly to Smart's effort, however. The *Critical Review*, in the first reference to Smart that I have found in its pages, remarked that the author "hath not given us the pleasure which we expected to find in this performance, in which there is more gratitude than genius, and more piety than poetry." The reviewer concluded, with something of a sneer, "we . . . are very glad to hear that he is *recovered*, and heartily wish that his muse were *recovered also*." The *Monthly Review* gave the poem the following notice: "As this poem seems to have been the genuine effusion of gratitude, it would be cruel, and invidious, to make it the subject of criticism; tho' otherwise, not the least exceptionable of this gentleman's performances. It is an instance, however, of the goodness of his heart, if not of the fidelity of his muse."

The only other critic who has bothered to mention this poem, so far as I have found, is Mr. Oliver Elton, in *A Survey of English Literature, 1750-1780* (N. Y., 1928). "Even in the unpromising *Hymn to the Supreme Being*," he remarks, "amid the stock phrases and characteristically vague grammar, there is poetic emotion," and he quotes the fifteenth stanza to prove his contention.

I think that the poem deserves more attention than these critics would lead us to suppose. Its poetic merit is not high, of course, when it is compared with Smart's best work, but this is not to say it has no merit at all. Its great value, however, lies first in the evidence it gives us of the nature of Smart's affliction, and second in the revelation of his emotional reaction to illness. He was stricken both physically and mentally: he says that he was unable to walk and that he could not bear strong light in his eyes; he also says quite explicitly three times in the poem that during the illness he lost his reason. The two attacks he had suffered previously had probably not been so severe, but it is evident from this poem that Smart's family bore with a great deal before they finally sent him into an asylum.

More interesting than these sordid details is the evidence of the poem concerning the religious nature of Smart's experience. Smart was singularly free from the "sense of sin" which weighs so heavily on many religious people. In fact, this poem contains the sole mention, so far as I have found, of the idea at all. But even here he is only momentarily ashamed of his "follies"; his essentially happy nature turns immediately to more congenial themes: "To love, to praise, to bless, to wonder and adore." Smart's religion was a religion of joy, and this poem, despite its literary shortcomings, is a valuable expression of it.

This poem was probably published in June or July, 1756 (it was reviewed in the July magazines), and Smart had apparently fallen ill the previous April. We have no exact information as to how long his recovery lasted, but there is reason to believe that he was ill again almost immediately. The long seven-year period of intermittent insanity and chaos in all his affairs had begun.

Rejoice in the Lamb

In 1939, Mr. William Force Stead published, under the title used here, a number of pages of manuscript written by Christopher Smart and at that time in the private collection of Colonel Cawardine Probert. The manuscript is incomplete, but the pages that have survived contain very lengthy portions of what are apparently two large compositions written during the period of Smart's confinement. One of these compositions is called the "Let" section, since every line of it, except the first two, begins with the word "Let"; in the other, every line begins with the word "For," and it is accordingly called the "For" section. Although the evidence shows that Smart was sometimes, at least, working on both of them simultaneously, it seems clear that they form two separate works.

The question of dating the various portions is an exceedingly complicated one, but it is reasonably certain that what we have in the manuscript is two separate portions of each of the two sections. The earliest in date of composition is a portion of the "For" section written between the summer of 1759 and the latter part of the summer of 1760. Then around August 1, 1760, Smart began the "Let" section and continued writing in it, at a rate of two lines a day, until around May 12, 1761. Meanwhile, he had either continued to write steadily in the "For" section or he had abandoned it and begun it again, for we have a portion of the "For" section which can be dated from c. February 21, 1761, to c. May 12, 1761; it had clearly been started earlier than February 21, for it begins with an incomplete alphabet starting with the letter H, but how much earlier we do not know. Again, we do not know whether Smart stopped writing in both sections around May 12, or whether some pages have been lost. All we have in the remaining pages of the manuscript is a portion of the "Let" section written, one line a day, from June 12, 1762, to January 30, 1763. Thus, *Rejoice in the Lamb* gives us in its two sections a unique record of day-by-day writing done by a poet who was under confinement as insane.

Of the two compositions, the "Let" section is much the more formal: in the first portion of it, Smart wrote consistently (with very occasional exceptions) two lines a day over a period of about a year; in the latter part, he wrote one line a day for something over six months. The poem begins:

> Rejoice in God, O ye Tongues; give the glory to the Lord, and the Lamb.
> Nations and languages, and every Creature, in which is the breath of Life.
> Let man and beast appear before him, and magnify his name together.
> Let Noah and his company approach the throne of Grace, and do homage to the Ark of their Salvation.
> Let Abraham present a Ram, and worship the God of his Redemption.
> Let Isaac, the Bridegroom, kneel with his Camels, and bless the hope of his pilgrimage.

In this manner the poem proceeds through its hundreds of lines, with a proper name coupled in each line with the name of some animal, bird, fish, insect, plant, or stone. The result is a gigantic assemblage of human beings joining with all the objects of creation in a mighty chorus of praise to the Creator. There can be no doubt that Smart intended this composition to be a poem, for it is cunningly and carefully wrought and Mr. Stead has shown that even the form is a deliberate attempt to adapt principles of Hebraic versification. There is a great deal of parallelism and intricate cross-reference from line to line. But there is evidence of mania, also, in this dogged repetition of the same theme and the same form through hundreds of lines and days, so that the final result is hardly a poem at all but rather a vast storehouse of image and allusion and detail upon which Smart was to draw in creating the poetry of his last eight years. Its chief value today is in the light it throws on Smart's enormous learning and his richly stored memory, both of which illuminate many corners of his later and finer work.

The "For" section is an entirely different matter. I do not believe that Smart intended this composition to be a unified poem at all. Rather, it appears to be a kind of diary or commonplace book in which he jotted down from time to time all sorts of ideas that occurred to him about himself, his family, his friends, public events, and what not, along with his opinions on scientific matters, spiritual meditations, bits of philosophizing, and gnomic utterances. The dating of the various parts of this section is extremely difficult and uncertain, for although a number of dates appear in it, we cannot date the intervening lines with any certainty because he does not appear to have written any fixed number of lines a day, as he did in the "Let" section.

The "For" section, however, is extremely valuable. In many places, a number of consecutive lines will form a fascinating little poem by themselves. More important, from this section comes almost all the information we have about Smart's reaction to his confinement. It gives us wonderful insights into his mind and character. We discover that like most good poets he was greatly interested in the advances science was making in his day, and that like most unhappy souls he found relief in prophesying better days to come. He followed public affairs, as well as he was able, with a keen and thoughtful attention. We are better able to judge his poetry after we have read through such a passage as that on the spiritual music, and have understood with what care he studied such details of his craft as rhymes and vowel quantities. Despite many puzzling lines, and an occasional pathetic and ridiculous one, this section of *Rejoice in the Lamb* provides a clear revelation of the personality of Christopher Smart. And there are few personalities which, under the stress of mental disease, would show such purity and goodness.

In presenting selections from this manuscript, I have chosen first a long passage from the "For" section and printed it exactly as written, in order to give a clear idea of the disconnected way in which Smart frequently jotted down his thoughts. Next, I have selected certain short passages which form consistent little units. In the third place, I have arbitrarily grouped under titles various lines selected from different portions of the manuscript. My purpose in making this last kind of selection and grouping is simply to provide more readable fragments. Anyone who is seriously interested in Smart should obtain the complete *Rejoice in the Lamb* in Mr. Stead's admirable edition, for it is indispensable to a complete view of the poet and his work. The original manuscript is now in the collection of the Harvard University Library.

A Translation of the Psalms of David

The volume from which the selections here printed are taken was published in 1765, two years after *A Song to David* had been issued.

They are placed before the *Song* in the present reprinting, however, because the whole translation was completed before the *Song* was published, and very likely had been finished before it was written. It is impossible to determine the exact order of composition of the *Psalms*, the *Hymns and Spiritual Songs*, and *A Song to David*, but they were all done during the last years of Smart's confinement and the first few months after his release. The only record of those years is to be found in *Rejoice in the Lamb*, in the later pages of which we are clearly informed that both the *Psalms* and the *Hymns* are in process of composition. The *Hymns* are mentioned in two entries, both earlier than any reference to the *Psalms*:

> The Lord magnify the idea of Smart singing hymns on this day in the eyes of the whole University of Cambridge. Nov.ʳ 5.ᵗʰ 1762. N.S. (xxix, 20)

> The Lord help on with the hymns (xxxi, 5. date, c. Dec. 26, 1762)

The first of these entries prompts the conjecture that when he made it Smart had just written his "Hymn xxix. The Fifth of November," and makes one wonder whether, with some notion of propriety, he had set himself the task of writing the hymn for a certain fast or feast on the day of its celebration. If so, this would mean that they were all composed during 1762, which would account for their being ready for the press in April, 1763, when they were announced. It would also mean that the second reference would correspond roughly to the time of composition of "Hymn xxxiii. St. Stephen" (December 26), and that with only two more to be written Smart saw the end of his labors in sight.

The references to the *Psalms* are more in number, and all occur in entries written during the first weeks of 1763. At the very end of 1762, Smart had written:

> Let Merrick, house of Merrick rejoice with Lageus a kind of Grape. God all-sufficient bless & forward the Psalmist in the Lord Jesus.

This must refer to another "translation" of the Psalms, done by Merrick and published shortly before Smart's own work appeared. The two were ultimately compared, to Merrick's advantage, when the *Critical Review* noticed them in 1765. Smart must have heard that Merrick was engaged on a rival translation, and this kindly reference to it is another of the many evidences of his good nature and charitable disposition.

On January 2, Smart wrote, "God forward my version of the Psalms thro' Jesus Christ our Lord" (xxxi, 14); and two days later, "I pray for the soul of Crockatt the bookseller the first to put me upon a version of the Psalms." Upon this last entry Mr. Stead has a valuable note: "The name Crockat or Crockatt occurs in Plomer's *Dictionary of Booksellers and Printers*, where the period of his activity is 1726-52. . . . Apparently Smart had had the idea in mind for a number of years without acting upon it, which again suggests that he was now achieving work which he had been unable to settle down to during the helter-skelter of his life before being confined."

Mr. Stead is right that Smart had not previously "settled down" to the job of translating the Psalms. But he had perhaps made a few essays towards it. There are two versions of Psalms in the *Student*, signed "T.E.P.," which sound very much like Smart; if they are his work, it may have been these that caused Crockatt to make his suggestion. At any rate we know from the dates given by Plomer that Smart had toyed with the idea years before his illness, just as the germ of *A Song to David* was suggested to his mind as early as 1746 (see Intro. p. 66). Besides this evidence, Smart wrote and published at least two Psalms in the intervening years. A version of "The 42nd Psalm" appeared in *The Universal Visiter* in October, 1756; and "The 100th Psalm, for a Scotch tune" was printed in *The Christian's Magazine*, supplement for January-June, 1761. In his translation as it was finally published, Smart did not use any of these earlier versions, but their existence shows us that the project had been in his mind for many years.

There are three more entries relating to the *Psalms* in *Rejoice in the Lamb*. In an entry which we can date January 11, 1763, the poet wrote: "I pray for a musician or musicians to set the new psalms"—a prayer that was abundantly answered (see Introduction, p. 50). Two days later he wrote, "the Lord forward my translation of the psalms this year," and on the following day, "I pray God bless all my subscribers." This last indicates that he had already begun to advertise, probably by word of mouth, his projected volume, a task that was to require over two years for its completion.

All this evidence from *Rejoice in the Lamb* shows very clearly that the translation and the *Hymns* were at least well started at the beginning of 1763, at the time when Smart was apparently released from confinement. When *A Song to David* was published on April 8, the following announcement was printed in the pamphlet:

This day are published, PROPOSALS for Printing, by subscription, A NEW TRANSLATION of the PSALMS of DAVID. To which will be added, A Set of HYMNS for the FASTS and FESTIVALS of the

CHURCH of ENGLAND. By CHRISTOPHER SMART, A.M. Proposals at large may be had, with a Specimen of the Work, and subscriptions are taken in, by the following Booksellers: Messrs. Dodsley . . . *etc.* . . . . And by C. Say, Printer, in Newgate-street; who has the Copy in his Possession.

We do not know, of course, that this copy was the complete translation as it was finally published, but we have every reason to suppose that it represented the bulk of the text. All this would indicate that much of the work on the *Psalms,* together with *A Song to David,* was done in a great burst of activity in the early months of 1763, activity largely stimulated by Smart's excitement at being released from his confinement.

As a final argument for the order in which the poems in question are presented in the present volume, we have the authority of Smart's own arrangement in the 1765 edition, *i.e., Psalms, Hymns, Song.* Whether this represents the order of composition or not, it is certainly correct artistically. Read in this order, these works exhibit a steadily increasing power in Smart's technical control of his medium, as well as a developing structure of religious thought which becomes more complicated and at the same time more clearly defined.

Smart's *Translation of the Psalms of David, Attempted in the Spirit of Christianity, and Adapted to the Divine Service* is, as its lengthy subtitle suggests, hardly a translation at all. Some of the versions are fairly faithful renderings of the originals, but many could be better described as variations upon themes suggested by the Psalter, and there are also many which amount to virtually original compositions. Smart's statement as to his procedure, given in a prefatory note, is quite clear: "In this translation, all expressions, that seem contrary to Christ, are omitted, and evangelical matter put in their room." This method has produced some rather surprising changes. For example, the hatred and desire for vengeance which is the subject of so many of the Psalms is not to be found in Smart's version, its place being taken by expressions of Christian love and forgiveness. There is no smiting of cheek-bones and breaking of teeth. When the Psalmist cries out against his enemies, "Destroy thou them, O God; let them perish through their own imagination," Smart prays, "Save them, Jesu, lest they perish / Thro' their own debas'd conceit." This example is typical of the entire work.

This evangelical interpretation of the Psalms was not a new procedure in English versification. The germ of such a treatment had first appeared in Archbishop Parker's *The Whole Psalter* (1557?), and was adopted in some measure by John Patrick in *A Century of Psalms* (1679). The writer who had carried the method farthest before Smart was Isaac Watts in his *Psalms of David Imitated in the Language of the New Testament*, 1719. Smart, however, is much more consistent and thoroughgoing than Watts. Watts often preserves the unsparing, self-righteous God of the Psalmist, but Smart has completely done away with this barbaric Jehovah and substituted the figure and teachings of Jesus. One should compare the Prayer Book version (the text Smart used) of Ps. vii with Smart's (p. 121) to see a fine example of his methods. Watts did not modify, in his version, the Psalmist's picture of the vindictiveness of God. Smart changes the whole meaning of the poem completely: the bow bent to shoot the arrow of vengeance is metamorphosed into the rainbow, the heavenly promise of mercy; the swords of an avenging God are turned into shepherd's crooks, and His darts and spears are beaten into pruning-hooks; even the phrase, "Behold, he [the wicked] travaileth with mischief," becomes, most surprisingly:

> Behold a virgin has conceiv'd
> By congress undefil'd
> And lost Jeshurun is retriev'd
> By an almighty child.

Perhaps the most daring of all Smart's modifications is found in Psalm liv, where David's prayer for strength against his enemies becomes a free rendering of Christ's agony in the garden. This kind of extreme alteration makes Smart's version a quite different thing from the usual versified Psalter. It cannot be called a volume of original religious poetry, but there is certainly more of Smart than of the various Psalmists in it.

Smart's rather arbitrary practice of writing exactly one stanza for each verse in the Prayer Book Psalter (there are only two exceptions in the entire book) made necessary a great deal of expansion, and it is frequently the "evangelical matter" which accounts for it. The poet had remarked in his prefatory note, that "the reader will find sundry allusions to the rites and ceremonies of the Church of England." These are fairly numerous, and they offer interesting sidelights not only on the personality of Smart but also on his method of assimilating the material of his text. The emotion of faith, as expressed by the Psalmist with the words, "My trust is in the tender mercy of God for ever and ever," is most logically translated into the emotion of faith as it springs up in the heart of the translator:

And rooted in the church I place
My trust in Christ's eternal grace.   (Ps. iii, 9)

"And so I will go to thine altar" becomes

And so prepared will I be seen
Thine eucharist to take.   (Ps. xxvi, 6)

Similarly, petitions for the deliverance of Israel become prayers for the laity and clergy of the Church.

The expansion necessitated by Smart's method permitted a free rendering of the book into a collection of poems which seem often the production of the translator rather than the original author's. But it also exposed Smart at every turn to the temptation of padding, the curse of most versifiers of the Psalter. The better translators have met the problem by using short meters and by making no effort to follow the divisions of thought in the divisions of their stanzas, or by omitting material at will and rearranging in a completely arbitrary fashion. Smart's rendition, on the other hand, contains almost always more material than the original.

The remarkable thing is that with all this expansion, Smart is very seldom guilty of mere padding. Such useless extra lines as "to dress the vine-clad elm" in Psalm vii are really surprisingly rare. A stanza which will illustrate some of the methods of expansion normally used is the following. The original runs: "Confounded be all they that worship carved images, and that delight in vain gods: worship him, all ye gods." (Ps. xcvii, 7.)

Shame on the seeker after signs
That vanity and vice enshrines
And serves the prince of hell;
Hear at his word, ye painted stocks,
And worship him, ye chissel'd rocks,
And fall as Dagon fell.

This is simply an elaboration of the original theme; nothing extraneous is introduced. The additional material is implied in, or flows naturally out of, the simple words of the text. Yet each new bit that Smart adds sheds a further light on the subject, presents it from a slightly different point of view, or explains its nature in a new way. Noteworthy is the parallelism in lines four and five. This sort of doubleness of statement, which is always much more than mere repetition, is a marked characteristic of most sacred Hebrew poetry. It represents in reality a way of thinking, and Smart's use of it here, where it is not immediately suggested by the text, is significant. It is important to notice, however, that although Smart's manner of *seeing* and *thinking* with regard to this particular bit of imagery is distinctly Hebraic, his manner of *speaking* (his actual vocabulary and syntax) is definitely not.

Often the expansions do not elaborate the text in this way, however, but are used in an attempt to bring into a clearer light the simple material of the psalm, without adding to that material. One feels again and again that Smart has found the imagery of the text complete and in need of no explanation; in such cases he seems to try to present that image in the most brilliant light possible, heightening and making more vivid with the extra words which his stanza form permits him. For this purpose he naturally relies largely on the concrete verbs and nouns with which the language is so plentifully supplied. Psalm lxxx offers a good example. This is the psalm which contains the beautiful simile of the vine (the Children of Israel) which the Lord has planted and cultivated and then left. Now, says the Psalmist, "The wild boar of the wood doth root it up: and the wild beasts of the field devour it" (ver. 13). Smart takes this verse, the first half clear and concrete, the second vague and general, and by clothing the whole in strong nouns and verbs and using two adjectives which contain as much action as verbs, gives the following lively and accurate lines:

> The furious boars with greedy tusk
> The ranges overturn,
> And goats and foxes to the husk
> The luscious bunches churn.

Often in Smart's version a general statement will be taken apart, and for one inclusive phrase he will substitute a group of phrases each presenting a specific part of the whole. For example, in Ps. lxxxix, 39, the sentence, "Thou hast overthrown all his hedges and broken down all his strongholds," becomes

> Around his borders are infring'd
> And all the tow'rs he barr'd;
> The moats filled up, the gates unhing'd,
> The strong munitions marr'd.

Here again the effect of brilliant clarity is achieved by the use of concrete nouns and verbs.

Sometimes for a general idea or situation only one specific example is substituted, in cases where the clear depiction of a single instance will heighten the emotional effect. A fine example of this method is shown in the following (Ps. xlviii, 6):

For fear took hold upon them there,	Fear came there upon
And anguish working on despair	them, and sorrow:
Confounded man and steed;	
Such are the terror and the cries	as upon a woman in
Of some base harlot when she dies	her travail.
Of an abortive seed.	

Another method of expansion used by Smart is the introduction of images and figures not in the original text nor even necessarily implied but which yet fit into the general effect. Their fitness arises from the fact that Smart selects them with an eye for the nature of his subject rather than for the wording of the individual verse of his text. Thus, "Thou makest us to be rebuked of our neighbours" (Ps. xliv, 14), becomes

> Each neighbour licens'd to contest
> Our bounds, his venom spurts.

The introduction of the vivid serpent-metaphor definitely heightens these lines. A more extended image introduced in this fashion is seen in Ps. lxiv, 8:

Yea, they their dealings shall impeach	Yea, their own
With their own tongues, and make a breach	tongues shall
Upon the webs they spun.	make them fall.

A very fruitful kind of expansion is found in Smart's use of expository material from Hebrew history and customs. In handling this device, as in others we have noticed, it will be found that he always seeks to interpret the abstract thought of the Psalmist by means of a concrete image. A good example is this, from Ps. cxix, Mëm, 2:

I through thy spirit am discreet	Thou through thy command-
Beyond my foes and their deceit,	ments hast made me wiser
Beyond my rivals wise;	than mine enemies: for
For I thy word about me bear,	they are ever with me.
As bracelets on my wrist I wear,	
And frontlets on my eyes.	

Here the bracelets and frontlets refer to the custom among the Israelites of wearing phylacteries, *i.e.*, lockets which contained bits of the law written within them; a custom traceable to the exhortation in Deuteronomy, vi, 8: "And thou shalt bind them (these words, which I command thee this day) for a sign upon thine hand, and they shall be as frontlets between thine eyes" (cf. also Ex. xiii, 16, and Deut.

xi, 18). Of a similar nature is the modification in Ps. cv, 14, in which the phrase, "but reproved even kings for their sake," becomes

> And for the virtue of their wives
> He mighty kings reprov'd.

This bit of explanatory material can only refer, it seems to me, to the incident of Abraham's sojourn with Abimelech (Genesis, xx), a story which Smart was later to make the subject of an oratorio.

Finally, there is the general elaboration and expansion resulting from combinations of these various methods. One example will serve to show the kind of result Smart obtained in this way. It is from lxxxii, 6-7:

I called your origin divine,	I have said, Ye are
And prais'd the lustre of your line	gods: and ye are
Ye bore your heads so high,	all the children
As sons of God, and nothing less,	of the most Highest.
Ye were so guarded of access,	
So haughty of reply.	
But ye shall share the common lot	But ye shall die
With them whose worldly goods ye got,	like men: and fall
The wretches ye enslave;	like one of the
And he, whose angel comes by stealth,	princes.
Shall take your princedom, pride and wealth,	
And sink them in the grave.	

Besides the elaborate modifications of the material of the Psalms, there is a further element which contributes to the seeming originality of Smart's "translation." This is the poet's attempt to write in what he considered the Horatian manner (see Introduction, pp. 67 ff.). It is the mingling of the Hebraic splendor and license with the "unrivalled peculiarity of expression" which Smart admired so much in Horace that is responsible for passages like the following:

Though ye the bitter bondage wept,	Though ye have lien among
And midst Rhamnesian tripods slept,	the pots, yet shall ye be
Hereafter is your own;	as the wings of a dove,
Ye shall as turtle-doves unfold	that is covered with silver
The silver plumage winged with gold,	wings, and her feathers
And make melodious moan.	like gold.
	—Ps. lxviii, 13

Smart saw the effectiveness of this strange union, according to his own taste, in this translation of the Psalms. In his original religious poetry he also used these two elements which he had so successfully blended, as will be seen in the *Hymns and Spiritual Songs* and *A Song to David*.

For anyone acquainted with the Prayer Book or the Authorized Version, a discussion of the intrinsic merit of any verse translation of the Psalms in English may seem little profitable. Ordinarily, in the work of any of the dozens of versifiers who have set themselves the task, if one can point to an occasional development of the thought or here and there single out examples of felicity in expression the effort seems justified. Smart's work is better than this. We have seen that it may almost be regarded as a collection of original poetry. Certainly the value of the work is not the value one expects in a translation. Smart's *Psalms* are not translations: they are Christian meditations suggested by a reading of the Psalter.

Their value is threefold. The reader approaching them for the first time may be most excited by the light they throw upon *A Song to David*, and certainly the student of that great poem will find much enlightenment in them. Other readers, however, may prefer to consider them alone. Read simply as a series of Christian poems they reveal an interesting personality and an intense religious experience. But their greatest value lies, it seems to me, in their intrinsic merit when considered purely as poetry. One must admit, of course, that they are very uneven in quality, and that blemishes are all too frequent. But when all deductions of this sort have been made, there still remains a great deal of brilliant writing.

Hymns and Spiritual Songs

Thirty-five "hymns and spiritual songs for the fasts and festivals of the Church of England" comprise the second section of the large volume which Smart published in 1765. These poems, perhaps the most valuable of his work aside from the *Song*, have suffered almost complete neglect from the time of their publication until the present. In the only contemporary review of the volume which I have found,[1] there is no mention of them. In 1825 Smart's daughter, Elizabeth LeNoir, made an effort to recall some of them to the attention of the literary world by printing them in an appendix to the two-volume collection of her own *Miscellaneous Poems*. In her prefatory note, she remarked that the *Psalms* and *A Song to David* are very poor stuff, but added: "Of the Hymns here selected, she has a different

---

[1] *Critical Review*, September, 1765, xxv, 310. In this article Smart's *Psalms* are compared with Merrick's, to the advantage of the latter.

opinion, conceiving that they possess so much originality, ardent piety, and true poetic fire, as cannot but render them acceptable to readers of taste and sentiment." She then reprinted eight of the poems, but not without considerable alterations in which she did her blue-stockinged best to make them "acceptable" to those eminently respectable readers of hers. Since Mrs. LeNoir's poems did not command much attention from the literary world, her filial endeavors did not succeed in restoring her father's reputation.

The late nineteenth-century admirers of the poet were apparently unaware of the existence of the *Hymns and Spiritual Songs*. In 1900 Thomas Seccombe mentioned them in a sentence of his *The Age of Johnson*, and in 1928 Oliver Elton referred to "his *Hymns*, some of which . . . have their own beauty, and also that touch of oddness which in Smart is inseparable from the beauty" (*Survey of English Literature, 1730-1780*, ii, 84). Mr. McKenzie has discussed them briefly (*Christopher Smart: Sa Vie et Son Oeuvre*), indicating certain parallels in thought and material between them and *A Song to David*. The reprinting of a few extracts in Mr. Blunden's edition of the *Song* has been the only effort, I believe, to make any of these poems generally available to the modern reader, although Ainsworth and Noyes have quoted many fragments from them in their excellent *Christopher Smart: A Biographical and Critical Study*.

The poems included under this general title are a series of lyrics designed to be read or sung upon the various principal days of the Church calendar. They comprise a fairly complete "Christian year," and it is interesting that a collection so modeled should precede Keble's similar volume by a full half-century. The plan is of course not entirely new in English literature. More than a century before Smart's volume appeared, George Wither had produced *Hymns and Songs of the Church* (1623), the second part of which contains a group of hymns for special days, beginning with Advent and roughly following the calendar of feast-, fast-, and saints'-days. The verse is bad, and there is no indication that Smart ever saw the volume. Nevertheless, Wither got a patent from the king that his *Hymns* should be bound up with his *Metrical Psalter* for the use of the Church, and it is possible that Smart had the idea of his collection from this book.

There are examples of individual hymns for special days in the work of many writers of religious verse, notably in Herrick's *Noble Numbers* (1647), Crashaw's *Steps to the Temple* (1646), and Herbert's *The Temple* (1633). Jeremy Taylor's *Festival Hymns* represent an incomplete calendar, from Advent through Whitsunday, but they can hardly have been intended to be sung. As a complete calendar of respectable poetry, however, Smart's book stands alone between Wither and Keble. In my opinion it is decidedly better than either, although some readers may prefer the pleasant flowing verses of the later man.[2]

The religion of Christopher Smart, of which these hymns give the most comprehensive statement, has been discussed in some detail in the Introduction to the present volume, and need not be re-analyzed here. However, there is one point that is of sufficient importance to need some expansion. This is Smart's concept of the tri-partite nature of man. It grows out of his interest in angelology, about which subject he utilized all the material he could find. In the *Psalms* he frequently added angelical lore to the text before him, and his strictly original verse is even richer in this material. There is good Scriptural authority, either canonical or apocryphal, for his ideas concerning the angels of the Presence (Hymns i, vi, and xxxiii), angels as heavenly messengers (Hymns ix and xxiv; *Song to David*, xix), angels joining with men in acts of worship (Psalm cxi; Hymns iv and xxiv), and angels as national guardians (Psalm cxxv, xviii, xxii, and lxviii; Hymns xxiv and xxvi). A more original idea is that each individual has his tutelary angel. He had suggested this in Psalm xvi, 9, when he translated "for he [God] is on my right hand" with the phrase "his good angel guides my hand." He considered this spiritual guide not so much an outside influence, however, as an essential part of man—one element, in fact, of man's triune nature. There is a hint of this in Psalm xli, 12, where the Psalmist's "shall set me before thy face forever" becomes "shall take my soul to dwell Where now my angel stands." Smart must have considered this change to represent "evangelical matter," for he seems to have derived it from Matthew xvi, 10: "Take heed that ye despise not one of these little ones; for I say unto you, that in heaven their angels do always behold the face of my Father which is in heaven."

That this theory developed in his mind into a clear doctrine of trichotomy (a heresy, incidentally) is shown conclusively in his poem on the Holy Trinity (Hymn xvi):

> Man, soul and angel join
> To strike up strains divine;
> . . . .
> For angel, man and soul
> Make up upon the whole

[2] I think it probable that Keble had read at least *A Song to David* and perhaps also the *Psalms* and *Hymns*. There are some interesting parallels.

> One individual here,
> And in the highest sphere;
> Where with God he shall repose,
> From whose image first he rose.—St. 5 and 6.

A recognition of this element in the poet's belief makes readily understandable his otherwise puzzling description of David as "man, soul and angel without peer" (*Song to David*, xv). The last two lines quoted also explain what was to Smart a perfectly logical basis for his opinion. When he says in the *Song to David*, xlii, "Man's made of mercy, soul and sense," he reveals in a few words a great deal about his conception of the threefold nature of man. Here "sense" corresponds to "man" in the passages cited above: it is the rational, earth-bound, three-dimensional part of one. "Mercy," corresponding to "angel," is that part of a human being which is divine, the purely spiritual essence, through which alone one may approach the throne of God; and by the designation "mercy" it is shown that this part of one partakes in an absolute sense of the nature of Deity (cp. Hymn vi, *The Presentation*, st. 16). Between these two is the "soul," a receptive and communicative agent, bringing to the "sense-man" nature intuitive glimpses of the eternal and the divine, and judging the flights of the "angel-mercy" by the aid of human reason. In these lines from Hymn xi, 22, the point is emphasized by a careful juxtaposition of the two words which connote intuition and reason:

> And each *man* in his *spirit knows*
> That *mercy* has no bounds.

Stylistically, the *Hymns* follow lines already developed in the *Psalms* and discussed at length in the Introduction. Material definitely Hebraic in origin is frequently poured into a sort of Horatian mold, and there are many examples of the consciously "peculiar" phrase. At times Smart even alters the natural order of whole phrases for the purpose of emphasis.

The most interesting technical feature of these poems, however, is one which, in the Introduction, I have compared with counterpoint in music, and which should now be examined. It arises from a sense of arrangement, which Smart developed to a fairly high point. It will be helpful first to glance at the Hymns as a whole, for the group is artfully arranged in a unit by the simple and ancient device of linking, much as are the lovely stanzas of the fourteenth-century *Pearl*. In the last stanza of Hymn i are the lines,

> Christ his *blessing* universal
> On th' *arch-patriarch's* seed bestow,

and the second hymn opens with the line, "When *Abraham* was *blessed*." Hymn ii ends,

> This is my HEIR of GRACE,
> In whose *perfections* I rejoice.

The poem which immediately follows begins, "GRACE, thou source of each *perfection*."

This method is carried through the entire book. Sometimes the links are not quite so obvious, as when the mention of "Peter's tears" in the last line of Hymn vii suggests as the opening line of Hymn viii, "Hark! the cock proclaims the morning." The subtlest link is that between Hymns x and xi. The first of these, on "The Crucifixion," ends with the word "sleep"; and "Easter Day," which follows, begins with the word "Awake." But the entire group are knitted together, one after another like flowers in a wreath, and when the reader comes to the last line of the last poem,

> Till all nations have concurr'd
> In the worship of the WORD

his mind returns immediately to

> WORD of endless adoration,
> Christ, I to thy call appear;
> On my knees in meek prostration
> To begin a better year.—Hymn i, stanza i.

The garland of the year is a perfect circle.

Within the individual poems Smart quite often arranged his material to achieve a similar tightly unified structure. In Hymn i, for example, there is a very formal arrangement. Here the statement of the first theme is followed by a statement of the second (st. 1-3). Then follows an elaboration of 1 (st. 4) and of 2 (st. 5-6). These two themes are woven together in stanzas 7 and 8, and out of them comes the third theme, which is elaborated in the final stanzas. A similar treatment is used in Hymn ii, with the addition of certain contrapuntal effects.

An interesting example of the frequent "cross reference" of his lines is found in the last stanza of Hymn ix ("The Annunciation"):

> Praise him faith, hope, and love
> That tend Jehovah's dove;
> By men from lust repriev'd
> As females best conceiv'd;
> To remount the man and muse
> Far above all earthly views.

The two middle lines are very strange, and it is just possible that the printer has got them in the wrong order. As they stand, however, the thought is expressed backwards. The lines mean: "As women have conceived the best offspring when their children were begotten by men who had been reprieved from lust." The lines still seem odd, however, until we notice that they refer back to "the three Who sang in Mary's key," mentioned in the preceding stanza. These three were Hannah, Sarah, and Elizabeth. In the case of the last two, their husbands were very old when their children were conceived, yet these children were Isaac and John the Baptist. Hannah of course considered herself barren before the birth of Samuel. There is a further reference back to the lines about Gabriel in the second and third stanzas of the poem, for before the birth of each of these men heavenly voices announced their advent to one or other of their parents. Woven around the main theme of the miraculous conception are the subsidiary themes of purity and mystery, of the "usual means and ends" seen in "nature's plainest course," and the great counter-theme of praise expressing itself in the songs of men and of angels. The chief virtue of Smart's composition (which for all its interest is not one of his finest poems) is that he has treated all these themes clearly and distinctly, yet all are bound inextricably together. He touches first one stop, then another, and sometimes two or three at once, yet the reader is never distracted from the real subject of the annunciation, for all are in perfect harmony with it.

From such experiments in arrangements Smart learned the deepest secret of his art, knowledge of which enabled him to touch at one small point the work of the greatest poets. He discovered that the words of genuine poetry do not merely "mean"; they also refer, and the extent of their reference is perhaps the surest test of their validity. I do not know whether he was aware that when the captain tells Hamlet,

> We go to claim a little patch of ground
> That hath no honour in it but a name

the points of reference in the two men's minds are miles apart; that the speaker is talking prose while Hamlet is hearing poetry; and that the universality of reference which flows naturally out of these simple words makes them an example of consummate art. It is certain, however, that such words as "born," "mann'd," "remount" (to mention only a few) did not find their way into the poem we have been discussing accidentally.

This elaborate arrangement and disposition of material, so that the words of a poem are constantly calling across whole stanzas and passages to each other, and are constantly summoning around the immediate idea a whole group of related and harmonious ideas from other parts of the poem, is displayed at large in *A Song to David*, where it accounts for much of the complexity and the splendor of the poem. Its use there is discussed in the notes.

There is a further device of technique frequently used by Smart which may be illustrated by many passages in the *Hymns*. It is that which some modern poets and critics have called "telescoping": the trick of compressing several images into one. Two examples will have to suffice here. The first is in this stanza from Hymn xii:

> To whom [Christ] belong the tribe that vie
> In what is musick to the eye,
>   Whose voice is "stoop to pray"—
> While many-colour'd tints attire
> His fav'rites, like the golden wire,
>   The beams on wind flow'rs play.

The immediate image in the last three lines is a bed of anemones in a shady part of a wood, where the sunlight comes down between the leaves in small rays. The sunbeams look like golden wires, and from this Smart makes his metaphor of the Aeolian harp, which he points by the words "musick," "play," and the deliberate choice of "wind flow'rs." The symbol which rises out of this image and this metaphor is simply Smart's favorite theme of universal praise.

A better illustration of telescoping is found in the eighth stanza of one of Smart's loveliest lyrics, Hymn xxxii, *The Nativity*, a poem which also reveals the ingenuity of Smart's intricate arrangements of material. Here he writes:

> Spinks and ouzles sing sublimely,
>   "We too have a Saviour born";
> Whiter blossoms burst untimely
>   On the blest Mosaic thorn.

Smart is thinking of the Glastonbury thorn, which bloomed at Christmas and which was traditionally said to spring from the staff of Joseph of Arimathea. But the word "Mosaic" connects this image with another blossoming staff, the rod of Aaron, which burst into bloom in the tabernacle as a sign of the selection of the Levites to be priests (Numbers xvii). This latter event being taken as an adumbration of the ministry of Christ, the reference becomes clear.

All these elements—the heavy use of material and methods derived from Hebraic poetry, the attempt to achieve in English something of the strange felicity of Horace, the baroque elaboration produced by complex arrangement of ideas, and the telescoping of images into tightly packed units—make of the *Hymns and Spiritual Songs* a fascinating study in poetics. But they should have a wider appeal than this, for the technique is not so difficult as to obscure for the general reader their more ordinary virtues. Few collections of religious verse offer more in richness of description, beauty and variety of melody, and range of emotion.

A Song to David

This poem, unquestionably Smart's masterpiece, was first printed on April 6th, 1763, and was reprinted only once during the eighteenth century, when Smart added it to his volume of *Psalms* in 1765. Like many other great poems it met with a very poor reception. Mason's remark in a letter to Gray is typical of the contemporary attitude: "I have seen his Song to David and from thence conclude him as mad as ever." After Browning's championship of the poem over a hundred years later, criticism swung to the opposite extreme, and Rossetti proclaimed it "the only great *accomplished* poem of the last century." Both these extreme opinions rest on the assumption that the poem is the product of insanity, and there is a moral for the critic in their quaint contrast: the one represents the final stultification of the neo-classic impulse; the other is the wild exaggeration of a romanticism gone to seed. Most readers today would agree with the anonymous reviewer who wrote in the *Times Literary Supplement* (April 6, 1922): "To us there is in its strange beauty and tenderness much unevenness, some obscurity—though no more than in many of the greatest of the world's poets—and not a hint of insanity or derangement." At any rate, we can no longer presuppose the author of *A Song to David* to have been an inspired madman (or, as Mason thought, simply a madman) and read the poem in the light of that prejudice. It will be better to read the poem first and judge of the condition of its author's mind when it was composed from the evidence there presented.

Nevertheless, *A Song to David* is what some people call a "difficult" poem. It is no poem for an idle hour, for it makes very serious demands upon its readers. It is complicated to an extraordinary degree. The following notes, it is hoped, may clear up some of the difficulties and possibly remove some of the obscurities. At least it may be shown that the unusual features of the poem are quite logical and comprehensible. One of the causes for the "obscurities" in the poem is that Smart brought to his task a mind richly stored with information gathered from a variety of sources, some of which are not at all widely known. Mr. Stead, in his admirable edition of *Rejoice in the Lamb*, has demonstrated beyond question that Smart was possessed of a phenomenal memory and that he ransacked it for material to insert into the long manuscript composed during his illness. Hundreds of people whom he had met at one time or another, an even greater number of characters he had read about in the Bible and elsewhere, and a prodigious multitude of animals, birds, fish, reptiles, plants, and even stones whose English, Latin, or Greek names he had come across years before in the works of a variety of "natural historians"—all these, together with a strange assortment of "facts" gathered from scientists, pseudo-scientists, and mystics, are brought together in the strange medley. To a much lesser degree, this recollection of details gathered from many sources is characteristic of *A Song to David*. There is a veritable "road to Xanadu" leading to the poem. In the following notes, some of the landmarks on that road will be pointed out and their contributions recorded. Here it must suffice to name the more important ones. Naturally, Smart draws heavily upon the Bible, especially the accounts of David's life in the books of Samuel. He uses the Genesis account of the creation in stanzas xxx to xxxvii, and the whole poem is enriched by material from the Psalms and from various other sacred books, both canonical and apocryphal. He also remembered a surprising number of details from a rhapsodical book called *An Historical Account of the Life and Reign of David, King of Israel*, written by Patrick Delany, the friend of Swift, and first published in London, 1740-1742. (My references below are by volume and page to the fourth edition, London, 1769.) Smart had read this book at least as early as 1755 (he refers to it in a footnote on the opening lines of *On the Goodness of the Supreme Being*), and it is not likely he had a copy by him when he composed *A Song to David*. Certainly he had never seen many of the animals, birds, fish, and other creatures mentioned in the poem, nor had he looked upon the landscapes his imagination constructs from hints given by the naturalists and travelers whose books he had read. When the reader, therefore, encounters the beautiful image

> And Ivis with her gorgeous vest
> Builds for her eggs her cunning nest (st. liii, 4-5),

he need not suppose, with Mr. A. Larkyn Williams, that *Ivis* should be emended to *Iris* on the ground that "it is surely more probable that the copyist mistook 'r' for 'v' than that Smart coined a meaningless term." (See Mr. Williams' letter in T.L.S., March 27, 1924).

Smart printed *Ivis* in both editions of his poem, and he even inserted a footnote to explain it: "a humming bird." Although neither Mr. Stead nor I have found the naturalist who is responsible for the term, there can be no doubt that the poet who knew the swordfish was called "xiphias" also had good authority for naming the humming bird "Ivis."

With such a background as I have suggested, of which his acquaintance with the Bible is the most important element, Christopher Smart set about writing *A Song to David*. He called it "a Poem composed in a Spirit of affection and thankfulness to the great Author of the Book of Gratitude, which is the *Psalms* of David the King" (in an advertisement of the first edition printed in *Poems on Several Occasions*, 1763). Certainly he could hardly have chosen a subject more congenial to his temperament or more suitable to his peculiar abilities. Early in his career he had been attracted to the figure of David as a possible subject (see Introduction, p. 66), and it is obvious that his study of the Psalms increased his admiration for the king as a poet. Furthermore, he read David's work as the "Book of Gratitude," finding that it stirred in him the deepest emotion of his religious life. Nothing could be more natural than that he should take the life and work of David as the central idea around which to construct his rhapsody on the meaning of religion. The main outlines of that religion have been discussed in the Introduction; along with the direct references to David, they constitute the principal matter of the poem, and an understanding of them will make *A Song to David* easily comprehensible on the first reading. In the major and minor themes which are woven around them, there is nothing particularly strange or difficult. The real difficulty of the poem, the extraordinary complexity which has puzzled readers, lies in Smart's technique of expression. Here also is the real power of the poem, in the sheer intellectual and artistic ingenuity with which the main themes are stated, elaborated, varied, and intensified by the manipulation of a number of minor themes around them.

In the larger problems of structure, or architectonics, Smart had early experimented with the climactic building up of a series of concepts which embody certain similarities; and his favorite use of such a method is found in the series which traces through the varied kingdoms of life. This has been noted in the early Seaton poems, in the *Hymn to the Supreme Being*, and in the *Psalms* and *Hymns*. It is the chief structural characteristic of the *Song*. The whole poem is a well-ordered sequence of such climactic series, joined by brief transitional passages, and grouped in an order which itself builds up to a terrific climax at the end. Smart has outlined the structure of his poem quite clearly in the "Contents" prefixed to it, and this analysis will be used as a guide when we come to examine the poem in detail. The point to be made here is that Smart was quite conscious of what he had done and was justly proud of his accomplishment when he wrote in the advertisement referred to above: "This Song is allowed by Mr. Smart's judicious Friends and enemies to be the best Piece ever made public by him, its chief fault being *the exact Regularity and Method with which it is conducted*." (Italics mine.)

Several critics have drawn attention to some of the architectonic features of the poem, and their studies may be summarized before turning to an examination of the arrangement of thought-sequences. Sir Edmund Gosse, in his essay on the Song (*Leaves and Fruit*, N.Y., 1927) has remarked on the orchestral effects of the poem, doubtless guided by the many references to music. Of the stanzas on the pillars of knowledge (xxx-xxxviii) he says, "Each is like a fresh blast upon the trumpet." He notes the repetition of the word "Adoration," which "from this moment (st. li) incessantly recurs with the blare of some brass instrument in an orchestra. And the writing from this point onward has an orchestral effect, as of a choral symphony, unseen figures of angelic ancestry joining in a loud unison of voice, harp, and clarion. . . . Presently the tumult of the symphony declines, and the flute is heard above the trumpet." Near the end of the poem, "once more the transport breaks forth and the brass instruments are dominant." This is of course impressionistic criticism, and it stems directly from Browning's rhapsodies, but it is important for calling attention to the musical analogies in the structure of the poem.

Much more sound and thorough is Signor Federico Olivero's investigation of the architectural symbolism of the *Song*.[1] This critic likewise takes a hint from Browning, one which he develops with considerable ingenuity. He writes: "In *Parleyings with certain people of importance in their Day* Robert Browning compares the poetic work of Smart to a large house full of uninteresting rooms in which, nevertheless, there is a single chapel of miraculous splendor. And the *Song to David* is indeed something of a temple in its precise, symmetrical, architectural structure. The poet himself has indicated the disposition or architecture of his work in a prefatory note. After a brief invocation to David, which may be compared to the steps by which one ascends to the lyrical temple, the façade appears, on which the figure of David is shown, as if in twelve statues in various atti-

---

[1] Cf. the essay "Il 'Canto a Davide' di Christopher Smart" in his *Studi Britannici*, Torino, 1931, pp. 105-126. All quotations are in my own translation.

tudes. . . . We enter thence into the temple . . . the radiant images that adorn stanzas xviii-xxvi give the impression of nine leaded windows, of rich colour and fantastic design, representing the subjects of David's poetry . . . ; we can imagine these windows arranged thus: four on each side of the church and a rose over the entrance. After a passage in which the poet exalts David, as if in two statues placed at the beginning of the nave, contrasting his strength and his sweetness . . . we see seven pillars, finely carved, which symbolize the wisdom of God as it appears in the seven days of creation. . . . The presentation of the precepts of the decalogue is wound about like a series of bas-reliefs on the walls of the church, . . . After having insisted on the profound sweetness of the precepts expressed in the lyric magnificence of the Psalter the poet prefigures, as in radiant pictures on the walls and the ceiling of the temple, the sense of adoration toward the Creator which he discerns in nature . . . and then turns to observe it in the operation of the senses . . . in stanza lxx he exalts the triumph of a chaste spirit over itself. He presents then—as in five shining mosaics in the apse—the emblematic images of Beauty, Strength, and spiritual Splendor, his observation of each being founded on reality; each finds its perfection in David, who stands forth—as in five statutes on the pinnacle that crowns the church—in triumphal attitude, the fundamental thought being reached in the exaltation of David as a prototype of the Saviour." This again is of course the kind of analysis one makes to please oneself. It is perhaps too precious for most readers, but it serves to call attention to such use of architectural imagery as there unquestionably is in the poem.

Signor Olivero performs a more permanent service to students of Smart's technique when he points out the extraordinary accuracy of arrangement of details. "In this lyric each image is not independent of the others, but they respond from stanza to stanza in a harmony that echoes long and far; it is not a rapid succession of unrelated pictures, but these images, which at a superficial glance appear disconnected, are disposed—although each forms a picture in itself—with skillful artifice into an intricate garland. The poet proceeds by comparison and contrast, which finds a counterpart in the progression of the thought, with perfect symmetry. Thus in stanza 75 he insists on the idea of *speed*, in stanza 76 on the idea of *force*; he considers each quality in animals; respectively in quadrupeds, birds, fish; thus the horse for speed (lxxv, 1) corresponds to the lion for force (lxxvi, 1), the ostrich [and, we should add, the glede] (lxxv, 2-4) to the eagle (lxxvi, 4), the swordfish (lxxv, 5-6) to the whale (lxxvi, 5-6).

. . . In stanza lxxxiv, 1-3, the image of *light*, exemplified in the splendor of the heavens, in the sun, stars, and comets, finds correspondence in the aurora borealis in st. lxxxv, 1; to the idea of *sound* expressed with the trumpet in lxxxiv, 4, responds the song to God, the thunder, the *hosanna*, the *amen* in lxxxv, 2-5. The image of the halcyon who builds her nest . . . on the sea, which conveys the idea of calm on the ocean in spring (st. liv), corresponds to the figure of the siren nursing her baby (st. lv), which adduces the same idea of serenity upon the water. Especially noteworthy is the elegance of the groupings—vines and oranges (lviii)—spice trees, peaches, and pomegranates (lx). Exotic trees, flowers, and fruits correspond to each other from strophe to strophe from st. liv to st. lxix: the cedars of Lebanon (liv, 1), the palm, the jasmine (lvi, 1, 4), pineapples (lxix, 2), sugar cane, cocoanuts (lviii, 1, 2), spices (lx, 2—lxviii, 1, 6). The images, grouped according to a certain affinity among themselves, are further arranged with well studied gradation and . . . the passage from one group to another is scarcey perceptible because of the distant echoes which chime to each other from strophe to strophe and give unity to the composition."

Finally, Professor Raymond D. Havens, in a valuable article on "The Structure of Smart's *Song to David*" (*Review of English Studies*, April, 1938) has shown how ". . . the poem is constructed throughout on one or another formal pattern. This attention to form extends even to the general divisions, which are made up almost entirely of stanzas grouped in threes, or sevens or their multiples—the mystic numbers. The *Song* begins with three stanzas of invocation, which are followed by fourteen (twice seven) describing David, by nine (thrice three) which give the subjects of which he sings, and by three recounting the results of his singing; then comes a group of nine consisting of an introductory stanza, seven devoted to the seven 'pillars of the Lord,' and a concluding stanza; then an introduction, a group of nine stanzas that summarizes the Biblical moral code, and a conclusion; then a stanza introductory to the three groups that follow, each of seven stanzas dealing with adoration; and finally five groups of three which treat of earthly delights and of the greater delight in each field to be found in God."

From a very careful analysis of the structure Professor Havens concludes that the poem "was constructed with unusual attention to parallelism, formal design, and pattern—to the ordered beauty of classic and neo-classic art." This is very true, and this analysis (with a very slight modification in the grouping of stanzas xlix-li, inclusive), together with Smart's "Contents," will be followed in the explanation of the arrangement of thought-sequences now to be given. In the manipulation of his ideas, Smart worked as logically and with as great wealth and variety of invention as in handling the basic structure and the decorative details of his poem. In the interweaving of themes and counter-themes, the poem is like an elaborate fugue.

Stanzas i-iii

The poem opens with an "Invocation," in which the two main themes of the entire composition are announced: David is hailed as the supreme poet and servant of God; and side by side with this is the theme of praise as an expression of gratitude. These two are to run through the whole poem, with the principal emphasis throughout stanzas iv-l on the first of them, and through stanzas li-lxxxvi on the latter. There is in these three stanzas a faint foreshadowing of one of the minor themes to be developed later in the poem, that of the tri-partite nature of man.[2] This reappears in the development of the second section (st. xv, 2) and in the recapitulation at the end of the third (st. xxvii-xxix).

Stanzas iv-xvi

This section deals, as Smart has indicated, with "the excellence and lustre of David's character, in twelve points of view, prov'd from the history of his life." That he attached great significance to this arrangement of twelve virtues may be seen from two passages in *Rejoice in the Lamb*:

> For there be twelve cardinal virtues—three to the East— Greatness, Valour, Piety.
>
> For there be three to the West—Goodness, Purity & Sublimity.
>
> For there be three to the North—Meditation, Happiness, Strength.
>
> For there be three to the South—Constancy, Pleasantry, and Wisdom. (xi, 60-63)

In another place he goes into greater detail, associating the virtues not in groups with the points of the compass but individually with the tribes of Israel and with certain of his contemporaries:

> For there be twelve cardinal virtues the gifts of the twelve sons of Jacob.
>
> For Reuben is Great. God be gracious to Lord Falmouth.
>
> For Simean is Valiant. God be gracious to the Duke of Somerset.

[2] Cf. notes on Hymn xvi, "Trinity Sunday" (p. 287).

For Levi is Pious. God be gracious to the Bishop of London.
For Judah is Good. God be gracious to Lord Granville.
For Dan is clean—neat, dextrous, apt, active, compact. God
be gracious to Draper.
For Naphtali is Sublime—God be gracious to Chesterfield.
For Gad is Contemplative—God be gracious to Lord North-
ampton.
For Ashur is Happy—God be gracious to George Bowes.
For Issachar is Strong—God be gracious to the Duke of
Dorsett.
For Zabulon is Constant—God be gracious to Lord Bath.
For Joseph is Pleasant—God be gracious to Lord Bolingbroke.
For Benjamin is Wise—God be gracious to Honeywood. (xviii,
21-33)

These virtues are not associated arbitrarily with the twelve sons of
Jacob: the associations are suggested either by the meaning of their
names (Genesis xxx), by the words of Jacob's blessing (Genesis xlix),
or by some such obvious fact as that the Levites were the priestly
tribe (hence, piety as their peculiar virtue). The evident reason for
Smart's description of David's character in terms of these twelve
virtues is that David may be shown as the embodiment of all that was
finest in the Israelites—the epic prototype of his people.

The development of this section is done with the utmost formality,
one stanza being devoted to each virtue. This is straightforward ex-
position, and naturally there is very little counterplay of themes.
There is also little difficulty in the material itself. Most of it is derived from Samuel, but certain ideas seem to have been suggested
by Delany, and may strike the reader as a little strange. For example,
there is no mention of divine inspiration ("the seraph in his soul")
in Samuel's account of David's plan for the temple (st. vii). Delany,
however (II, 5) describes David as "filled with the image of a glorious
and magnificent temple, impressed upon him by the immediate influence of the spirit of God," and in a footnote refers to I Chronicles
xxviii, 11-12. The last three lines of Smart's stanza refer to David's
actions when he was informed by Nathan that God would not permit him to build the temple, but that it would be built by his son.
Delany discusses this episode at some length (II, 5-14), devoting most
of his space to David's prayer of thanksgiving and praise (*i.e.*, "to
bless the welcome news") for the promise. David's *gratitude* is the
point stressed by Delany. In stanza xvi there are two ideas which are
made clearer by a reading of Delany. The first three lines refer to

the sin of David with respect to Bathsheba and Uriah, of which Delany says: "millions have been lost in these labyrinths of guilt; but none, sure, in any more intricate and perplexing than this! . . . millions have fallen, have sinned, as *David* did; but who ever repented and recovered like him? Revolve his whole life before this evil accident; it is almost one train of a wise, a generous, a pious, and a valiant conduct! Revolve his whole life, from the hour of this guilt, and you will find it little else than one train of humiliation, and repentance before God." The last two lines of the stanza contain an idea not mentioned, I believe, in the Bible, but Delany is again the source: "And that David was not wanting to his son, upon this subject [friendship], may very reasonably be concluded from the many excellent precepts, and fine reflections upon friendship, scattered through his *Proverbs.* [II, 326.] . . . As critics have considered the first nine chapters of the *Proverbs*, only as a preface to what is properly called the book of *Proverbs*, the attentive reader will find all the precepts, from the beginning of the fourth chapter to the end of the ninth, to be only recitals of David's instructions to his son *Solomon.*" (II, 299.) The final stanza of this section (st. xvii) in which, according to Smart, "He [David] consecrates his genius for consolation and edification," makes a transition to the second major section of the poem. Michal and Abishag are, respectively, David's first wife, and the Shunammite woman who nursed him in his last illness. In the Bible Abishag is nowhere referred to as David's wife, but Delany states very positively that she and David were married (II, 287), thus suggesting the present parallel to Smart.

Stanzas xviii-xxvi

In this section Smart summarizes the subjects of David's poetry, which are, according to his "Contents," "The Supreme Being, angels, men of reknown, [and] the works of nature in all directions, either particularly or collectively considered." Many of the images in the last six stanzas of this section are derived, quite naturally, from Psalm civ.

It is in this section that he begins to use his method of introducing minor themes into the development of the theme immediately dominant. Here, against the background of David's nature poetry, appears the little theme of the contrast between the natural and the cultivated, which runs as an undercurrent through the rest of the poem. It is a result of Smart's early speculations on the various manifestations of praise, and of his perception of praise rising spontaneously from natural objects as well as from reasoning man. In the present stanzas it is pointed by such juxtapositions as "They that make music, or that mock," "The quail, the brave domestic cock," and the contrasted groupings in the other stanzas. This motif is treated with a very nice contrapuntal effect in stanza xxv, where Smart, by an ingenious arrangement, has contrived to state his theme four times but with regularly alternating reference. The first two animals are wild, but while one is merely taking a natural delight in life the other is "plodding his task." Similarly the two domesticated animals are presented, the rabbit working away at her home and the kids indulging in pure enjoyment. This little theme appears and reappears in later sections.

Stanzas xxvii-xxix

These three stanzas are devoted to the results of David's singing, or, as Smart puts it, "He obtains power over infernal spirits, and the malignity of his enemies; wins the heart of Michal." In the brief working out of these subjects, there is a suggestion again of the "Angel, soul, and man" concept which Smart had announced in stanza xv, and which is developed in Hymn xvi and elsewhere.

Stanzas xxx-xxxviii

This passage on the intellectual life has given pause to critics since the poem's first publication. Its central meaning, according to Smart, is that "[David] shows that the pillars of knowledge are the monuments of God's works in the first week." This is perfectly clear, but Smart's habit of making reference to several concepts outside, yet consonant with, the principal theme makes the section very closely packed with meaning. Smart believed in a completed universe, created in the traditional seven days of divine activity. The sum of all possible knowledge, therefore, would be comprehended in the knowledge of the works created in each of the seven divisions, and it is this knowledge which Smart found in David. He takes as his symbol for this idea the traditional "pillars of knowledge," which are referred to in Proverbs ix, 1 (a passage he probably thought, with Delany, to have been written by David): "Wisdom has builded her an house; she hath hewn out her seven pillars." He therefore represents the divisions of creation in the description of carvings on the pillars.

But there is a subsidiary sequence of thought running through these stanzas and it is marked out by the Greek letters which serve as names for the columns. They are Alpha, Gamma, Eta, Theta, Iota, Sigma and Omega. It must be said at the outset that so far no completely satisfactory explanation has been offered for the poet's choice of letters. If they are an anagram, I have been unable to solve it. Commentators on the Proverbs have suggested for the seven pillars such interpretations as "the seven planets," "the seven days of the week," "the seven sacraments," "the schools of the prophets," *etc.*, but Smart's letters are not the initials of any of these groups. All readers of the poem have been puzzled by these letters, but no one since the poet's day has offered any explanation. When the poem was first reviewed by an anonymous writer in *The Monthly Review* (April, 1763, vol. 28, p. 320), however, the letters were commented on as follows: "These, we conjecture, are made choice of, as consecrated for the following reasons. *Alpha* and *Omega*, from a well-known text in the Revelation. *Iota, Eta,* and *Sigma* because they are used to signify our Saviour, on altars and pulpits. *Theta,* as being the initial of God; and *Gamma,* as denoting the number *three,* held sacred by some Christians." On the face of it, one is inclined to accept this interpretation as most probably the one in Smart's mind, but the evidence is not entirely conclusive.

Several facts lend credence to the belief that this explanation is correct. We know that Smart read this review. (See notes on stanza lv below.) If the reviewer erred in his interpretation, it is probable that Smart would have refuted the assertions and given his real meaning, either in some advertisement or in the second edition. It is possible that the anonymous reviewer discussed the matter with the poet. We know that some of the writers on *The Monthly Review* were acquaintances and intimates of Smart;[3] the three bits of interpretation offered in the article (on this passage, on stanza lv, and on stanza lxvi) are ingenious beyond the scope of the ordinary reviewer; and the whole tone of the review in this matter is one of confidence in the results. Finally, no other explanation of the letters has been offered which is satisfactory at all.

On the other hand, there are certain objections to the acceptance of this interpretation. It does not explain the order of the letters. Why, for instance, if *Iota, Eta, Sigma,* are to be so interpreted, do they occur in the order *Eta, (Theta), Iota, Sigma*? On metrical grounds, each fits one place as well as another. We may justly inquire, also, if this interpretation be right, why Smart did not incorporate this explanation also into the notes to the second edition, as well as the allusion to the 'large quadruped' in the note to stanza lv. Finally, the interpretation is somewhat makeshift, a fact that lends it less credence when one considers the almost mathematical regularity and logical construction of the poem as a whole. Such is the evidence. It seems

[3] Cf. the list given in Walter Graham's *English Literary Periodicals.* New York, 1930.

to me that the case for the anonymous reviewer's interpretation is the stronger, but the problem cannot be regarded as solved.

Two salient facts, with regard to Smart's methods of composition, however, emerge from this discussion. The first is that his device in this instance is not immediately successful. The second is that it is obviously quite deliberate. Here again, Smart was trying to add a minor theme, trying to increase the reference of his lines. He is writing on the subject of the intellectual life, using as his main themes "knowledge" and "the works of creation." He has adorned these ideas with the imagery of carved and decorated columns, and has related the whole passage quite definitely to his central subject, David, in the phrase, "such is thy science" (stanza xxxviii). But there is an additional theme, that of the curious names of the columns. If the anonymous reviewer's interpretation is correct, then it becomes clear that this subsidiary theme is the repeated names of the Deity, carrying the implied idea that all knowledge springs from and is comprised in the concept of God. As the reader peruses this discussion of human wisdom he is constantly reminded of the mystic names of the Father of all wisdom.

In the last stanza of this section, a little theme is brought forward for a moment which is to reappear later. It is the strength and sweetness of David's "harp" (*i.e.*, his poetry), symbolized in the lion and the bee. This little motif is developed beautifully in the concluding stanzas of the poem; lxxvi, 1-3 with lxxvii, 1-2, and lxxxiii, 4-6 with lxxxiv.

Stanza xxxix

A brief transitional passage, leading to the subject of the moral life to be developed in the next section. It contains one of the most beautiful statements of the doctrine of the Holy Trinity in our poetry. It also anticipates the combination of the teachings of God (Jehovah) and the teachings of Christ to be developed in the following section. There is also here a subtle reference to David. In the coming stanzas Smart intends to present David as a great moral teacher. He was probably aware that some readers might consider David less qualified for the task than he himself did, so he here reminds us that no mortal man is perfect.

Stanzas xl-xlviii

Smart now presents what he calls "an exercise upon the decalogue," which is in reality a discussion of the moral life of man, with David as the supreme example of the moral man. To accomplish this, Smart conceives of David as the link between Moses and Christ, the descendant of one and the ancestor of the other. Thus in David's life he finds the mingling of the Mosaic and Christian ethical codes. But there is more of Smart in these stanzas than of David, as we shall see. This section has been considered dull by some critics (it is entirely omitted in the *Oxford Book of Verse*), but it seems to me one of the most interesting sections of the poem, for the light it throws upon Smart's character and his religion. In his *New Translation of the Psalms* he had made a very thoroughgoing Christianization of the Hebraic material, and much of the same thing is evident in his dissertation on the moral life.

The first commandment, since it is the bedrock of both creeds, is presented simply in the revelation to Moses, with no specifically New Testament comment upon it (st. xl). Smart omits the second commandment, "Thou shalt not make unto thee any graven image," and this is rather surprising, for it would have provided a good opportunity for one of his strictures on the Roman Church. He very wisely kept such controversy out of his poem. The third commandment, "Thou shalt not take the name of the Lord thy God in vain" appears in stanza xli transformed into the Christian teaching, "Thou shalt not call thy brother fool" (Matthew v, 22).

Stanza xlii brings in again the theme of the tri-partite nature of man in the phrase "mercy, soul, and sense," words that correspond to "angel, soul, and man." The purity and goodness of man is evidenced by his being designed for peaceful pursuits, and this is pointed by the contrast with the unclean snail (cf. Leviticus xi, 30) and his brother, the whelk, which Smart, with an Horatian revival of an obsolete form, calls a wilk. This is preparatory to the main theme of the stanza, which is the fourth commandment, "Remember the Sabbath day to keep it holy." This Smart characteristically presents in a Christian version, with an idea derived from Luke xiii, 15, where Jesus, defending his healing on the sabbath, points out that even Pharisees loose their oxen and asses and give them rest and refreshment on the holy day. Smart had remarked in *Rejoice in the Lamb*, "For the merciful man is merciful to his beast, and to the trees that give them shelter," and his tenderness towards animals is charmingly illustrated here in his recollection that they, too, have a right to share God's day of rest.

In stanza xliii the subject is the fifth commandment, "Honour thy father and thy mother, that thy days may be long upon the land which the Lord thy God giveth thee," and is illustrated by Christ's submission to the will of His Father. The next two stanzas are among the most interesting of the group. Smart comes here to discuss the two most gross crimes, murder and adultery, but his natural delicacy does not permit him even to mention them. Instead of "Thou shalt not kill" we are given a passage which might have been written by a modern psychiatrist (if he were a poet), an exhortation to the creative use of the passions rather than a flat prohibition. The syntax of the stanza (xliv) is difficult. The verb *is* in line 1 is the predicate for the following subjects: *love, joy, hope's eternal fort, care*, and *rapture*. The last three lines may be paraphrased: "Care (in the sense of vigilance) is thine, to arouse thee from lethargy, in order that thou mayest curb concupiscence with fear (*i.e.*, in the fear of the Lord); and rapture is thine to transport thee." In stanza xlv, the only hint of the commandment, "Thou shalt not commit adultery" is in the line, "Remember thy baptismal bond" (". . . renounce . . . the carnal desires of the flesh . . ."). Woven around this is a little dissertation on refraining from that which is unnatural and unsuitable, with illustrations from the teachings of both Moses (Deuteronomy xxii, 10, 11) and Jesus (Matthew ix, 17).

The negative Mosaic commandment, "Thou shalt not steal," becomes in stanza xlvi the positive Christian injunction to practice charity. There is an echo from Romans x, 15 in the opening lines and a paraphrase of the Golden Rule in the last three. Smart has a charming remark on this subject in *Rejoice in the Lamb*: "For Tully says to be generous you must be first just, but the voice of Christ is distribute at all events" (xii, 24).

In a similar way, the ninth and tenth commandments are enunciated with Christian overtones in stanzas xlvii and xlviii, the former stanza being noteworthy for the pointed aphorisms with which it is concluded. (For the New Adam, cf. I Corinthians xv, 22 and 45.)

Stanzas xlix-li

At this point my grouping differs slightly from that of Dr. Havens. I take these stanzas as another group of three, serving as a transitional passage between the portions of the poem that are chiefly devoted to David and the sections devoted primarily to the great central theme of praise. This group, in other words, represents the central division of the thought of the poem. Up to this point the poet has been primarily concerned with his first major theme, *i.e.*, the presentation of David as the ideal man, the "man after God's own heart." We are constantly reminded that these studies of the natural man, the man as artist, as thinker, and as moral being all refer to him. Thus immediately after the "pillars of knowledge" stanzas Smart writes "O David, scholar of the Lord! / Such is thy science." Likewise the "exercise upon the decalogue" is definitely attached to David in the first stanza of this present transitional group: "O David, highest in the list / Of worthies." From stanza lii onward to the end, the theme of David is subordinate to the second major theme of the poem, the great theme of praise arising from a sense of gratitude. This group of three stanzas is therefore the most important transitional passage in the poem. The others (stanza xxxix and stanza lxiv) are only little bridges between two sub-divisions *within* a major division, and are given only one stanza each. This more important link is given three.

Smart accomplishes his transition by showing that David, in his function as moralist, teaches that the highest of all virtues is "the transcendent virtue of praise and adoration." Again Smart uses the familiar minor theme of "man - soul - angel." This is pointed in stanza xlix by the phrase "highest in the list of worthies" and by the reference to the "documents of men"; by "the gen'rous soul" in stanza l; and by the "ranks of angels" with "David in the midst" in stanza li.

Stanzas lii-lxiiii

The poem has now reached its great central theme, which is to be predominant through the remaining portions, and from this point onward the writing soars to heights unreached by any other religious lyric in the language. The theme of praise, which now comes to dominate all others, has been foreshadowed frequently up to this point, however. It was announced in the invocation, and it has been suggested repeatedly, much as the four-note motif in Beethoven's fifth symphony keeps recurring against the background of more immediate matter. (x, 3; xvi, 5; xx, 5; xxii, 6; xxxv, 3; xxxvii, 3; and xlvii, 2.)

Smart calls the first section of the "adoration" passage "an exercise upon the seasons and the right use of them," and he develops this theme in twelve stanzas arranged in groups of three corresponding to the twelve months grouped into the four seasons. Here Smart's method of packing into his lines specific reference to subsidiary themes appears at its most elaborate. There are in these stanzas at least five themes being developed simultaneously, all different yet all in harmony with one another.

The first, the theme of praise, is done most formally and obviously. "Adoration" occurs in the first line of the first stanza in the group, in the second line of the next, in the third line of the third stanza, and so on through the first six stanzas; the device is then repeated in the second group of six. The presentation of the other themes is done less artificially.

The second theme is that of the progression of the seasons from early spring to the dead of winter, which has already been mentioned. This is of course quite natural and predictable. The other themes in this passage are not so exactly implicit in the subject, but they are quite consonant with it. One of these is the idea of home, of peace and security in the domestic scene. This is suggested by the humming bird's nest, the mermaid caring for her baby, and, with special appropriateness in a poem about David, in the description of the children of Israel at peace in Canaan (st. lvi and lvii); it is also to be noticed in such phrases as "the social laugh" and "For adoration counts his sheaves / To peace, her bounteous prince." Finally, there is the phrase "the fencèd land" (lx, 4), which occurs frequently in descriptions of the Promised Land in both the Bible (where it is usually "the fenced cities") and in Delany. This theme is brought in again and connected with the principal symbol of the poem, David, in stanza lxxi, at the end of the series on the senses.

Closely related to this theme of peace and security in the home are two more of the subsidiary themes. The first of these is the contrast between the natural or wild and the domesticated, which has been noted in earlier sections of the poem. Here it is pointed out in the grouping of the images which in almost every stanza are arranged to show this contrast. Thus in stanza liii cultivated plants appear in the first three lines, wild birds and flowers in the last three; in lv the wild animals of the first three lines are seen in contrast to beasts in the ark. In stanza lvii the "pink and mottled vault" is the sky and the "opposing spirits" are storm clouds as symbols of warfare with the tribes living in and around the Promised Land; this image is contrasted with that of the boy peacefully floating in his canoe, reading and watching the fish. Stanza lv calls for some special comment. In the first edition, Smart had no note on this stanza. However, the reviewer who wrote on the poem in the *Monthly Review* (see above, p. 302) commented on it as follows: "Our Poet's allusions also, in this little piece, relate frequently to subjects too little known, and far fetched. Thus, 'For adoration beasts embark,' &c. We remember to have somewhere read, a strange story of a certain quadruped which puts to sea on a piece of timber to prey upon fish. But we have no account of such embarkation in any natural Historian of credit."

Smart apparently read this review, for when *A Song to David* was reprinted in 1765 he solemnly inserted the following footnote: "There is a large quadruped that preys upon fish and provides himself with a piece of timber for that purpose, with which he is very handy." I must say that this seems to me a piece of rationalizing on the part of the author. It seems obvious that Smart, when he wrote the lines, was not thinking of any such obscure quadruped, but merely of the animals in Noah's ark, and the parallel between their safety there and the safety of the eggs in the halcyon's nest. The insertion of this dubious footnote (in an attempt to placate the reviewers?) is the only indication I have found in his later work of lingering traces of his illness.

The second theme that is closely related to that of the domestic scene is one that traces the growth and development of a man. The stages of one's life from conception to manhood are pointed in the first six stanzas of this section: "eggs," "infant," "playsome cubs," the "wean'd adventurer" playing with his toys, and the "coasting reader" (which we have seen is an image taken from Smart's own boyhood). The theme thus specifically marked out is implied through the remaining stanzas, pointed by references to the "pilgrim," the laborer, *etc.*

Smart has contrived in this section to treat artistically his theme of the seasons and the right use of them, and to make it reinforce his great theme of praise. To these he has added the consonant ideas of the growth of man, of his peace and security within the home, and of the contrast between the sense of praise that is inculcated by training and that which rises spontaneously from nature. When such an intellectual feat is accomplished, as here, in exquisitely musical verse and adorned with harmonious and beautiful imagery, it is difficult to withhold from the author the highest praise.

Stanza lxiv

In this brief transitional passage, Smart moves from the first to the second section of his division on adoration. It is natural that David should be brought forward again, and natural that the control of passions should be mentioned, for the next section is to be "an exercise upon the senses," and how to subdue them.

Stanzas lxv-lxxi

Each of the five senses has a stanza devoted to it (in the order: touch, sight, hearing, smell, taste), but since Smart is apparently holding to his grouping of threes and sevens a little padding out is necessary. Stanza lxx therefore, as Dr. Havens says, treats of "the purification and sanctification of the senses"; but stanza lxxi has, so far as I can see, nothing to do with the senses. It is used to pick up again one of the minor themes from the preceding section and to re-introduce David ("O man of God's humility") but it does not fit precisely into any of the schemes we critics have figured out. We can be thankful for it as the exception which we can use to prove our rules.

In this section again there are some of the minor themes we have noted before. For example, the contrast between that which is cultivated and that which is natural appears in st. lxv, where the "scholar bulfinch" is placed against the "daring redbreast"; in the next stanza the scientific naming of the constellations is contrasted with the artless shine of the glowworm. The phrase, "The Lord's Philosopher," in this stanza calls for special comment. It seems somewhat obscure and strained at first sight, but Smart's astonishing memory apparently fished it up from one of Delany's footnotes: ". . . Doctor Patrick thinks, that the Greek word *Sophos*, which was originally the title of astronomers, might be derived from *Zoph*, which in Hebrew signifies a Prophet" (1, 16). Smart's phrase then becomes a happy epithet for David, and his use of it serves artfully to re-introduce the central symbol of his poem.

Stanzas lxxii-lxxxvi

The last triumphal series of the poem Smart called "An amplification in five degrees, which is wrought up to this conclusion, That the best poet which ever lived was thought worthy of the highest honour which possibly can be conceived, as the Saviour of the world was ascribed to his house, and called his son in the body." Here the central theme of David becomes dominant again, and all else is subservient to it. Each of the five "degrees" has three stanzas, the first two beginning with a positive adjective while in the third stanza the same adjective in the comparative degree is applied to David. There is in these fifteen stanzas very little of the extraordinary complication of theme we have noticed in earlier sections of the poem. There are echoes of many ideas previously mentioned, but for the most part the poem sweeps onward to its conclusion with nothing to distract from the transcendent figure of David. In this final summary of the character of the poet-king, Smart stresses again those elements of the religious life which were to him the sum of it all: David's gratitude, his faith, his prayer, his pure heart, and his salvation through Christ. Some readers may consider this an indulgent view of David, but they have only to reflect that in this poem, as in most great works of art, the real subject is the author. Smart had an intense religious experience, and this poem is his most triumphal expression of it.

The various analyses of the thought and imagery of *A Song to David* all point directly to one basic fact, an understanding of which is essential to any student of the poem: "the exact Regularity and

Method with which it is conducted." We are not accustomed to much complexity of thought or technique in the lyric form. But here is a poem packed with meaning, presenting a wide variety of ideas all knitted firmly to a single theme. Furthermore, the presentation of these ideas is itself complicated to a high degree by an extraordinary use of interlocking imagery, and a contrapuntal arrangement of themes. The exotic splendor of Hebraic coloring is heightened by a Horatian "peculiarity of choice diction." But it is one of the marvels of our literature that in all this complexity, in all this extended manipulation of an exceedingly difficult medium, there is not one false note. There is nothing else in English quite like *A Song to David*.

Minor Poems, 1761-1768

"The 100th Psalm" was published while Smart was still under confinement, and I have included it here as evidence of some literary activity during that time rather than because it has any particular merit. Dr. Dodd, the editor of the *Christian's Magazine*, apparently interested himself in the unfortunate poet, for he published not only this piece but also an "Epitaph on a Young Clergyman [Mr. Reynolds] at St. Peter's in the Isle of Thanet" in the magazine for August, 1761, an "Epitaph on the Rev. James Sheeles" in January, 1763, and reprinted the "Epitaph on Master Newbery" in March, 1762. He subscribed to Smart's *Psalms*, and in December, 1765, printed three pieces from the book (Psalms cxvii, cxxiii, and cxlii), apparently by way of advertising the work. In the complete translation, "The 100th Psalm" is replaced by a better version; this first attempt, however, has a certain importance. Together with the "Epitaph on a Young Clergyman," it shows that at least at intervals during his confinement Smart was able to write publishable verse.

He was released early in 1763, and on April 8 he published *A Song to David*. On the heels of this came a pamphlet entitled *Poems by Mr. Smart*, a copy of which Boswell sent to Sir David Dalrymple on July 30. This pamphlet contained the fable, "Reason and Imagination," together with "Ode to Admiral Sir George Pococke," "Ode to General Draper," and "An Epistle to John Sherratt, Esq." This last is interesting chiefly because of Smart's comments on the last days of his confinement, during which friends visited him and began to arrange for his release. It is clear that he attributed his freedom to the Sherratts, the ever-faithful Rolts, and Miss A. F. Sheeles of Queens-Square, the "sublime, transcendent maid" for whose brother (presumably) Smart wrote an epitaph. Aside from the Rolts, nothing else is known of these people who befriended the poet. However, the *Critical Review*, in a contemptuous notice of *Poems by Mr. Smart*, sneeringly remarked, "Did our criticism of Mr. Smart's last production [*A Song to David*] require any farther elucidation, we might produce the fact of his inscribing a poem to John Sherrat, Esq., and his encomiums upon one Rolt, whom the world has unanimously damned both as poet and historian" (July, 1763, vol. 16, p. 72). From such a sentence it is clear that the people who finally obtained release for Smart, and who thus made possible the poetry of his last eight years, were the kind of poor and simple people whom the sophisticates love to berate as "common." It is significant that it was they, and not the Johnsons or the Newberys or even Smart's own family, who welcomed his return to sanity and freedom.

By November of the same year (1763), Smart had issued another pamphlet, called *Poems on Several Occasions*. This one contained another fable, "Munificence and Modesty," a translation of "Epitaph from Demosthenes," and a group of occasional pieces: "Female Dignity, to Lady Hussey Delaval," "Verses from Catullus, after Dining with Mr. Murray," and epitaphs on Henry Fielding, The Rev. James Sheeles, and the Duchess of Cleveland (Smart's early benefactress, who had been dead for twenty years). The titles and dedications of many of these pieces and ones in the earlier pamphlet indicate that during his first year of freedom Smart was badly in need of money, and was trying by various means to recall former patrons and attract new ones.

The same impression is given by his next publication, another pamphlet, entitled *Ode to the Right Honorable the Earl of Northumberland . . . etc.*, which was published in July, 1764. This small collection contains, in addition to several more pieces of flattery addressed to prospective or actual patrons, three of the loveliest of Smart's secular lyrics. They are almost the only pieces from all his minor poetry of the last period that have hitherto been reprinted, and they deserve wider circulation. That Smart's occasional gift for deft light verse had not deserted him during his long period of intermittent insanity is admirably illustrated by "Where shall Caelia," which stands in pleasant contrast to the gentle melancholy of the other two lyrics.

The texts of Smart's two oratorios are, I am sorry to say, uncommonly dull. The recitatives are interesting, if at all, chiefly for the use of a conversational blank verse. The form is pliable in Smart's hands, and offers a nice contrast to the Miltonic blank verse of his earlier period. For the most part, however, *Hannah* and *Abimelech* are poor reading. It is only in the lyrics that they come alive on the printed page, as here and there a line lifts for a moment with the music Smart was master of in his better days.

"On Gratitude. To the Memory of Mr. Seaton" is here reprinted from the holograph copy in the Henry W. and Albert A. Berg Collection in the New York Public Library. This is presumably the manuscript from which John Drinkwater printed the poem in his *A Book for Bookmen* (New York, 1927), with some curious and unfortunate misreadings. The Drinkwater version is the only example of the poem hitherto in print, and no other manuscripts have been catalogued. Although the holograph is undated, the poem has every earmark of having been written during the latter years of Smart's life, and it is pleasant to think of the poet, in the midst of his afflictions, gratefully remembering the man whose bequest had made possible his early triumphs. The corrections Smart has made in this holograph are such as to suggest that he was not copying a poem previously composed, but that we have instead his actual first draft. If this is true, it gives us a very good idea of the speed, and often the carelessness, with which he wrote. The manuscript is reproduced opposite p. 122.

The Works of Horace

Since this great translation, together with the important critical "Preface" to it, has been discussed at length in the Introduction to the present volume, it is not necessary to say much about it here. To anyone interested in neo-classic poetry, the entire translation is worth serious study, both for its faults and for its many virtues, but it is hoped that the selections given will indicate something of its originality and force. That lines like "What stomachs have clowns to their broth?" and "Scoff o' the plaited coronet's refulgence" should have been fashioned in the age of Johnson is remarkable, but the surprise of single lines is less significant than the satisfying freshness of the whole work. Smart's memory has never been hurt, as he feared it might be, by his early prose version, and if this verse translation were as widely known the memory of its author would suffer even less.

The bibliography of the translation is simplicity itself. It was published once only, in a beautiful four-volume edition which is now to be found only in a few specialized collections, such as the Patterson Collection of Horace in the Princeton University Library, whose copy I have used. So far as I know, only two short odes have hitherto been reprinted, and I can find no critical comment on the book, either contemporary or later.

The dedication of the verse Horace to Sir Francis Blake Delaval brings to mind another well-to-do family whose patronage probably eased the difficulties of Smart's declining years. They were the sons of "old Delaval of Northumberland" and his wife, the former Rhoda Apreece. Smart's connection with them began after the liveliest member of the family, John Blake Hussey Delaval, arrived in Cambridge in October, 1746, enrolled at Pembroke, and engaged Smart as his tutor. Delaval did not remain a student long, however. On December 27, 1746, Gray wrote to Wharton in one of his numerous gossipy letters: "poor dear Mr. Delaval indeed has had a little Misfortune. Intelligence was brought, that he had with him a certain Gentlewoman properly call'd Nell Burnet, (but whose Nom de Guerre was Captn. Hargraves) in an Officer's Habit, whom he carried all about to see Chappels & Libraries, & make Visits in the Face of Day. the Master raised his Posse-Comitatus in Order to search his Chambers, & after long Feeling and Snuffeling about the Bed, he declared they had certainly been there. wch. was very true, & the Captain was then locked up in a Cupboard there, while his Lover stood below in order to convey him out at Window, when all was over. however they took Care not to discover her, tho' the Master affirm'd; had he but caught her, he would soon have known, whether it was a Man, or a Woman. upon this Mr. Del: was desired to cut out his Name, & did so: next day Dr. L: [ong] repented, & wrote a Paper to testify he never knew any Hurt of him, wch he brought to Dr. Whaley, who would have directly admitted him here [i.e., at Peterhouse] if Stuart had not absolutely refused. he was offer'd about at several Colleges, but in vain. Then Dr. L: call[ed] two Meetings to get him re-admitted there, but every one was inexorable & so he has lost his Pupil, who is gone, I suppose, to lie with his Aunt Price [Apreece]."

This episode ended "poor dear Mr. Delaval's" career at Cambridge, but it did not end the friendship with Smart. When he and his older brother Francis decided to get up a performance of *Othello* five years later in London, John Blake (who was to play the part of Iago) sought out his former tutor and prevailed upon him to write a prologue and an epilogue for it. The next news we have of the quondam student is his creation as Baronet in 1761. By 1763 he was married, for in that year Smart inscribed his poem "Female Dignity" to Lady Hussey Delaval. Two years later the translation of Phaedrus was dedicated to their little son, Master J. H. Delaval. By this time Sir John was M.P. for Berwick, a position he held until 1774 and had again from 1780 to 1786, two years before his death. In 1765, Sir John and his lady each subscribed for a copy of Smart's *Psalms*, along with Sir Francis and their youngest brother, Edward. The 1767 dedication to Sir Francis is evidence of the continuing efforts of the Delavals to assist the unfortunate poet. The friendship and patronage of this distinguished family over a period of twenty years is but another indication of the essential good nature and appealing personality of Smart.

Hymns for the Amusement of Children

It is noteworthy that a fair proportion of Smart's later work was designed for children. Indeed, after the publication of the *Psalms* volume in 1765, Smart turned his attention almost exclusively to the production of books for children and young people. The oratorio, *Abimelech*, is the only work of Smart's last five years that is addressed to an exclusively adult audience. The Horace was designed to appeal to readers of all ages, and the remaining works were all intended specifically for very young children. They were three in number: a translation of the fables of Phaedrus, 1765; the *Parables of Our Lord and Saviour Jesus Christ*, "done into familiar verse, with occasional applications, for the use and improvement of younger minds," and published in 1768; and finally the *Hymns for . . . Children.*

The fables of Phaedrus are not particularly good to start with, and they do not provide Smart with the kind of material he handles well. The translation is a serviceable one, but of no real significance in Smart's career. Since it is easily available in a modern reprint, I have not thought it necessary to include any specimens from it.

The *Parables* are somewhat more interesting. The whole collection is done in octosyllabic couplets, and the verse often descends to the level of pure doggerel. Nevertheless, it is frequently good. It is interesting to note in this book many examples of the Horatian "peculiarity of diction" which is so characteristic of Smart's greater poetry. Even when writing for children, he could not resist the startling phrase: "the cry of Abel's veins"; "O Salem! Salem! whose fell rage / *Assassins* each prophetic sage"; "And there his servants shall partake / The mansions, that the branches make." An occasional neat epigram enlivens the verse, and the poet's characteristic notions and prejudices sometimes lend a quaint charm to his "applications" of the sacred stories. This, from the parable of the Wise and Foolish Virgins, well illustrates the whole book:

In these ten virgins Christ recites
Five senses in two diff'rent lights.
The wise are passions kept on guard;
The foolish ones are mercies marr'd.
The touch, the taste, the sight, the smell,
The sense of hearing will rebell,
Not kept from wand'ring and mischance
By all attentive vigilance:
So they that every sense degrade,
What time the thoughts of death invade,
On any crutch, however mean,
In spite of Christ the word would lean:
Hence idleness itself subsists
On spiritual oeconomists.
Invidious folk with evil eyes,
Bad tongues, and list'ners unto lies,
Who keep not the Lord's body chaste,
Gluttons, that mar th' intent of taste,
Those that defile the human breath
With oaths and curses unto death,
And spoil that incense God desires,
Which through the lips to heav'n aspires;
Wretches like these would all to *Rome*
And go to them that sell perfume,
And to the *man of sin* apply,
There pardons and indulgence buy:
But Christ against the fools, that put
Their trust in man, his door has shut.

A short while before his death, Smart composed another book for children, the *Hymns for the Amusement of Children*. It was published by Carnan, Smart's brother-in-law, on December 27, 1770, and had apparently been written during the preceding year. This little collection, which now exists in only two recorded copies (see my article, "Christopher Smart's *Hymns for the Amusement of Children*," *Papers of the Bibliographical Society of America*, vol. 35, first quarter, 1941) is the least known of all his writings, yet it unquestionably deserves the attention of all who are attracted by the poet. It is his final word upon the meaning of religion, and any study of his religious life must be incomplete without some consideration of this volume. Technically, to be sure, these verses have little interest. There are occasional traces of the earlier peculiarity of Smart's prosody, but for the most part only the simplest phrases, rhythms, and structural patterns are employed. It is rather the spirit of this little book that is important. The sonorous grandeur of *A Song to David* is not here; neither is the assertive brilliance of some of the *Hymns and Spiritual Songs* or the mystic fervor of others. This last book is written in a mood of resignation and quiet peace. After the thrilling realization that he had created a masterpiece and the subsequent denunciations of those who could not understand him, Smart found his final comfort in the conviction that

> There's God in ev'ry man most sure,
> And ev'ry soul's to Christ allied.—Hymn ix, p. 12.

At the end he meant those lines to apply universally, without reservation.

Out of his suffering, Smart learned the real meaning of forgiveness. The burden of poem after poem is in these lines from Hymn xii:

> To give my brother more than due,
>   In talent or in name;
> Nor e'en mine enemy pursue,
>   To hurt or to defame.
>
> Nay more, to bless him and to pray
>   Mine anger to controul;
> And give the wages of the day
>   To him that hunts my soul.

In *Abimelech* (p. 6) he had prayed that memory, "the mother of the Muse," would "shape all my sorrows into song." In the *Hymns for . . . Children* his prayer is answered, and the chief impression left by the book is of a gentle sweetness distilled from pain. There is a seriousness in these verses of a kind not found in his earlier poetry, a seriousness which is given added strength by the simplicity of its expression, but there is no resentment and no hysteria.

It is natural that there should be many references in this book to the poor, with whom Smart spent his last days. The verses are filled with admonitions to the young readers to be generous with their worldly goods. The prayer in Hymn iii is typical:

> Then guide, O Christ, this little hand,
> To deal thy bounties round the land;
> To clothe and feed the hungry poor,
> And to the stranger ope my door.

Hymn xxxvii repeats the same theme:

> I just came by the prison door,
> I gave a penny to the poor:
> Pappa did this good act approve,
> And poor mamma cry'd out for love.

> When'er the poor comes to my gate,
> Relief I will communicate;
> And tell my sire his sons shall be
> As charitably great as he.

It is pleasant for a lover of Smart to be able to record that such expressions were not, even in the days of his final poverty, prompted merely by his own need. Fanny Burney has left a note in her diary which shows that Smart was not selfish in his preachments on charity: "In a letter he sent my father not long before his death, to ask his assistance for a fellow sufferer . . . he made use of an expression which pleased me much 'that he had himself assisted him, according to his willing poverty.'"

It should be remembered always in judging these last verses of Smart that they were written for children. As children's poetry many of them have decided merit. Preeminently they have the virtues of simplicity and directness. There is in some of them an apparent artlessness, a simplicity of diction combined with the most startlingly accurate arrangement of thought, which gives them a quality very like that of *Songs of Innocence and Experience*. They are like clear water in a brook, and it is usually only children whose speech is so lucid. In many there is also evident an understanding of the psychology of childhood: for example, in the charming arrangement of ideas in Hymn xxv (on Mirth). Judged purely as language, this poem is almost like the speech of an unusually wise and graceful child.

A Note on the Portraits

The large portrait of Smart which appears as a frontispiece to this volume now hangs in the Library of Pembroke College, Cambridge. It was formerly in the possession of the late Frederick Cowslade, the last direct descendant of the poet, and the last member of the family to own and publish the Reading *Mercury*. It is usually called the Cowslade portrait, but will be found occasionally referred to as the "Reynolds" portrait, because of a rather vague tradition that it was painted by Reynolds. It was apparently painted at some time before Smart's breakdown and shows him at the height of his worldly "success."

The smaller portrait facing page 74 was first reproduced in the American printing of William Force Stead's edition of *Rejoice in the Lamb* in 1939. The original has been, apparently since the eighteenth century, in the possession of the Falkiner family in Dublin, descendants of Smart's younger sister. As this book goes to press, however, the present owner of the portrait, Miss Irene K. Falkiner, informs me that she is negotiating the sale of it to the National Gallery in London, who will presumably become its permanent custodians. The portrait is reproduced here from the original plate, through the kindness of the Henry Holt Company. Since it shows Smart in cap and gown, and since it presents the face of a man much younger than the subject of the Cowslade portrait, the assumption is that it was painted while Smart was still in residence at Cambridge.

There is a third known likeness of Christopher Smart, a small oval mezzotint, showing only head and shoulders, which appears in some copies of Hunter's so-called *Collected Poems of Christopher Smart*, 1791. It appears to have been engraved from the Cowslade portrait, although it differs in certain slight details.

A Selected Bibliography

I. Smart's Principal Publications

1. *The Horatian Canons of Friendship. Being the Third Satire of the First Book of Horace. Imitated.* . . . London, 1750.
2. *On the Eternity of the Supreme Being. A poetical Essay.* . . . Cambridge, 1750 (second edition, Cambridge, 1752; third edition, Cambridge, 1756).
3. *The Midwife: or, Old Woman's Magazine* (3 volumes, dated 1751, 1751, and 1753, London).
4. *On the Immensity of the Supreme Being. A Poetical Essay.* . . . Cambridge, 1751 (second edition, Cambridge, 1753; third edition, London, 1756).
5. *Poems on Several Occasions.* . . . London, 1752.
6. *On the Omniscience of the Supreme Being. A Poetical Essay.* . . . Cambridge, 1752 (second edition, Cambridge, 1756).
7. *The Hilliad: an epic poem.* . . . London, 1753 (another edition, Dublin, 1753).
8. *On the Power of the Supreme Being. A Poetical Essay.* . . . Cambridge, 1754 (second edition, London, 1758).
9. *On the Goodness of the Supreme Being. A Poetical Essay.* . . . Cambridge, 1756 (second edition, Cambridge, 1756).
10. *The Works of Horace, Translated Literally into English Prose.* . . . London, 1756.
11. *Hymn to the Supreme Being, on Recovery from a Dangerous Fit of Illness.* . . . London, 1756.
12. *A Song to David*, London, 1763.
13. *Poems. By Mr. Smart.* . . . London, n.d. [1763].
14. *Poems on Several Occasions*, London, n.d. [1763].
15. *Hannah. An Oratorio*, London, n.d. [1764].
16. *Ode to the Right Honourable the Earl of Northumberland, on his being appointed Lord Lieutenant of Ireland.* . . . *With some other Pieces*, London, 1764.
17. *A Poetical Translation of the Fables of Phaedrus, with The Appendix of Gudius*, London, 1765.
18. *A Translation of the Psalms of David.* . . , London, 1765.
19. *The Works of Horace, Translated into Verse*, London, 1767.
20. *The Parables of Our Lord and Saviour Jesus Christ.* Done into familiar verse, with occasional applications, for the use and improvement of younger minds. . . . London, 1768.

21. *Abimelech, An Oratorio.* . . . Sold at the Theatre . . . n.d. [1768].
22. *Hymns for the Amusement of Children* [London, 1770]. (Only two copies have been reported of this work. One, in the Bodleian, is a copy of the third edition, London, 1775. The other is a copy of an American edition, Philadelphia, 1791, in the American Antiquarian Society Library, Worcester, Mass. The Luttrell Society has recently issued a facsimile of the Bodleian copy [B. H. Blackwell, Ltd., Oxford, 1947] with an introduction by Edmund Blunden).

II.   Principal Works about Smart

1. *The Poems of the late Christopher Smart* . . . to which is prefixed An Account of his Life and Writings. . . . Reading, 1791. (The "Account" was written by Christopher Hunter, and the work was published by Francis Newbery.)
2. G. J. Gray: "A Bibliography of the Writings of Christopher Smart, with Biographical References," *Transactions of the Bibliographical Society*, vi, 295 ff.
3. Edward G. Ainsworth and Charles E. Noyes: *Christopher Smart, A Biographical and Critical Study*, University of Missouri Studies, Columbia, 1943.
4. K. A. McKenzie: *Christopher Smart: sa vie et ses oeuvres*, Paris, 1925.
5. William Force Stead: *Rejoice in the Lamb*, London & N.Y., 1939.
6. C. D. Abbott: "The Date of Christopher Smart's Madness," *PMLA*, xlv, 1014-1022.
7. Leonard Whibley: "The Jubilee at Pembroke Hall in 1743," *Blackwood's Magazine*, ccxxi, 104-115.
8. Federico Olivero: "Il 'Canto a Davide' di Christopher Smart," *Studi Britannici*, Torino, 1931.
9. Robert Brittain: "Christopher Smart in the Magazines," *Transactions of the Bibliographical Society, The Library*, March, 1941, n.s. xxi, 320 ff.
10. Roland B. Botting: "Christopher Smart in London," *Research Studies of the State College of Washington*, March, 1939.
11. Claude Jones: "Christopher Smart, Richard Rolt, and *The Universal Visiter*," *The Library*, xviii (Sept. 1937), 212-214.
12. Roland B. Botting: "Johnson, Smart, and the 'Universal Visiter,' " *Modern Philology*, xxxvi (Feb. 1939), 293-300.
13. Roland B. Botting: "Christopher Smart's Association with Arthur Murphy," *JEGP*, xliii (January 1944), 49-56.

14. Laurence Binyon: "*The Case of Christopher Smart*, Pamphlet No. 90, *The English Association*, December, 1934.

15. Robert Brittain: "Christopher Smart's 'Hymns for the Amusement of Children,'" *Papers of the Bibliographical Society of America*, xxxv, First Quarter, 1941.

16. Raymond D. Havens: "The Structure of Smart's *Song to David*," *Review of English Studies*, xiv (April, 1938).

17. Roland B. Botting: "Christopher Smart and the *Lilliputian Magazine*," *English Literary History*, ix, 286-287 (Dec. 1942).

18. Roland B. Botting: "Gray and Christopher Smart," *Modern Language Notes*, lvii, 360-361 (May, 1942).

19. Gerard E. Jensen: "Concerning Christopher Smart," *Modern Language Notes*, xxx, 99-101 (1915).

20. Cyril Falls: *The Critic's Armoury*, London, 1924, pp. 110 ff.

21. Edmund Blunden: (ed.) *A Song to David, with Other Poems, by Christopher Smart*, London, 1924.

22. Robert Brittain: "An Early Model for Smart's *A Song to David*," *PMLA*, lvi, 165-174 (March, 1941). (An incorrect attribution to Smart of a poem by Merrick. See no. 23 below.)

23. A. D. McKillop: "The Benedicite Paraphrased: a Reply to R. E. Brittain," *PMLA*, lviii, 582 (June, 1943). (Correction of no. 22 above.)

General Index

Index of First Lines